NOTRE DAME REVIEW

NOTRE DAME REVIEW

NUMBER 19

Editors
John Matthias
William O'Rourke

Senior Editor
Founding Editor
Steve Tomasula
Valerie Sayers

Managing Editor
Angela Hur
Executive Editor
Kathleen J. Canavan

Sparks Editorial Asst.
Renée E. D'Aoust

Contributing Editors
Francisco Aragón
Matthew Benedict
Gerald Bruns
Seamus Deane
Stephen Fredman
Sonia Gernes
Kevin Hart
Orlando Menes
James Walton
Henry Weinfield

Editorial Assistants
Sandy Dedo
Mary Dixon
Lisa Gonzales
Nathan Gunsch
John Joseph Hess
Lily Hoang
Jennifer Malidor
Janet McNally
Tom Miller
Rebecca Pennell
Dani Rado
Matthew Ricke
Dustin Rutledge
Mark Stafford
James Wilson

The *Notre Dame Review* is published semi-annually. Subscriptions: $15 (individuals) or $20 (institutions) per year or $250 (sustainers). Single Copy price: $8. Distributed by Ubiquity Distributors, Brooklyn, NY; Media Solutions, Huntsville, Alabama; Ingram Periodicals, LaVergne, Tennessee; and International Periodical Distributors, Solana Beach, California. We welcome manuscripts, which are accepted from September through March. Please include a SASE for reply. Please send all subscription and editorial correspondence to: *Notre Dame Review*, 840 Flanner Hall, University of Notre Dame, Notre Dame, IN 46556. *The Notre Dame Review* is indexed in *The American Humanities Index* and the *Index of American Periodical Verse*.

CONTENTS

Now and Then *poetry* **1**
Mark Halperin

Missing; Man in a Dream State *poetry* **2**
Debora Greger

The Maquiladoras *poetry* **6**
John Koethe

Tobias and the Angel; Enneads *poetry* **8**
Paul Kane

Love Beneath the Napalm *story* **13**
James D. Redwood

Violin *poetry* **24**
John Peck

Graphology 100: Salt Systemics *poetry* **28**
John Kinsella

Reverberations *poetry* **32**
Steve Timm

The General Silence; Reconstruction *poetry* **35**
Simeon Berry

Your Thin Grandmother *story* **37**
Frances Sherwood

A Fragment of Culture II *poetry* **50**
Regina Derieva

Highland Town *poetry* **51**
Claudio Rodriguez

Fence on the Border; Sonata on Original Sin *poetry* **53**
Sheryl Luna

Birthday on Mt. Washinton *poetry* 58
Keith Taylor

Guardian Raptors *poetry* 59
Maria Terrone

Ember; Anthem *poetry* 60
Paulann Petersen

Interment; Counter-Fable *poetry* 62
Martha Zweig

1953: James Dean Walks the Streets of New York All Night;
The Ventriloquist and His Dummy *poetry* 64
Bill Meissner

Small Blessings *story* 66
Ed Falco

Interviewing the Gods *poetry* 80
Jeffery Bahr

To a Drowned Man; The Summer My Mother Acknowledges My
Sister as Hysteric *poetry* 81
Michelle Margolis

Off For the War/ Home From the War *poetry* 83
Daneen Wardrop

Blue Study; Yellow Study *poetry* 85
Kirsten Kaschock

Shadows and Distance; The Wanderer *poetry* 89
Brian Swann

from Barrens *poetry* 92
Tom O'Connor

Letters on a Reprint of Robert Duncan's *Letters* *review* 97
Stephen Fredman

Transparent Things *review* 104
James Walton

Rhymes with History: Joe Francis Doerr and Kevin Ducey *review* 107
Robert Archambeau

"This Delicate Balance": Two Books by Diane Thiel *review* 113
Kathryn Kruger

Editors Select 117
Contributors 121

NOW AND THEN

Mark Halperin

Wasn't the present to be that knife-edge
on which the past and future tottered,
cleanly dividing them, with no saving up
or weighing consequences, not this
effort against that result? Wasn't the past

to contain no more than old habits,
and love to be not simply prelude to grief,
source of soiled hopes that beggared,
riddled and despoiled the view? Remember
a bridge, a rise from which the square

opened in snow, the marble, angel-topped
column in the distance and a dome?
Remorse could wash you one last time
and each parting seem the final one,
unique in its own diminished future.

Then, now—the present became one
life you left off for another, a changing
coastline of new sounds, the wilderness
we only visit and a foreign country where
time goes on unveiling endless variations.

MISSING

Debora Greger

I. Not There

There was no one in the house I'd borrowed
except the twilight of far-off Florida—

that purple you don't see anywhere else,
and then it's gone. Where were you?

There was no one, only the night at the window,
the shade undrawn. A moth opened its book

to the same dusty page as always. What
was about to happen? Close the book!

A ghost of the subtropics, a pale pink gecko,
was looking up the word for food.

Through its skin, I saw a small blue heart.
Twin sacs of blue air emptied and filled.

The headlights of a car saw through it
and swept the room: no one was there.

No frog barked from a tree in the afterglow
of a thunder shower. Oh, love, I remember

that student of ours whose boyfriend came
from the desert to visit. She said she woke one night

to find the door of the apartment open.
He was standing there, watching rain fall

in that relaxed and ruthless way it does in Florida.
Though she would marry and divorce him later,

in sleep she'd missed him, while he'd been missing
the kind of rain he'd never known.

II. *Not Here*

You weren't here. We didn't breathe the same air.
Mine held a note of smoke, as if prunings burned

in the vineyards. Or had the foothills turned to flame?
Outside my window—no, much farther off,

your absence rose like some foreign city.
It stood in water, admiring its reflection,

even in decay. Like you, it hadn't slept yet,
though its barges bore the burdens of a new day

past the old customs house and the church
of Santa Maria del Salute: Venice needed Coke

and Xerox machines. And stacks of artichokes—
or at least their hearts afloat in lemon juice

so they wouldn't darken, exposed to the air.
I didn't know I could love a city the way I loved you.

A dredge scooped up mud for breakfast,
but Venice wouldn't wake from its dream of water.

A water taxi opened the Grand Canal like a book.
Its pages were green, edges deckled with foam.

In every slip and slap I read the long marriage
of city to lagoon. Each watery, salty kiss devoured.

How far away you were: I wrote zero after zero
down a page of the deepest green water.

MAN IN A DREAM STATE
—John Muir, 1867

Debora Greger

Today at last I reach Florida,
the so-called "Land of Flowers."
Here, just a few yards away, it was—
flat, watery, reedy, with strange moss-dressed trees
in the distance.
                              The steamer found her way
among reed islands like a duck.
Visiting this state in dreams, I had come
upon close forest, trees in flower yet bent,
tangled by vines with even brighter blooms,
all of it flooded by sunlight.
                              But such was not the gate
by which I entered the promised land.
Salt marsh more sea than land; groves sunk
to the shoulder in sedge and rush;
land not rising in hilly waves and swells
but stretching out like water.
                              We were discharged,
without breakfast, onto a rickety wharf
a few steps from a rickety town.
There I bought bread without asking a single question,
making straight for the gloomy shade.
At the first dry spot I threw down my flower press
on something like a deserted muskrat house,
and applied myself to my meal.
                              Not a mark
of friendly recognition, not a breath,
not a spirit-whisper of sympathy came
from anything around me. I lay on my elbow
eating my bread, listening to the strangeness.

A rustling sound behind me—
had my mind been healthy, my body not starved,
I should only have turned calmly to it.
But at once I could feel the stroke
of a long notched tail, rows of teeth
closing around me, just as in pictures I had seen.
I do not know the measure of my fright in time or pain.
But then my man-eating alligator
became a tall white crane, handsome as a minister
from the spirit world.
                                        Ministers tell us only man
is immortal, plants are soulless, etc.;
but my first palmetto told me grander things
than ever got from human priest.
                                        Yet I gave up hope
of finding food or bed, searching only
for a dry spot large enough to sleep on,
safely hidden from freed slaves. All creatures
of these trackless woods had a home but I.
On that far-off dry plain, a stone for a pillow,
Jacob must have been happier.
                                        Yet I slept,
waking next morning wet with dew,
and breakfastless. Could this meal be dispensed with,
I doubt civilization would see me again.
Ask the owl, the noisiest
of all my unseen witnesses.

THE MAQUILADORAS

John Koethe

They oversimplify our lives,
These stories, stripping them of context and detail,
Recasting each one as a journey, moving from the country
To a factory on the border, from a rural home

To one that I'd imagined, to this place
That I inhabit, locked in the idea
Of a room, a home, a city street, the country
Where I live and I was nineteen once

And where I find myself a subject of two states,
Of two distinct domains: a private one
Of furniture and poetry, pottery and silent monologues
While shaving in a mirror, thinking through

A turn of phrase, the course of an emotion,
Tracing the trajectory of a thought
That takes me to the kingdom of a single mind
Where what I think and feel and say all seem the same.

We all live in the other one. On the news
Last night a woman in New Jersey
And a man in Pennsylvania read my mind. More dead
Filled up the screen as someone read their names

Instead of mine, which would have been the same.
More Walmarts in Chicago, on the sites
Of some abandoned factories, while the doors keep closing
On the maquiladoras in Tijuana and Juarez

Through which the money flows, and flows away. Who says
That life is change, and change is for the better?
It can look that way when looked at through the blinders
Of an individual life, one constantly embarking

On a journey of its own, of everyone's,
From adolescence through late middle age. Nineteen
Was nothing special and I wouldn't want it back,
Yet sometimes when I think about the years to come

I see almost as many as the ones since then.
I feel a vague and incoherent fear, a fear
Of waking from time's dream into an even stranger place,
As different from today as now is from nineteen,

Without a sense of where I am or where I'd been before—
Which is always here, in my imagination.   When I ask myself
What home was really like the answer is sheer fiction,
As I picture to myself an endless summer

Sky above a Culver's or a Dairy Queen,
A school, the Hansen-Onion funeral home, the modest
Mansions on the quiet, shady streets
Of a small Wisconsin town time left unchanged.

Tobias and the Angel

Paul Kane

> And Raphael was sent to heal them both, that is, to scale
> away the whiteness of Tobit's eyes, and to give Sara the
> daughter of Raguel for a wife to Tobias the son of Tobit;
> and to bind Asmodeus the evil spirit.
>
> —Tobit 3:17

Was it enough to walk with him
beyond the dry hills of Nineveh,
enough to roast fish together
on the banks of the Tigris?

I knew him as a countryman but
not for what he was, unknowable,
a voice in the stricken night, crying
"I am brethren, I will bind you to me."

Such a distance to travel, under
a milky sky, with dust in the air, sharp
pebbles underfoot, birds raucous in trees,
and the puzzlement of his eyes.

What more could I take in but that
tone, that surety hanging like a cloud
about him? Even my dog staggered
in his presence. What question could I frame?

Blindness he could cure, yet one day
half-blind himself he and I carried a table
through a doorway and up the long
passage, as if we both might thereby see.

Later, a vision of my father, of gall
anointing his upturned face, of whiteness
pilling away from the corners of his eyes
and he falling upon my neck and weeping.

I had no such tears to offer, knowing
so little what time brings, the sacred
affliction, the unsought recompense
on the outskirts of the waking town.

And what of Sara and the dark angel?
I was mad to wed her, trembling
on the threshold desiring either her flesh or
my death, I could not distinguish that night.

In twos and threes and then decades
at a time, the years passed as I prospered.
Was it enough to attend to his words
now that words are no longer enough?

ENNEADS

Paul Kane

He was unlike all others, other
than all those he made appear the same:
a blackened pine tree scarred by lightning,
singled out for a knowledge never
forgiven, struck by blazoned power
intolerable—the light whitening
around him, falling like a shower
on us, who first heard our secret name
and rose at its burden's lightening.

But then others came, and then more, such
that we despaired to know our true place—
there were so many with so little
to give, and they took much, far too much
for us or him to sustain, so down
that spiraling staircase of riddle
he went, speaking strangely and around
the central point, creating a space
all his own, all edge, with no middle.

We followed him to that edge and then
no further, for there was nowhere else
to go. We turned back only to find
he had turned his back on us, and when
most we needed him—or thought we did—
till suddenly there occurred a sign
for us that neither revealed nor hid
a truth, but showed what was false:
a disease of the eye—he'd gone blind.

How the blind see! Poet, prophet, man
of utter insight, the blinding stroke
turns the world inside out, draining shape
and color from form until the hand
reaches out to grasp the silhouettes
fading in the light, but they escape
in formlessness, the mocking objects
of our desire to believe. He spoke
of this, as of an inner landscape.

From then on, we knew our sole duty
was to open our eyes and for once
see as he saw us, unobscured by
form, sheer life visible, the beauty
of nothingness—and to find then form
as a coating that displays just why
we are opaque and cannot perform
the least service to ourselves: this blunts
self-regard—our life become our lie.

As you would expect, the death was hard
on us all, though surely least on him
who welcomed it as a sloughing off,
the body a skin of no regard,
though we buried it and mourned our loss—
but the voice we missed most, lilting soft,
then with harsh rebuke, as if to toss
aside some mask and unmake us limb
by limb, alien to ourselves, cast off

into shallows, where wallowing in
swamps of pity we picked ourselves up
in the end, purified by knowledge
of baseness. O, what a state to win
on this earth! But now who could debase
himself, walk out to the very ledge
and beyond? Before what god deface
the countenance of pride, how disrupt
the casual tide of sacrilege?

We had no answers, who only had
questions, and those unanswerable.
And the rhetoric of inquiry!
We could not stand our voices, the sad
mimicry and despair that laced
our words, until the iniquity—
the wheedling pretense—came to be faced.
Amidst decay, what was durable?
What could we wrest from our nullity?

And then we knew, we had understood
more than we knew, for in leaving us
he had left us ourselves, fraught with all
our diminishing flaws—yet we would
go on, like birds repopulating
a barren pond: seeds, parasites fall
as they breast the waters, negating
the emptiness around with surplus
of life. Do you grasp now why we call?

LOVE BENEATH THE NAPALM

James D. Redwood

Mr. Tu leaned forward on his haunches, and with the aid of a trowel, gently dug out a weed which had insinuated itself between two pansies and threatened to choke them. It was late afternoon. A sharp breeze broke from the Helderberg Mountains seven miles away. Winter was coming, and he greatly missed his native village of Long Dien, which would now be entering the long hot dry season. Mr. Tu did not look forward to the death of his flower garden and the eight long months of wait before he could bring it to life again. He shivered in his thin, second-hand flannel jacket, a gift from Mrs. Hai-li, the Chinese owner of the Golden Dragon Restaurant on the corner of Peach Street and Route 138 in downtown Schenectady. She paid Mr. Tu thirty dollars a week to tend the two square boxes which stood beside the stone dragons in front of the restaurant.

"Hello, Uncle," a voice said to his back, in Vietnamese. Mr. Tu arched his neck in surprise. It had been months since anyone had spoken to him, aside from Mrs. Hai-li, and more than a year since he'd heard his own language. He turned.

The girl gave a sharp little cry and stepped back. She placed her hand over her mouth and stared at him, her eyes wide. Mr. Tu's jaw crinkled as he flashed her the resigned little smile he gave everyone. If he had not been peering down at a nice bauhinia flower on the An Loc battlefield when the bomb hit, his eyes would have fried like eggs and he would never have seen the look his face always inflicted on strangers. But then he noticed how much the young lady standing over him resembled Le. She had the same lush black hair, the same doelike, almond-shaped eyes, the same playful smile of a kitten toying with a coil of hemp, now that she had recovered from her shock. Even the tilt of her shoulders was the same as she leaned forward again. Mr. Tu's heart pattered joyfully.

"Why, hello, Little Sister," he said, struggling to keep his voice from quavering. Mr. Tu then spotted the man beside her. He was American, and had looked away, of course.

"I like your flowers," she said. "Wait, Phil," she added in English, tugging her companion's sleeve. The American was big, blond, and handsome, though in Mr. Tu's opinion not as handsome as he himself had once been. Mr. Tu sensed the man's irritation at being stopped from the way his fist tightened around the restaurant door handle.

"Come on," the American growled. "I'm hungry. You can squawk with

13

this guy later."

The girl blushed at her companion's comment and stepped back from Mr. Tu again. The implication that their tongue resembled the talk of chickens would have caused Mr. Tu to blush as well if the plastic surgeon who'd repaired his face after An Loc had left him any color to work with. This man reminded him unpleasantly of his induction training in 1971. The American advisers at the Thu Duc Military School had mocked his beautiful language, made fun of his eyes, his skin the color of Cham drums, his inconsequential stature. Their innuendos about the inadequate size of the Vietnamese male member filled him with humiliation and rage. Mr. Tu glanced at the beautiful girl again. Had she taken this blond ape because of the bulk of his penis?

"Hoa?" the ape said, nudging her arm. His voice whined with impatience, and Mr. Tu felt perversely tempted to goad him.

"So your name is Hoa," he said conversationally, leaning back on his haunches. He tapped his garden box with his trowel. "It's a name I like." He was tired of hearing only the Chinese word for flower.

The girl laughed like a wind chime tinkling nervously in a breeze, and the sound filled Mr. Tu with delight. Mrs. Hai-li carped at him constantly and gave him nothing but scowls.

"I can see that," Hoa said. Mr. Tu was impressed at how quickly she picked up on his implication. This girl was smart as well as pretty, just like Le. Mr. Tu sighed at the memory of his fiancée. He'd met her in 1970, shortly after his father died and he moved to Saigon. Le was studying at the Faculté des Lettres and living with an old aunt in Gia Dinh. Back then Mr. Tu was something to look at, and their courtship blossomed like his pansy patch in summer, until the day he was called up for duty.

Hoa crouched down beside him.

"Did you garden back…there?" she asked.

The word *there* coursed through Mr. Tu's veins like a spring flood rushing along the Mekong. He watched as she indolently ran her fingers through the dirt of one of the flower boxes and then carefully straightened out a pansy which had bent in the breeze from the Helderbergs. *A girl from the earth*, he thought with satisfaction, *a true Vietnamese*. Yet what was she doing with this American?

"Not after I went to Saigon," he replied. "The ground wasn't suitable, you see. And—"

He stopped talking. The girl had suddenly snapped her head back over her shoulder. The American was staring at the street. Mr. Tu was disconcerted at the interruption but looked on.

A red Thunderbird convertible with the top down chugged along the street toward them and screeched to a halt just beyond the Golden Dragon. Russet-colored maple leaves whipped up by the little car fluttered to the ground beside a clapboard house across the street. Two teenaged girls in the front seat, a blonde and a redhead, turned their heads and whistled at the handsome American. Hoa leaned toward Phil but then froze. The scowl which had overspread his face when she began to talk to Mr. Tu melted into a big smile. The redhead, who was slightly overweight and had a half-empty bottle of liquor in one hand, jutted her breasts forward in a gesture which Mr. Tu found both vulgar and inviting.

"Hey guys, wanna party?" she crooned, swaying in her seat.

She winked at Phil, who burst into a laugh.

"Later, girlie," he called, giving her a friendly wave. "Save it for dessert."

The redhead giggled, and the convertible took off. Mr. Tu's brow darkened as the woman beside him bit her lip and glanced down at her own tiny breasts. Suddenly she jabbed Mr. Tu's trowel into the potting soil and almost tore off one of the pansies. She threw the trowel down and looked away. Mr. Tu hastily leaned forward to fix the flower, but it flopped forlornly on its side, its neck broken. His heart yearned for the girl. He shared her humiliation as though it was another mark of their national disgrace, like the size of his penis.

The American leered at the Thunderbird as it disappeared up the street. The wind whipped through the man's hair like an autumn breeze through wheat. Mr. Tu sighed. Phil was just the kind of loon who would appeal to a superficial woman like the tramp in the convertible. Such swine never lifted their snouts out of the muck. Mr. Tu eyed Hoa longingly. How could the tow-headed lout *ever* understand this lovely girl who'd seen through his face to the very heart of him? Only the Vietnamese appreciated the pearl within the oyster. But still he was uneasy.

Phil glanced down, and his face tightened in a frown.

"Come on," he said coldly, tapping Hoa's shoulder. "That's enough. Let's eat."

Hoa barely looked at Mr. Tu now.

"Goodbye," she said, but her voice was distant. Mr. Tu gazed regretfully at her as she rose to her feet. He was hoping for another smile, just like Le's, and felt a pang of disappointment when instead she turned and edged close to Phil. Yet he knew she had to keep up appearances, and he took comfort from the fact that she held her body rigid beside the American. Mr. Tu thought of the many conquests of his youth, when women had dropped into his lap like persimmons from an overladen tree. Of course she was standoffish, reluctant to look at him! No woman likes to struggle with her affections. But she was beginning to fall for him, Mr. Tu felt certain. He could tell that from the way she'd laughed at his little joke about her name. He had a sense of these things. They were both Vietnamese, after all, linked by bonds invisible to the Americans. Mr. Tu felt suddenly exhilarated. His soul had peeked through his blistered skin at her like a crocus through the snow. As he leaned back on his haunches again and watched them enter the restaurant, he realized he was in love.

"Let's row out to the middle of the pond," Le said, grabbing his arm.

It was March, 1972. Mr. Tu, twenty-three and crisp in his new lieutenant's uniform, removed his white kid gloves, folded them neatly in half, and slipped them into his pocket. He turned to her and smiled possessively, like all acknowledged lovers, and led her carefully along the dock which jutted into the crescent-shaped water lily pond on the grounds of the Botanical Gardens. It was the trysting place of lovers, but the disastrous Lam Son offensive of the year before had thinned the ranks of males, and solitary females could not take pleasure in a spot like this. Tu and Le had it all to themselves, briefly. He had to report to his unit the next day. A new North Vietnamese offensive was rumored.

When they reached the end of the dock, he unmoored a rowboat, got in, and assisted her to board. He seated her in the stern, sat down amidships, fixed the oars in the rowlocks, and shoved off.

"How I shall miss you!" Le cried, leaning towards him. Tears glittered in her eyes like sun-spotted diamonds glancing off the surface of the lily pond. Their marriage had finally been set for the following month. Le had waited patiently for two years with the old aunt in Gia Dinh for Mr. Tu to finish his training. Now they would have to wait some more.

A doleful-sounding vespers bell clanged in a nearby Buddhist monastery, and Mr. Tu felt a weight upon his heart as heavy as the iron from which it was cast. The bell seemed to toll their final moments together. The sweet scent of jasmine and rare orchids from the greenhouse on the far side of the island toward which they were heading only added to his sadness, and he pulled at the oars with long desolate strokes, like a mourner lugging a funeral barge.

"Don't think about it, my dearest," he said bravely, but Le burst into a torrent of tears. Mr. Tu quickly rowed beneath the Japanese bridge which crossed over to the island and stopped beneath one of its arches. Here she could indulge her sorrow in peace. He made the boat fast against the bank and seated himself beside her. He kissed her eyes, her lips, drank in the warmth of her body, the panting of her breath. She was beautiful, and he was happy and sad at the same time.

"My big strong soldier," she wailed. "How I shall worry about you!"

Mr. Tu nodded grimly and drew her close. In their two years together in Saigon other women had tempted him to kick over the traces, as was only natural with a man of his looks, but Le had managed to hold the reins tight and keep him on course. Never had they imagined she might lose him to the war.

"You will take care, won't you, darling?" she said, her voice choking.

"Of course," he responded, trying to sound cheerful. He hoped she would not notice his trembling, however. He thought of his father, who'd been caught in an airstrike while out tending his rice field on a foot-powered paddy pump. All they found of him afterward was a white powdery residue which looked like the chalk dust on the erasers at the Long Dien village school. Mr. Tu gripped the gunwales hard to stop his shaking. His unit was headed into the Iron Triangle, the jaws of the tiger. Le would have plenty to worry about, and so would he.

"Oh, my handsome one!" she exclaimed, collapsing on his shoulder and breaking down completely. Mr. Tu slumped in his seat. His carefree days were over. She fluttered against his chest like the last bird before winter...

The wind snapped off the Helderbergs again, and Mr. Tu shuddered and shook off the sad memory. He heard a noise and looked up. Mrs. Hai-li stood over him, staring down.

"What are you still doing here, blockhead?" she asked, her voice shrill. "Take yourself off."

She craned her neck and scanned the sidewalk for customers. Business had fallen off lately, and she blamed it on Mr. Tu's face. People lost their appetite when they saw him. The sidewalk was empty.

She turned back and frowned at him.

"Shove off now, that's enough for tonight," she said, waving him off the stoop with the back of her hand. "You'll frighten the whole neighborhood if you stay here after dark."

Mr. Tu rose reluctantly to his feet. He longingly eyed the restaurant door and thought of the girl Hoa seated somewhere behind it. Would he ever see her again?

"And don't forget that trowel," Mrs. Hai-li barked, pointing to the tool which was barely visible in the dim light. "If it rusts in the damp air, the replacement will come out of your pay."

Mr. Tu attempted to bite his lip. He leaned over and picked up the trowel, gazing fondly at his beloved pansies one last time as he did so. Their ugly little mugs reminded him of his own, and they comforted him in his distress as Mrs. Hai-li continued to berate him even while he trudged sadly away. Why had fate linked him to such a doltish shrew? Once he wouldn't have given her a second thought, but now he had to march to her tune, all because of An Loc. Truly his lot was a hard one.

When he stumbled into his darkened garret a few minutes later and switched on the light, the drabness of his lodgings further dampened his spirits. Rodents pattered behind the plaster, and the wind howled through a window gap covered with cheap masking tape. Boys who lived in the neighborhood had thrown a rock through the window soon after he moved in and then laughed at Mr. Tu's pink hairless skull when it peeped through the jagged hole. Mr. Tu shook his fist at them, but they just laughed harder and strolled away in a leisurely fashion to show they were not afraid of him. Afterward Mr. Tu kept his head covered with a New York Yankees baseball cap, but he still felt aggrieved. The boys were Vietnamese.

The wind whistled through the window crack again, causing Mr. Tu to shiver and fluttering the candle which stood inside a tiny spirit lamp on top of his bureau. He thought how nice it would be to have the girl from the restaurant to warm his bed, and then he stared at the photograph beside the spirit lamp. Le smiled alluringly at him from a painted Chinese background, a sprig of *mai* blossoms in her hand. He'd taken the photo himself, and at the time he was very proud of it. But after he parted from her that last day in Saigon, with the North Vietnamese inexorably closing in, Mr. Tu succumbed to the superstition that cameras took away a person's soul...

"This is my favorite part," he whispered, leaning over in the crowded movie theater and touching Le's sleeve. It was April 30, 1975. On the wide screen in front of them a tall Chinese warlord, girded for battle, strutted about his palace bedroom, gesticulating wildly at his wife, who stood scowling in the middle of the room, her fists tightened in a bunch. In the far corner the warlord's favorite concubine lay weeping.

"Yes, *thuong anh*," Le said, nodding. She kept her eyes glued to the screen. "Just let me watch, will you?"

Mr. Tu thrilled with pleasure when she called him her beloved one, words he had not heard since that sad afternoon in the Botanical Gardens three years earlier. Given the way she'd greeted him that morning, he would not have expected it.

She'd shrunk behind the statue of the Virgin Mary in the deserted square outside the National Cathedral to protect herself from the unknown mutant who kept calling out her name and insisting he was her fiancé. Mr. Tu was hurt and chagrined until she remembered his voice. But Le too had changed. She was dressed in a pricy western mini-skirt, her hair curled in false ringlets, her mouth and cheeks painted red as a *Hat Boi* actress's. Still, he had recognized *her* immediately.

A rocket screeched by overhead, close to the theater, and Mr. Tu instinctively ducked. When it hit, his and Le's seats, as well as those of the other patrons who'd come there hoping to escape the war, shook in their sockets, and several people cried out in alarm. Le glanced at him anxiously, and Mr. Tu put his arm around her shoulder to comfort her. They clung to each other and watched the conclusion of "Endless Passion," quaking whenever another rocket hit.

Mr. Tu spotted Hoa from the far side of Liberty Street, late in the afternoon, near closing time. She was sitting in a chair by one of the tall library windows, reading something and basking in the rays of the declining sun. The gardener darted between some fast-moving cars and gained the other side of the street. He peeped in at her from several feet away, his heart pounding. With her head bowed over a magazine, her face at an angle, she reminded him of Le even more than she had the evening before. She was dressed in a leather mini-skirt that reached above the knees, and although from the tilt of her head he could not tell if she was wearing makeup, her hair was curled in exactly the same way as his fiancée's. Mr. Tu's heart beat faster as he scurried toward the entrance.

After the movie, Le had insisted on going back alone for some traditional clothes to make it easier for her to blend in with the hordes fleeing the capital. Mrs. Lanh, the madam, was fed up with men and would surely create a scene, she said. She would not be long.

He waited for her on the crowded dock which jutted into the Saigon River at Newport, where the big American ships used to land. Artillery shells pounded the city, and a pall of thick black smoke ringed the metropolis like a funeral wreath. Mr. Tu ran back and forth along the dock, glancing frantically about, mouthing out her name, trying to avoid the bodies trampled in the final rush to freedom and now lying crumpled beneath some crude woven mats. He started peeking to see if Le was among them, but stopped when the third body he came to had a face as mutilated as his own. A boat horn blasted behind him. People yelled at him to come on. Slowly, reluctantly, her name still on his lips, with tears struggling to form beneath the dead skin beside his eyelids, he turned away...

The librarian date-stamping books behind the checkout desk glared at him as though his face might set off the security alarm, but Mr. Tu glanced only briefly at her as he pushed back the door flap and strode intrepidly toward the stacks. Departing patrons whisked by him, some of them with books crooked under their arms, and paid him hardly any mind. Yet Mr. Tu started to tremble when he saw the row of sunlit windows up ahead and spotted her, poring over her magazine still. Hoa was seated all alone. His feet began to drag, and he froze in his tracks. The dust particles which danced in the air all along the bookshelf separating them seemed to Mr. Tu's distracted mind to be playing with her hair, which had lightened to a beautiful shade of auburn in the glow of the sun. He had difficulty breathing, and might have stayed there forever, just watching her, if a young man impatient for a book on the shelf beside him had not roughly ordered him aside. The man was rude, contemptuous, as though Mr. Tu's face gave him the right to be that way. Mr. Tu winced beneath his skin grafts and stepped uncertainly forward.

"Hello," he murmured, coming up to her. He was embarrassed when she didn't hear him. "Hello," he repeated, so loudly this time she jerked her head up from the page.

"Oh, hi," she said mechanically, and Mr. Tu's heart faltered. Didn't she remember who he was? No one could forget a face like his.

"So you come here also," she added, but her tone was flat, devoid of interest. She gazed at a bookshelf behind him. Mr. Tu knew he should leap at the opening which lay before him like a dropped handkerchief in the movies, but just at that moment his Adam's apple snarled up his windpipe and his courage flagged. The girl shrugged and lowered her eyes again. She flipped the magazine page, and Mr. Tu heard the paper snap as if she was angry at it.

He shifted awkwardly on his feet. Now that he was standing over her, he didn't have the slightest idea what to say. Hoa remained silent.

"May I join you?" he asked at last, indicating a chair across from her. She flicked her hand, impatiently it seemed, and Mr. Tu settled in and tried to make himself comfortable. But instead he became quite nervous as he stared at the beautiful bowed head and the tantalizing body opposite him, which had stiffened since he sat down. Occasionally, she glanced up at the bookshelf again, but not at him. Mr. Tu started to sweat, and the thought that she might smell him filled him with horror. His mouth went dry, and what finally emerged from his throat was little more than a croak.

"Aren't you glad to see me, Miss Hoa?"

She looked at him and smiled slightly, for the first time. Mr. Tu was encouraged.

"Oh, you remembered my name."

"How could I forget it?" he blurted out.

Her face immediately darkened, and Mr. Tu's hand jerked spasmodically on his chair arm. He was going too fast. She was trying to sort out her feelings for him, and he had to proceed cautiously.

"I work with flowers, remember," he added, trying to sound casual.

"Ah, yes. So you do." But she shrugged a second time.

Mr. Tu decided to hazard a smile, but stopped midway, afraid his defective face muscles might turn it into a sneer. For a moment he almost envied his father's fate. No one had been indifferent to the little pile of dust which was heaped up in the middle of the old man's rice field and which was virtually indistinguishable from the powdered fertilizer USAID had given him to increase his crop yield. It was the talk of Long Dien village for months.

The sound of raucous laughter suddenly came from behind the bookshelves, and Hoa popped her head up once more and frowned in its direction. The laughter was followed by giggling, then the hurried whisper of voices, one male, one female. Hoa looked across at Mr. Tu, visibly upset. He summoned up all his courage and flashed her the most engaging smile of which his blackened lips were capable. His smiles had cheered Le through many a troubled time. Hoa trembled slightly, and Mr. Tu felt emboldened. But his skin crinkled like a strip of tanning leather when he spoke again.

"Would you like to get a coffee somewhere?" he squeaked. He sank back down, embarrassed.

She twitched as though someone had yanked a rope around her neck.

"With *you*?" she said, her voice barely above a whisper.

She quickly shook her head, but Mr. Tu did not lose heart. He'd picked up the breathlessness of her reply, the rapid twittering of her fingers on the page. Women were programmed to demur, then to yield. He waited.

"I can't," she said, glancing anxiously at the bookshelves yet again.

Mr. Tu waved his hand as though her refusal was only to be expected. He tried to fix her with his eyes, those beautiful unscarred eyes which the gods had spared from the napalm at An Loc. Le had melted at the sight of them.

"Well," he said, attempting to keep his voice steady, "the Stockade

Diner's just up the street."

She peered at him.

"But you're so...different," she said.

Mr. Tu's heart finally sank within him. He thought of Mrs. Hai-li, who never looked him straight on, as though his face might blind her like a solar eclipse.

"You think I'm ugly, don't you?" he said feebly, unable to look at *her* now. He felt as insignificant as a mound of dust.

The laughter resumed behind the bookshelves. Hoa's magazine abruptly snapped shut, and Mr. Tu lifted his head. The girl darted to her feet and moved away from him.

"You're *Vietnamese*," she said, her voice filled with sudden scorn. Her eyes were glued to the book racks. Mr. Tu's jaw dropped as far as it was capable.

"But...so are *you*," he stammered, his face contorting itself into something resembling a look of confusion.

She glared down at him and shook her head vehemently.

"That was before," she said. "I want to forget all about that now, and you remind me of—"

A rustling came from the stacks, and Hoa paused in mid-sentence. Mr. Tu felt angry and hurt. He shot to his feet.

"Of *what*?" he said, his voice rising. He tried to grab her hand, but she drew away from him. "What do I remind you of?"

She didn't answer, for just at that moment Phil emerged from behind the bookshelf. Mr. Tu turned and spotted a wisp of red hair disappear in the direction of the checkout counter. Hoa flitted to the American's side. She scowled suspiciously at him and craned her neck in the direction of the exit. Phil grasped her roughly by the arm and twisted her around.

"Ow!" she yelped, trying to disengage herself. "You're hurting me!"

In spite of her curious remarks to him Mr. Tu stepped gallantly forward. Only her own people could help her in such a predicament.

"Be gentle with her, young man," he admonished, wagging a stern finger at the American.

Phil stared at him and then gaped at Hoa.

"What the fuck is this bird talking about?" he demanded. All of a sudden, Hoa wrenched free from him and turned on Mr. Tu.

"This is *our* business, so stay out of it!" she yelled. "And yes, you're right. You *are* ugly," she added savagely. "I would *never* go out with *you!*"

Mr. Tu was astounded. Never had Le treated him like this, nor any of the other ladies who had swooned over him in his youth. He drew himself up proudly in front of her.

"And I would never be seen with a whore like *you*, either," he snapped, tossing his head self-righteously and twisting his face into what he truly intended to be a sneer this time.

Hoa turned white and trembled all over. In a single bound she sprang to Mr. Tu, and with the swiftness of lightning she raised her hand and slapped him hard across the face. Mr. Tu's skin smarted as though it had been set on fire a second time. He felt dizzy, disoriented, and the tears which had been so many years in coming burst from his eyes at last. In his blindness the angry young woman with her fist still raised looked as though she stood at the edge of another world, beckoning for him to come back to her. Mr. Tu stretched his hand out and tried to call her name, but no sound emerged from his throat. He staggered against the chair he'd been sitting in and gingerly lowered himself into it. He bowed his head to calm his nerves. When he looked up again, a minute later, he was alone.

Mr. Tu's heart felt as thick and heavy as lead. His face burned fiercely still, and the pain, as it settled deep inside him, was much more intense than it had been the first time, when all he lost was a battle. A librarian began to switch off the lights in the stacks. She spotted Mr. Tu and started. Slowly he rose from his chair.

VIOLIN

John Peck

With all pasts and futures harboring in this present
then all, happiness and unhappiness, is a choice
if only because I have agreed to build here. Yet even
the most daring choose happiness alone, and thinking
will never get me through this, and feeling loiters in it—
only Great Harbor floats all of it, fresh, waiting.
Following descriptions of the North Pyramid at Dashur,
the Red Pyramid stripped of its red sandstone facing,
then photographs from recent expedition reports,
I found no speculations about precisely why
this pivotal structure slopes at forty-three degrees,
a matter of moment, perhaps or perhaps not, yet
I saw sand shelving along the base of the west face,
a ripply ledge smoothing along remnant facing
and blending with it— the same as on Plum Island,
barrier beach for piping plover and pale-belled sand shrubs
dropping its steep bevel sucked at for miles by surf,
the rolling sound momentarily sinking away in it,
its high edge fronting dune grass nervy against sun.
No Joseph among us to build granaries, no Jonah
to ironize destruction, no Jacob to hammer choice.
One third through the mere sixty years which saw the great
pyramids rise, this one, with the lowest inclination
at forty-three degrees, *cautious* some say to forestall
shiftings which skewed the vitals of the Bent Pyramid
somewhat earlier and three quarters of a mile off,
was the first achieved prototype. A slope which has me sense
greater mass and area than it commands. A discovery
about proportion and it may be an application
of lore no one yet has been able to read from the record.
This time the architect lifted the burial chamber
higher inside the mass—the squared cone of sunlight—
and for the first time aligned the coffin east-west
with tomb temple and the sun's track. Its capstone
pyramidion was of the same red sandstone,
not the gilded white stone or granite of later practice.

The entire casing bulged slightly outward much like
the faint entasis on a Greek column, though not
meant for Greek good looks, but rather for what would stand.
Altering the slope's angle rise by rise with
cord and peg, masons jesting with the overseer:
this innovation in masonry was not imitated.
Senefru, who enjoyed people, calling his staff *Dear Friend*,
the only king known for doing so, presided over
erection of the Bent and the Red pyramids, as well as
two others at Meidum and Seila, the start on Egypt's
Manhattan Project, four solar fusion battery casings
for his charged body, at three locations. He was buried
in this one if its hurried completion is any evidence.
Osiris's theology by then nosed ahead of the astral one.
An east-west journey at night with the sun in that god's boat.
Setting out through river reeds, their silken forgivingness.
On one side, barrier dunes thrusting up into solar acetylene
which tracks with me along their apex, while on the other
vast drenchings sink into the low slope. Four fiberglass
fishing poles shoot lines off into surf, their necks
bent studiously, their shanks in tubes rammed into sand,
their armchair owner dozing under a blue towel.
Four nylon zings of tackle as if sounding unison.
They baked loaves for him in the reliefs. He himself ran
a race in the Heb-Sed ceremony, as did his fathers,
all in renewal of their powers, his predecessor loping
hugely across the slab which seals a shaft at Meidum.
Though no tides any longer moisten the stones, those tunnels
smell of the sea. The burial of full-scale ships
began under his son Khufu near the vast piles at Giza.
My ears ring with a cricket-like susurrus that comes from years
of holding taut line out into the oncoming rush.
A certain age renders further ambition supernumerary,
my buried boats need no more cult. For all the forces
at play in this wide theater, its spaciousness declares
a propertyless state. May I now take up
the violin that nearly came to me at age ten,
my maternal uncle's gift? brought ceremoniously
on a special visit, yet it went back with him, the fact of it
raising an outsize grief in my mother for herself, perhaps.

Rest in peace and the mystery, with the silent thing in its case.
Or may I pursue this engineering further? surrogate
for the womanly body of that fiddle gone downstream.
Yet they were building spirit reservoirs, surge tanks
for seam voltage, soul-welding solar granaries, and one architect
had been chief priest. The hand tracking shadow at Dashur
from rod to rod for the foundation's first course of stones
may have held a lamp for priests in the last chamber
as rare privilege—for their ordained invocations
tested by many sequencings, happiness on alert
through ordeals, the chances awful and the aim real.
I woke with the sand grains of his destiny alive
across my maroon blanket, mustard golden spores
thrown over him by the king, a gift of land to that
Dear Friend. Deir of the geometries. His eye through the pile,
its red slope, the Forty-Three: design stabilizes the *mana*
of earth lofted into fire's force and held there,
steadies the dangerous changes. Guards against them
even before the end, so that a fine instrument
recharged and tuned during the royal run but at last
taken away may morph to mastery in some other walk
by another sea. May turn—mangled god—mischance into the path.
For this I sing: Deir of the triangle with plumb line
portable and pendulous in his eye's mind intending
this for the powers, the king and people, the realms
interlocking, past calamities, through dynasties dangling
in the shaky cycles of order.
                            I took from his case the still shiny
stream-bottom varnish of the thing and chin-clasped it
per his instruction, and before setting it back in the inky
blue plush drew one long wavery whine
from the G string, pushing up slowly with the bow.
Delight broke from his face. The dark closure not yet
having come across hers, she parted her lips, eyebrows
arching expectantly. Labored, nursed, caressed, that sound
could go on past the end of its own curve, such was
its Pythagorean hint even in my raw hand,
animal miracle among the ratios.
Next morning it was gone. This then sing:
that were I to walk that sand's bandwidth between desert

and facing stone, I would tread neither the waste
nor the monument, but one string stretched like the dune's world
behind my barrier beach, scrub and wiry foliage
nestled minutely into pockets of the in-between
and giving ear steadfastly to immensity.
That close to forty-three degrees is where the G-string
lands a bow's tilt, as a pro will testify.
That even the smudge across her happiness, and the murderous
touch of *creatura*, and the inept weight of fate,
dissolve where the soul burns and melts, where tone
and overtone release each other, and if all stabilized things vanish
in the furnace, truing the line and lighting the chant
give love to the fire. An immense fragrance rose
from the violin case's dyed velvet, the sealed wood,
strings, rosin, fogged bakelite of the chin cup,
the untreated inner wood of the curved body,
the equine substance of the glue, the fluted pegs,
ivory nut to tauten the pale sheaf of horsetail,
and a man's sweat and breath, when he opened these to me.
I have not imagined myself long in the burial chamber,
neither as carver nor priest, and only for a brief spell as builder
scanning the ceiling slab for telltale cracks. A vast
aroma lifted from that case among the bright faces.

GRAPHOLOGY 100: SALT SYSTEMICS

John Kinsella

Crystallography. Archway. Transgression.
Slip on the crust as underfoot a slick mud.
Underfoot a bottle unbroken down like
the box, house, even bricks: in channelling,
ditch diggers, to drain
into the Avon, a drainage bonanza, a sluicing
and discharge frenzy, a dance of gouging, cutting, ramming,
ripping, removing: so visitors might wonder,
an aesthetic. In the horror, pure beauty.
New Holland honey-eater curved beak picking at wattle, sucking
up brine and sap in the resonating flute. Aliens have sex there,
and from a gully
you might watch.
You might touch the opened earthquake parts.
You might facilitate. Beyond the traps,
the rabbits, the foxes.
The dam heavier, lighter than the Dead Sea. Flint stones,
struck rock chips kindred, corroding
if that's the word for it, transliterated.
How many stars guided under, a mass like rings outside the telescope,
haloes of expansiveness, the trees sparse on horizons,
inclement. Fragments of restitution, as if revenge
is a savage, resilient scrub, salt-tolerant,
begrudgingly succulent, poison to humans and stock.

History is absurdity. History is the scrub grappled out of its holds. History is the urge
to get the last tree out despite the tractor bogging down lower than its traction
point;
        history is overlay; history is rummage in the delicate lattice-work of salt, the
pluralism of crystals reaching out, so inclined to externals, a building erosion
that is so dialectic, if you want to play with words
when it gets so hot white blood cells
are not whiter. It's all white, glaring, burning,
like skin cells being stretched to breaking point, and then breaking.

The camera dulled down and no body-lines precise, not line
sharpened by excessive light: to fuck here is to risk
sterility.
                She-oak islands. So thin the fertility they manage,
small birds attracting eagles
with nowhere to nest.

Through the swamp grasses that spike in low-ground
chemical water, an oily film
tidal and Sargasso beneath the colorful horns of Christmas spiders,
the perky vauntings of stilted plovers, swathes of gnat anarchy, caught en-bulk,
but so singular, so crazy in their range, specific and motivated. Through swamp grasses
that are Christian in their rending, a castigating breeze that is only of the salt,
a low over crystals, a glare trough or soul movement
we can see, though maybe at dusk when shadows
run without trees, hearing it: midday sun
like shell casings, ejected twenty-two brass pedestals,
greening at the edges. And then nothing, so open to run across
attracts nothing.

As said to the army boys and their word orders of warning,
their words of combative dawning, the enemy over ridge
and under leaf, there's none of that left here now: stripped bare,
it's like a Freudian vacuum, a scouring post analysis,
a bursting out of the body that drains you dry
of all magnesium. Prophetically,
it's a madness, a journal entry on a journey
always inland, where seeing the edge of your expedition
is no comfort, always inland.

Out there, you can see who's approaching. Mulga parrot, zebra finch,
black-faced woodswallow, clamorous reed warbler... shadow paralepsy,
retrovirus in lively concentrated color array, so seemingly plural
in brevity, islands of samphire and introduced grasses, clever with insects. The magnetic
properties of salt are barely understood. A medium has more powers and ectenic forces
correlate: I left the argument so explosive with love
I went nowhere, and touched nothing: no walls, not sensation of salt panels

crunching underfoot. Kind of like swimming,
but caught up in voices. They were very much alive,
I was dead, even if swimming. A vast amount of energy was generated. I could see it,
feel it like the salt burning my skin. It wasn't touching me though, and I couldn't touch it.
You know,
the blood-orange effusion of sunset where vistas have been blown open,
where creeds and God colorations
watch faith into crops no longer connected to their origins.
A fusion reactor, cold if touch could be imagined. And the dead imagine
the other dead so full of life the sunsets
are sanguine. A connection has been shorted, and everywhere live wires kicking
off water, the sodden low ground in a drought-ridden zone. It says modernism was for
fascists and those who didn't have to work for a living. Post-moderns
are architects.

Salinity is not a problem. Salinity engenders no strategy. Sodium burns in air, in water. It
is popular. Chlorine cleanses swimming pools. Kills in war stories.
Uncle Harold was shot, his buddies elsewhere chlorinated.
And here, stable, innocuous. Little goes there.

Hansard. Dante. Johnny Cash. Ernie Bridge's pipeline. How I remember is a lens
and a mirror, is a solid dissolving and re-forming out of solution. My uncle, cousins, the
tractor—the kings of the tractor—the followers with skills
less useful, a mnemonic step in gum boots hacking with mud clots,
on the edge of paddocks sown for bread,
sown for fodder, wandoo fence-posts bleached
and anatomical: all the saids, obviousnesses. A tour.
I don't want to be anywhere else, and the health is a parody of growth. A profit
of healing. You could build over the lot and the ball of the earth
is about gravity and no more. Holding companies.
Riff-raff refrain in drunkenness, where no audience
but a nankeen night heron knowing crustaceans in the dam's abandoned
waters, even stream below feeding thirst-crushers. Palliatives and cheeky
red-capped robins, cheeky in its own fraternity, this bright male
jester. It's not. It's a comparison made from loneliness, or a desire for understanding.
You won't understand this. There's a place in our galaxy—our other place
in the galaxy—where palinodes remember us and spend all capital
at hand getting here. Arriving, they can neither be seen nor heard,

they congregate on the salt and have sex
because there's nothing else to do before they starve to death. It's the logical end
to a lifelong journey.

What's polished in the hubbub of family, of travel,
of earning a living. What garnishes creeks, spray residues, corneal grafts?
To love in all of that is so effusive, coming across as else-wise.
A jargon of tree stumps burnt out to generations.
Traps limbering on fencelines.
Marsupials co-existing and lost.
A day book, tallying of prices diversifying in pacts of ants: multiple varieties,
few discovered, items
of obstetrics and men birthing illnesses, as if the ache of a child's face
looking up isn't enough. These earners,
these map-pins and speculum-makers. Salt-births, spontaneous regeneration of flies:
and there's proof of this and that.

Avant-garde isn't the page. It's not carving up the
salt with the one-tine plough, or contour banks of argument,
it's flows and distribution outside the sheets, on the edges. We know this.
It's what you eat, what you do and don't say. Poets never have it, nor
the absolute metal of a plough, names we might recognise. Actinic. Hiding
the black.

REVERBERATIONS

Steve Timm

How can you speak without ears
the science of ergonymistry.
Oh father a limning of the reaching
of forgetting. The right
translation in the wrong
mouth. The hilarious alibi
like a leper dressed in cellophane. Sirens
rap. Logose. Ode to
—& from. *Of course.* Oh
to ear the foam cursing
veining the name of gravity
or its stoplight opposite. The trials
that time souls. Lone
souls alone in loneliness the lexi
con sez the walls of
talk back.

How can you not
back talk
sazz the ear in its lonitude. The moon
goes full one night
then it's clouds the next the next the next
(ask a german symp/hon/ath/ist). Your pain
is your pain. Uns
pea
kable
a method of clover to stretch
the death of winter
as though not a solitary
bird among the limp
leaf.

Not
as final as one'd think not
as onely as an end. Go along, boy, you brother me. Wolf
-boy stranded mid us humans
itchy ears like a deaf spy. Spry
holo thusiast set back the whole
bangshe gled
bun. Rare avid pion
eer tricking streams
for leads. The furled
reaches. The retched echoes
of the never herd.

Sweet nothings when/
sweet nothing-wens like
on a face in a folk
tale from somewhere
in Asia you can't remember
can you than. These are the doses
that top our drums. The roses
our dooms. Ellipsis
the devil's work ours to find
where the three quashed beats be
long. Where longing
beats. Beats all.

Utterly hopeful. They hand you
a ticket—Salt Lake City, Tuscaloosa
or is it Tangiers, Fish Creek, Nth Street. Oh, it
—it matters. The train the young woman
telling her hair the old
operalovers tacit helping
coats on the you the
I. It is not like going to work
it is not like enforcement. A cardinal in a heated
birdbath in the shallows
of a mild winter
neither. We each
claim our *nor* the sound
of in a language I for
get light.

THE GENERAL SILENCE

Simeon Berry

> More people had died in the Leningrad blockade
> than have ever died in a modern city—anywhere—anytime:
> more than ten times the number who died in Hiroshima.
> —Harrison Salisbury

Not the first time a Russian city was exiled into apotheosis. When the Red Army cast the White Army out of Odessa, they threw thousands overboard with weights. Divers saw them walking across the bottom of the harbor toward the city, waving their arms wildly against their chains.

Quieter here, in Leningrad—*Peter's cursed error* he built on the swamp while serfs ate baked clay instead of bread. *In an ancient book it is written:* the Panzer 103rd will founder, but the sideshow goes feral long before: the death-throes of the zoo elephant go on for hours, frozen sparrows leave their light bones in mid-air.

The silence is total, music left to those who walk upright, to Shostakovich, and the practicality of the concert notes: *The 1st violin is dying, the drummer died on the way to work. The French horn is near death.* Outside the auditorium, the stacked dead ring like metal when dropped.

Hunger psychosis, faces staring black with frost, the held gaze on infinite regress. A million gone in the streets. Dead crowds orchestrated by a blizzard's slow carousel. The painter can't help himself. Winter is ending, he has to stop the only other person in the park: *You understand. It is all strange, it is all alarming. But the sky is quiet as always.*

History is out of gear. For weeks after he drowns in the sub, the poet mails his wife letters. She hallucinates salt gritting the words, the envelope sealed with an indrawn breath. Vishnevskaya keeps watch by her stove with the circle of rats, thinking through post-mortem grammar: *Near death the diminutives, the suffixes increase. My little stove. My littlest door. My smallest one.*

RECONSTRUCTION

Simeon Berry

For the sake of argument, let's say you actually talked about those
who drank, like your Dad, how he moved through its liquid translations
from the speech of the drowned, and made your words light up

your lungs like tracers. Or why your brother kept his buzz-cut short,
cultivated a stare like a prisoner of war in a tiger pit, reconstructing
chess games while the rain wraps steel thread around the bamboo:

*King's rook, Knight four, Queen's pawn. You must be exact, you must know
it's all in the wrist,* how two shots of glazed vodka can unbalance
an evening. Or why, after five years of winning riding competitions,

you stopped when the fear of horses suddenly masked your fingers.
How anagrams grew to cover half of every page of notes you took.
I think I had only one chance to know: when you wrote the paper

on Mithridates and brought along the overdue book as evidence
of your passion, where you'd laid down neon over all the passages
describing how he sampled so many poisons they wouldn't kill him

when he finally wanted them to. I faltered, told you I used to fall asleep
by imagining myself sealed into a capsule the size of a coffin bed
and hurled out into space, into the perfect either/or. We stood

on the night pier with your immune king and my body ark, watching
the partial prints of jellyfish glow in the current, as if the water
had been gripped by someone who wanted very badly to live.

YOUR THIN GRANDMOTHER

Frances Sherwood

Thanksgiving was when she asked me. We were in the kitchen, she on a stool by my counter, I rinsing dishes to put in the dish washer and weary from making the pies—a pumpkin, a pecan, and a custard-coconut from a Bisquick recipe and doing the table á la *Family Circle*—corn cobs dressed as pow-wow Indians, their eyes bright red tacks, swatches of green felt wrapped around for miniature blankets, pilgrims from wooden spools found at the Goodwill.

"Like to drive me to the Women's Clinic, like tomorrow?" Nina asked.

Nina and her family—Mark, and their two sons, Dali and Duchamp—had been responsible for the turkey. They planned to roast it in a hole in their backyard Hawaiian luau-style. I could have told them our Massachusetts ground was too frozen in November for a pit, but no, like '49ers intent on gold, the two boys took turns with a pickax, the pale carcass wrapped in tin foil patiently lying on the ground beside them. At the last minute, they had to throw the cold bird into the oven turned full blast, burning the skin to a crisp, leaving the inside bloody raw, delivering it, Happy Thanksgiving, with a bottle of blueberry schnapps. I ate it faithfully. My husband, John, and my daughters, didn't.

"The Clinic?" Naturally, the men were in the den watching the game. Kids were somewhere and Francisco, Nina's tenant, had ambled over to join the guys with a hardy ho-ho. He had done the turkey thing, he said at his mother's, but was hungry for dessert, a night cap.

"I love you, Connie," Francisco cooed. "Like a Mother, and Nina. . . like a . . . ." He wiggled his eyebrows provocatively, grabbing cookies like a bear fattening up for a long winter's nap.

"Are you escorting at the Clinic, Nina, is that why you want me to go with you?"

"Not exactly."

I had read in the *Telegram Gazette* that The Young Christians were having a marathon picketing at the Clinic the day after Thanksgiving. Volunteers were needed to shepherd clients in from the parking lot.

"Counseling?"

"Nope. You're my friend, aren't you? Jesus Christ, Connie, it's post Roe versus Wade."

Barely post Roe versus Wade. We were in the early '90s. To Nina, history started in the late '60s, the heyday of the "Movement"—Berkeley,

Ann Arbor, Madison. The most I did during those exciting times was go to Catholic grammar school in my pleated skirt, participate in Spelling Bees. Now in Worcester, I helped out at the Rescue Mission, contributed conscientiously to the local PBS station during pledge week "Everything will be all right," we could hear one of her sons, Duchamp, singing from upstairs, but, of course, Bob Marley was dead of cancer. Duchamp, wearing a spiked dog collar, a reggae tam, and one dripping earring, looked like a grown boy nostalgic for dress-up games. Nina wore the other one of the pair of earrings, explaining that they were in son/mother matching outfits. My husband, John, was not amused. They're our next door neighbors, I had justified, be a sport.

"Is Mark using the car, Nina? Can't you use the bread truck?" It seemed that I wouldn't be able to get all the dishes in the dishwasher, would have to do it in two shifts.

"Mark is in a mood, and I won't be well enough." Nina was fiddling with her wire-framed glasses, rubbing the lens on her sweat shirt, holding them up to the light.

Mark was prone to depression through association, Nina genetically inclined. Every afternoon, after her bread route was over, she arrived on my doorstep to deliver the state of the union address, updating me on her battle with the Big D, no details withheld. Of course, there were times I was not in a great mood myself, but it never got to the dramatic extent Nina experienced. My daughters, Sophia and Theresa, teenage Curious Georges, using John's binoculars for bird watching, were able to keep tabs on additional doings and ditties next door since Nina and Mark did not bother with bourgeois amenities such as shades or curtains. Nina liked to say: My life is an open book, take no prisoners. My life was an open book, too, but not an exciting one. At six in the morning, if they were ambitious enough, my two girls could catch Nina and Mark hopping into their big, square bread trucks, twin, rusty red missiles. Side by side, barreling out to the bread warehouse, they picked up the loaves to deliver to supermarkets in the area before the first customer. Nina said she liked to work for her bread like a real person.

"Francisco will not be able to drive, either."

Francisco, the tenant, had joined the men in the den.

"Since when has Cat-man-do not been well enough to drive? What am I missing here?"

"Shell-shock."

I thought perhaps Francisco's sleepy ways had something to do with marijuana. The one time I tried it, at Nina's insistence, I wanted to lie down in the middle of the day. Anyway, Nina and Mark let Francisco, a Conceptual Artist, live free of charge in exchange for fixing up the basement. Which he was slow at because his creative time was best spent constructing installations of Styrofoam named after great lovers, Palo and Francisca, Eloise and Abelard, Romeo and Juliet, a series to be submitted to the Whitney Biannual. Nina had to explain to me what an honor that would be, and how talented Francisco was, for I, not knowledgeable about art, mainly viewed him as a serious keeper of cats—twenty, not counting drop-ins for meals and mating – he, himself resembling his brood mare, Beany, with his droopy underbelly and a sleepy, stupid smile.

"Cats don't care," Francisco once informed me. "They even do it with their kids."

"I didn't know Francisco was interested in 'Woman's Right to Her Body'." I could see something would have to be done with the turkey leftovers. I could chop them, fry them with onions and potatoes, make soup out of them, or throw them out the window.

"Hell, Connie, Francisco is the prime suspect." Tina gave me a satisfied little smirk.

I opened a cupboard, stared hard at my everyday china thinking of the years of meals, breakfast, lunch and dinner, eggs and sandwiches, casseroles, a steady march to the nearest graveyard. My husband was allergic to nuts, and my daughter, Sophia, was lactose intolerant, and Theresa was on Atkins. I read about diets in magazines. Nina said it was a state of mind, said I had to think thin.

"Are you saying I'm too over the hill for birth control, Connie? Francisco is really cute in the buff, you know."

"Is that so?" I was not a very good judge of male beauty. But I admired Nina's energy. My husband and I had been married for over seventeen years.

"It will only take an hour max; you can get back in time for your soaps."

"Thanks." I have never watched a soap opera in my life, except on Masterpiece Theater, and Nina knew it.

The roar of a touchdown emanating from the den, lapped into the kitchen. Nina pushed her glasses on the top of her head, gave me her nearsighted look. "Remember that Hemingway story, 'White Elephants,' when the guy is trying to convince the girl to do it, a little air in, out. No Biggie. Zip, zap."

"But, the guy in the Hemingway story didn't know what he was talking about, Nina, and the girl. . . The *girl* in the story was scared."

"Be a pal, Connie."

"There must be somebody else you can ask, Nina."

"You're my best friend, right? Right?"

"I am your friend.

"So what's the problem? It's not like you are doing it yourself."

"It's just that. . ."

"You practice birth control, right."

"Yes."

"Do you tell your priest?"

"Of course not."

"Well then."

I looked closely at Nina, trying to see pregnancy softening her face, filling out her body, but she was as thin and girlish as ever, her sharp face cutting the air like scissors through paper. She still wore bangs, a high pony tail, but most of all, she was eager, forever the earnest graduate student she was once. Keeping her dissertation, she recounted to me, during those precomputer days, in the fridge against fire, in a safety deposit box against theft, and under the bed to slip out at convenient moment to show off to admirers. Speaking of which, she slept with everybody on her thesis committee, which is, she confided, what people did in those days.

"Even the women?" I had asked, thrilled. Nina's area of study at Berkeley was Early Childhood Development and I couldn't imagine a womenless Dissertation Committee.

"Thighs were in," Nina went on. "We looked like drum majorettes in our miniskirts. A bump, a bump, a bump, bump, bump."

Despite the fact that she was my senior by a good ten years, Nina *could* be imagined as a majorette in white boots with tassels on them, or as a kid jump-roping red hot peppers till she fell from exhaustion, or as a Girl Scout honor bright, her beret slightly askew, a devilish glint in her eye. She put her coffee cup down on my butcher block kitchen table from Williams-Sonoma. Material things, she once told me, will possess you, and I knew she was right. She picked her furniture at St. Vincent de Paul, wore castoffs. All her possessions, which she said were merely temporary were recycled, and each item was rich in history, the rings on her table, the scuffs on her chairs, the spots on her mattress, her books from the library sale. My husband, John did not share my admiration, said he didn't know how they could live that way. Even the washer and dryer in the basement, in Francisco's "apartment" amid the cat litter containers, were from the used appliance store.

"God will reward you for your good deed."

"Sure."

I didn't sleep a wink that night. Around two, I slipped out of bed, drove to the Holy Cross campus in my robe, went to their church because all other Catholic churches in town were locked. But Our Lady, overseeing her corner of candles in serene alabaster, cloaked in baby blue, although available, offered small comfort. A guard asked what I was doing there.

"Praying," I answered.

I was praying for the usual things, Nina and her family, and also, a kind of dispensation, if you will, for I would be aiding and abetting the enemy, going against policy, practice, all that I had been taught and a good deal of what I felt. My last prayer was that I wouldn't see Father Michael or anybody else from my church.

My luck, the next day, there were some familiar faces among the Young Christians. Out in force, they were wearing choir robes, some dragging heavy crosses and others carrying big pickle jars of diluted catsup, or maybe it was real blood. Nobody could get through, although standing in the horseshoe shaped parking lot, not knowing whom to serve and protect, was a team of Worcester's Finest. The "Woman's Right to her Body Coalition," in a half crouch position, arms linked, legs together so that nobody could charge in from ranks of Young Christians to kill a doctor, surrounded the building and were chanting in unison:

"Hey, hey, what do you say? Coat-hangers make the day?"

As we approached a Young Christian, a middle aged man, lunged at us. "Murderer, murderer," he spat.

"Racist, misogynist fascist," Nina taunted back.

The Woman's Body Coalition chorused: "Five, six seven, eight, go home and masturbate."

Francisco looked like he wished he had thought of that earlier.

"Maybe we should go home."

"Shut up, Francisco," Nina said.

Francisco—Mr. Cool Cat, the ogre under the bridge, who goes there? Which is where it probably happened when Nina came down to do the laundry. Nina didn't fold anything, or believe in ironing. I wish I could be less obsessive about wrinkles. Anyway, they must have "done it" amid the dunes of cat crap and shadowed by the piled cardboard boxes, the cat condos. If they hadn't used the basement, it could have been the bedroom while Mark was out drinking in his bread truck, or sobering up in his "den," a bear's lair of baseball memorabilia. Mark was like a big bear himself, shaggy and handsome, and he could recite poetry, had studied the classics at Princeton, went to graduate school at Berkeley, same as Nina. In the summer he rested himself out back in the hole Dali and Duchamp had started to dig as a swimming pool—Mark and The Czarina, their pet beagle at incline on the sides of the pool in the shade of the lilac bushes which divided our yards. Our garden featured tulips in the spring, roses in the summer and lilies in the fall. My husband was a master gardener, wrote the gardening column that ran in several papers. Summer now seemed a million miles away.

Nina and I prepared to make a break, but the picket line was too thick and the crosses the kids were dragging looked like what they were—instruments of torture. Strains of song from the other group "we are young and old together/we are gay and straight together," wafted sweetly over our heads.

"I wish they would stop singing," Francisco moaned.

"Shut up, Francisco," Nina said.

"If we break through the picket line and accidentally brush against somebody, would that count as assault?"

"Shut up, Francisco."

Then, finally, two of the Woman's Right protectors left the human barricade they had formed against the wall of the Clinic, parted the line of pickets, saw us safely across to no man's land.

"It will be over before we know it," Francisco consoled us all as we entered the drafty, darkened hallway.

"Shut up, Francisco."

Then we were in the "reception" area, which had the feel of a locker room for an under-funded girls' sport in a rinky-dink school, a hefty and rather mature team, by the looks of it, the game lost.

"You have to take a number," a large white woman told us. "Up there." She looked like a Michelin man in her down winter coat.

Facing the rows of folding metal chairs was an unattended desk with a little number rack. White plastic disks with the numbers in bold red hung like the deli counter at Goretti's Supermarket. Nina was number 16. They were calling out 8. We settled in. Mark and Francisco were the only two men there and everybody looked at them with curiosity and approval.

"Are you sure you want to go through with this, Nina?" My stomach suddenly was betraying me. "One more kid is all, you already have the room. I could be the babysitter. Once babies come, people love them, they can't help it."

"Be a pal and stop trying to convert me, okay?" She showed me her pointy teeth. "Okay?"

"Okay."

"I've run with the bulls, posed nude for art classes, I've told you that."

"You have." She was an exceptionally brave woman.

Another time she told me that she had decided as a kid when she read

the Dorothy Parker line—"men don't make passes at girls who wear glasses"—that *she* would make the passes. In the end, she did not get her Ph.D.
because Mark arrived on the scene. Together they made bricks for the Peace
Corps in Barbados, followed by L.A., scriptwriting, then driving in four
furiously rainy days and nights to New York for years of editing legal documents third shift. Mark, who actually had a Ph.D. in American Culture,
became an academic gypsy, teaching here, there, and everywhere. Dali and
Duchamp were born in New Mexico and Montana, respectively.

Then last December, during a huge blizzard, John and I getting ready
for bed, I sitting at my dressing table putting on hand-lotion and night
cream, John plucking the grey out of his eyebrows in the bathroom, we
heard a clanking and chugging in the driveway next door. A car dragging a
muffler rolled in. A woman crawled out of the front, saw me looking out
the window, waved as if she had just pulled into Shangri-La, she her own
welcome wagon. I knew immediately that we would be friends. Soon, a
grand piano arrived. It actually had belonged to Nina's father, who was a
doctor. They cut the legs down so the kids could practice cross-legged on
the floor, and my daughters also observed Dali putting a garter snake down
his underpants.

"What's a little pain, Nina?"

"Shut up, Francisco."

The woman sitting in the row before us, gave us another look.

"It hurts?" Nina squeaked out.

"Damn straight," the woman said.

Mark and Francisco slipped down in their seats. They were holding
hands.

"Want a sip?" The woman handed Nina a thermos.

"What is it?"

"Vodka, honey. Take a shot."

"Will it help?"

"A candy bar will help."

"I'll go to the liquor store, buy some booze."

Nina gave Francisco a poke with her elbow, and he slumped back down
with a sigh, began to stroke his face. I will not say Francisco has a beard because beard would be a euphemism. More like patches, tufts, sprouts of fur
scattered haphazardly. Meanwhile, Mark had stuck his fingers in his ears as
if he were watching a scary movie and not to hear the creepy music lessened
the horror.

The woman gave me a once over like I had done something to cause
all this, then darted a glimpse at Mark and Francisco, because now the two

men were holding hands again and Mark was humming his favorite song, "Sunrise, Sunset" from *Fiddler on the Roof.*

"The thing is they will at least be giving me something for the pain," Nina said, "and if I mix that with alcohol, I might go into a coma."

"You wish." The woman turned back to her two children who were busy with their coloring books.

"I took a good shower this morning," Nina offered.

Compared to Nina I was obsessively neat. The last time I had seen Nina's upstairs bathtub it was full of clothes, books, ashtrays and newspapers, the curtains drawn, Nina's idea of cleaning house. My husband, John, won't set foot in Nina's house. Furthermore, he does not think that it is legal to have commercial vehicles parked in our residential neighborhood and, occasionally, threatens to call code enforcement on their bread trucks. Actually, he doesn't know that when the cops arrested Mark for disorderly conduct, he had hidden himself in the back of his truck, hunkered down among the metal bread racks shouted: "You won't take me alive." Nina wanted me to help her bail him out, and although I dreaded being one of the people who go to the police station, I went with her.

There were other times as well, one requiring a lengthy sojourn on the Psych Ward of Mass General and weeks of nightly AA meetings for him and Al-Anon meetings for Nina, which she said was a dating service, because everybody had everybody's phone number. Several men contacted Nina, she told me, which did not surprise me one bit. Mark had even been to a rehabilitation place. I envisioned it a kind of Betty Ford Clinic. Nina said it was more like a funny farm, the kind you'd read about in a Raymond Carver story with old guys out on the porch in rocking chairs crying in their 7-Up. Nina could make anyplace interesting just by her description.

At the moment, Mark, sober, a green-grey cast to his face, was in clean jeans and a grey sweat shirt that said Holy Cross, just the outfit for an abortion clinic. Francisco was in his painting clothes, not the white clothes of a painter who paints houses, but bohemian black. Black chinos and a black turtle neck into which he was retracting his neck. Are you a cat or a turtle, I wanted to ask.

"Sure you don't want to go to my doctor for this, Nina?"

Nina always went to clinics, didn't believe in private medicine, but, I thought, in this case, that she could compromise her principles.

"Connie, you always believe in comfort," she accused.

She was right. I spoiled myself.

"Hey," the large woman said. "She's not supposed to be coming out the front entrance. They have a back exit." She pointed to a woman coming down the hallway holding on to the wall for dear life and walking as if she had ten sanitary pads wedged between her legs, which she probably did.

"I need a fucking cigarette," Mark muttered, putting his fingers in his ears again.

"Don't worry, folks, no way am I going to be hobbling out like that."

But Nina came out worse.

And the trip home seemed forever.

And I prayed that nobody was about with the binoculars when we pulled up in Mark and Nina's driveway.

"Upsy daisy," Mark said, lifting his wife out of the car, grabbing the pillows I had brought. Nina, all bird-bone and beak, was carried with ease up the stairs and put her on the mattress in their bedroom.

"What happened?" Duchamp wanted to know.

"Mommy just had an abortion," Mark said.

Duchamp was wearing his spike bracelet, the one he had dipped in mashed potatoes and eaten from during Thanksgiving and he began hitting himself with it.

"Stop that this instant," his father said.

"If you need me," Francisco said. "I mean, if I can help, I'll be down in the dungeon."

"You've helped enough," I replied tartly.

"I guess, then, it's *au revoir* and *auf wiedersehen*, adios and *ciao*."

"What's wrong with Du?" Dali emerged from his room. Unlike Duchamp, Dali always wore a buttoned-up shirt, carried a kid's brief case to school. A prodigy, he had built a giant Lego city in the basement, fixed the mother board of their secondhand computer himself. When of legal age, he was going to change his name to something like Newton, he told my daughters.

"I better see to the boys." Mark went down the stairs.

Then, quite suddenly it was quiet. Looking through Nina's window towards my own bedroom, instead of concentrating on Nina, I remembered that Sophia was conceived shortly after I met John. He said we were going to get married someday anyway. It just put up the date by about three or four years. We were married in his church, the Greek Orthodox, the whole service chanted. John told me that the first time he heard an organ in church he nearly jumped out of his skin. On Greek Easter when he was a kid, they all had to go outside the church, run around it six times.

"You were right after all, Connie. It wasn't like in that story by Hemingway, when the guy says, they just let a little air in. They take the air out, do it with a vacuum, The Hoover Maneuver."

"Mom, would you like to have some tea?" Dali poked his head around the door.

"Thanks, Dal, that would be great."

The poster above Nina's bed, mattress rather, was Che Guervera. At one time every campus bookstore in the country sold them. Poor fellow died of an asthma attack. How many Saturday mornings had I spent in the Emergency Room of St. Vincent's Hospital with Sophia's asthma's attacks. Once, when I didn't think it was that bad, John had been the one to rush her to the hospital, save her life, something I'll never forgive myself for, and for which John will always be my hero. On my bedroom wall there are prints by Romare Bearden of women ironing, washing dishes, which I framed myself at the Ye Olde Framers Workshop. They reminded me of my mother.

"It *was* a vacuum cleaner," Nina looked better as she sat up and drank the tea Dali had brought her. "but it felt like fire going in. Like the flame thrower we saw in the World War I *Masterpiece Theater.* I thought I was going to die in the trenches."

"You didn't." I squeezed her hand.

"There you are up in the saddle staring at the holes in the asbestos. Somebody comes by, swoops away the bottle, but you see it, Connie, shreds, patches, a bucket of blood."

"I'm so sorry, Nina," was all I could think to say.

"It's not your fault, Connie."

"Shh." I stroked her arm. I wanted to say something, but I am not good with words, although at U Mass I started as a French major, had taken two years in high school, was supposed to spend my junior year in Paris. One day they changed the classroom of my French III class and it being the rule in the department only to speak *Français*, I spent three days unsuccessfully trying to find the correct room. Finally, I went into the woods around the observatory, sat on a bench and had a good cry. John came along on his way to his Business Administration class. I don't know why, but I suddenly burst into tears right there when I was supposed to be strong for Nina.

"Not the waterworks; come on Connie." She laughed, coughed, winced in pain, had to put the mug of tea on the floor by the side of her mattress. I got some Kleenex out of my purse so she could blow her nose, went to the bathroom and looked, to no avail, for a washrag to wipe her face. When I came back into her bedroom, Dali and Duchamp had dragged in their sleeping bags and were setting up beside the mattress. The Czarina had ensconced herself in with Nina on the mattress, her head on a pillow. The dog began to snore, and under the covers, wiggle her tail, feet, give little yelps.

"Do dogs dream?" Duchamp asked.

"For sure," Nina answered.

"A nice warm house," I offered.

"Running away," Dali chimed in.

"Eating mud," Duchamp suggested, for he, too, ate mud, paper. My daughters had seen him.

"Getting petted," Mark, who had snuggled in on Nina's other side, added.

It was getting dark; I had to go home, see about dinner. Tiptoeing down the stairs, out of the house, I closed their door quietly, got in my car and drove into my own driveway. My story was to be that I had gone to the Mall to do Christmas shopping. That was what you are supposed to do the day after Thanksgiving. Now, I would have to smile mysteriously as if all the secrets in the world were hidden in the trunk of the car. Fortunately, John did not look up from the TV when I came in. They were doing a football score rundown.

"Sophia, Theresa," I called.

"They went to a flick, a Frenchy, *Entre Nous*."

Both my girls, still in high school, already spoke better French than I ever did. Sophia was born in Amherst, when John was finishing up his degree. Teresa came into being without premeditation, too, but, at least, by then we were married. No Teresa, no Sophia? Unthinkable.

"What's for dinner, Constance?"

Not being able to face the turkey, I opened the cupboard and took out a can. I heated the chili in the microwave, grated some cheese over it, and put the whole concoction on toast, with a sliver of pickle on the side.

"*Là pièce de résistance*," I said setting the tray down in front of John in the den.

While he ate, I put the dirty dishes from breakfast into the dishwasher, cleaned the counters, sponged down the stove, played the phone messages back. My mother, who had spent Thanksgiving with my sister in L.A., was going to do all her Christmas shopping when she arrived to stay with us in Worcester. She had raised the two of us alone, and now we couldn't spoil her enough. My reading group was meeting on Wednesday, a message said. The book was *Ya-Ya Sisterhood*. There was a meeting for Concerned Catholic Mothers.

"Milk," John roared.

When I brought it in, and leaned down to place the glass on the coffee table, he lifted my skirt up, gave me a little whack on the *derriere*.

"You still have a gorgeous ass, Constance."

I knew what was to follow.

"So how about it?"

"I'm not in the mood."

"Oh, so we have moods here, too, do we. Suit yourself."

I went back to the kitchen, sat at the counter. A full moon illuminated the dead leaves which flooded Nina's swimming hole. I thought I saw the wisp of a little ghost, fragile as smoke, float up and out of Nina's bedroom window. Then, I saw a shadow which materialized into Francisco skirting the swimming hole and dodging the bare bones of the lilac bushes.

"Francisco." The last person in the whole world I wanted to see.

He plopped himself down on a stool, opened my cookie jar and took out a cookie in the shape of a pilgrim hat. Above us, I could hear the exercise bike in the bedroom going a mile a minute.

Francisco reached for his second cookie, a turkey.

"It could have been Mark's. *Anybody*, Connie," he said.

"I don't want to hear another word out of you, Francisco."

"Whatever."

"Nina is a big girl. Bigger than you think."

"She's not a giant, is she?"

"I'm splitting to Seattle."

"Good for you."

He ambled out with a handful of cookies, disappeared into the hedges. I set the dishwasher, went into the living room. In front of the house, the sidewalk, tinged with frost, gleamed with malice. I left the front lights on for the girls, dragged myself upstairs. Mark was already in bed. I put on my nightgown, the one with roses all across the front, the one I made myself, got in beside him, turned off my light. Across the room, I could see the family pictures stuck in the dresser mirror curlyqueing up at the edges. There were some from our trip to Greece, the four of us standing in front of the Parthenon. There was one photo of me and John, and for some reason, the lighting, something, our legs were faded off. Not a leg to stand on. I would have to destroy that picture, for I looked fat in it. Already I had weeded through the albums. I wanted to be remembered thin. Your thin grandmother.

"Have you always been faithful to me, John?" I said this out of the blue. The shells in the glass lamp by his side of the bed seemed to shift.

"I just want to know. It's okay . . ."

When he turned to me at that moment, I realized that his eyebrows grown together at the bridge of his nose were too grey to pluck, that his eyes held fear. Dear God, the terrain had been smooth a moment before, and I had planted land mines.

"You don't have to tell me," I said quickly, wanting to swallow back my dumb words.

"I *want* to tell you."

I braced myself.

"Connie." He took my head in his hands. "How could I be unfaithful to you, to the girls, to the family. I would see the Virgin Mary before me if I did anything to hurt you. I have too much self-respect."

I didn't know if the sudden sinking feeling was relief, or utter dismay, because for some reason I felt like crying. But I didn't; of course I didn't. I had cried at Nina's. That afternoon, before Mark, the boys and The Czarina came upstairs to keep her company, she whispered, as if she had won the game after all, "I want to feel bad, but I don't. I'm a player, Connie, I'm still a player."

A Fragment of Culture II

Regina Derieva

then the character started being ruined,
hearing got worse, vision fell off.
But what to do if in Sparta
there were no temples or gardens?
But there was the law, otherwise there'd be
the precipice where they threw out the trash.
The pigeons pecked at millet
and the girls strutted wearing beads.
And the girls wanted money,
like birds of peace on a placard.
The person who tied together a common broom
spent an age in someone else's dressing gown.
And the authorities gave out homemade beer
and the guards leered crookedly
in the deserts, where the young men
marched in formation for the prospects of Sparta.
The world was built up anew
and took up almost the whole map.
Life became better, but nature
ran wild and couldn't get used to it.
The blind sullenly walked the map,
the sea answered the deaf.

Translated from the Russian by Richard McKane

HIGHLAND TOWN

Claudio Rodríguez

No air's so healthy
as in these places, but I haven't
come to recover from anything.
I come to grasp what deed
trembles in the light, what dark revolt
demolishes life in us today.
Here there are flags no more,
nor walls, nor towers, as if now
everything could withstand the thrust
of earth, the plundering
of sky. And our vision's
swept away, our bodies are
a free market, our voices, dwellings,
and love and years,
doors for one and a thousand to come in.
Yes, so rootless as always,
as we walk along the old streets today,
our heels are stained
with fresh grape, and we hear
those waters overflowing I know well,
the ringing riverbed of hearing.

It's alliance: this mountain
air with the tension of company.
And to know what distance
spreads from man to man, from one life to another,
what planetary range separates
two heartbeats, what vast expanse
looms between two looks
or from a mouth to a kiss.
What use are so many sordid
maps of towns sharply etched
beside rivers, founded
on separation, on rocky
pride?
Never houses: barracks,

never streets: trenches,
never a day's wage: a soldier's pay.
What good has so much fortress
been, deep moat, rugged battlement,
walled enclosure?
Fear, defense,
self-interest and vengeance, hate,
loneliness: here's what's made us
live in vicinity, not in company.
Such is the cruel scene
they left us to inherit. How,
then, can life here be fortified
if it's only alliance?

I'm facing your walls,
frontier town which the sky
never stops disturbing.
Old ambition admired
now only by tourist or archaeologist,
or somebody who fancies crests and coats-of-arms.
This is no national monument,
but the light on the high plains is,
the fresh air watering the dry lung,
filling and making it
sheer offerance renewed, a homeland
in open fields. Here there are no coasts, sea,
north or south; here everything's the stuff
of harvest. And if in a while
the time to go arrives,
good-bye to the strong ring
of air and gold of alliance, good-bye to the high hill
not a bastion, but company,
so long to so many men
unfreed until today. For everything
around is surrendering and there are no frontiers,
nor distance, nor history.
Only ravenous space and October's night dew
above these high fields
of our land.

—Translated from the Spanish by Louis Bourne

FENCE ON THE BORDER

Sheryl Luna

It is in the bending, in the pain,
the way old paint scrapes off wood,
and the way mothers light our way through time
on their way to small frailty.

And there's a halo about the painted head of Jesus
on the yellow wall of *Our Lady of the Valley* Church
where teachers make a pittance and live richly
in their work among brown faced children.

There's a burlap robe on the pilgrim
walking in sandals up Mount Cristo Rey
when the sunset blurs a perfect pink,
like the palm of god pressing down on the bent heads
of men and women who learn prayer amidst a harshness
I have yet to know. The barrio is full of narrow streets,
adobe homes, and sweet smelling yucca flowers
bud in the air like a rainy night.

There's a way the sand clings to the wind
and the sands brown the sky in a sadness
that sings some kind of endless echo of the border
where the chain-link fence stretches for miles
and miles and the torn shirts of men flap
from the steel like trapped birds.

The river is narrow and appears slow.
The cardboard shanties of Colonias unveiled
among the vast open desert like ants.

The faces of the poor smiling and singing
as if sunset were a gift; the desert blooms
red and white flowers of the thinnest sparest cacti,
as if ground-hogs lived coolly in the shadows of the earth.

And here, on Cinco de Mayo the cornea of god
glints faintly in a thin rainbow;
the hands of god rest over the blue hills,
the song of god in the throats of sparrows.

Bless You.
Bless You.

This is the way the border transfigures greed,
shapes it into something holy,
and road runners stand alert; even the pigeons soar
with something akin to the music of the spheres,
and Spanish flutters through the smoke,
and there is a strange burning through our small lives.

SONATA ON ORIGINAL SIN

Sheryl Luna

It was all gone: memory, time, trees.
The sea was imagined. Music
a fog, and although unwhole,
I'm quiet night. No red cauldron,
no lightening eye, no quick Jesus:

dance of mosquitoes, whirr of crickets,
the moon's fated face. The order of nature
streaks sky, rain falls to music, smoke
rises. Work, rest in the stab
of love. Hold yourself like a warm
blanket. The saving always slow. Your Guarded song
a space of self along borders.

Love is gone in work. Gone
in a pin-striped suit, the appearance
of slick shoes. Gone in the way we mouth
nothing to one another. Guarded back. Watch it. Watch it.
Stiff chin. False hair color. Hide it all.

Your body and eye. *Paint your eyes,*
my grandmother tells me.
Buy a girdle.
Are Death and beauty bought?

Speechless and slanted in the walk,
I jog now, feel my joints loosen
to the tune of suns.

Death and beauty bought in faces,
in handshakes, in flatteries and hurried steps
to buses in slick towns, where women
wear lip gloss and highlight hairs, the electric
pang of music running through veins.

You played trombone like a wounded animal.
I am remembering snow on your hair in the yard,
the trees too capped with it. And then you came
like a ceramic doll smiling, a music box, set
to play the same tune for years, until the break
that Fall.

Original sin fell from our lips. Now
I am cracked in red lipstick.
An old maid counting and loving stars
alone. Carpe diem! Old lantern, black and costly,
antique chevy. The rust of poverty like lost love,
empty fiberglass pools.

My face a butterfly rash. Lupus, then a lover lost.
Then came the ash. Oboe slowness——. The way
you walked your dog each night
over the ridge. Arroyo empty. Gutted.
Chain-linked razor-wire fence always mended
and tended. The weeds overgrown. The ache,
muscle sore to the bone. This is the way of borders.

A slow series of breaths rising, falling. The way things
thirst. Tree without green, window
with no curtain, dog left to die.

We have to know
how to play. Pour like water,
patter as rain.
Beethoven was deaf.

Be Light in the silence, light in the noise.
I hold my rosy cheeks, my butterfly shape.
In the mirror I more than peer.

Time is breath smoked away. We were young
and flowered. Once, we were silent
in a perfect trance of sleep.

Endless deep throated voices of rage
turned to snow one night. The voices of women nearby rose
lighthearted with the sparrows.
I mourn the way we were too afraid to kiss
beneath the oaks, the moon laughing,

the moon crying. Us at the center of the small
universe. We two stars lingered in the bodied voice
of time, rising from dirges and requiems
like dancing stars, or the chaos of a blood sonata.

BIRTHDAY ON MT. WASHINGTON

Keith Taylor

At 51 I'm satisfied to be
the slowest hiker on the slope,
satisfied to stop somewhere below
the summit's restaurant and parking lot
where others are pleased to see
the view from the highest place
on this part of their planet, mountains
falling off around them, blue and green,
in all directions. I'm satisfied
to keep my hike pristine,
if artificially so, satisfied
to sit at the bottom of a sea
of rock covering the quarter mile
to the top, to sit above the last
alpine meadow, beginning to bloom
just this month—purple lapland rosebay
as backdrop to diapensia:
small, white, threatened by the noisy world.
And I feel something
more than satisfaction—not
"euphoria," but that direction—
when a ruby throated hummingbird
zooms up the rocks, circles
my head looking for blossoms, darts down
over cliffs and krummholz balsam fir,
then dives for the flowered slopes below.

June 4, 2003

GUARDIAN RAPTORS

Maria Terrone

*"More than three million migratory birds... bald eagles
and raptors... pass by Detroit each year on their way to the
Mississippi or Atlantic flyways."*
—Nature Conservancy magazine

The raptors are cruising
   the city, hanging with gangs—
the raptors'-in-training
   own damned angels, guardians
against kindness and
   uninvited dangers of light:

the way an explosion of sun
   on a junkyard bumper
can trigger memory, spinning
   a child into view who laughed,
once, into a camera's flash.
   The raptors distract, swoop down,
smother the glow to ash.

   Contrary to popular belief,
proud angels did not fall to hell,
   but soar, still. You can see them
by the millions above the city,
   unfurling a canopy of rust-dark wings,
watching with fierce and brilliant eyes
   over the not-quite-damned
who cling to craggy stoops,
   gathering for the kill.

EMBER

Paulann Petersen

Let the sun rise and set
farther and farther south.
Let the days faster and faster
shrivel into dusk.
Sometimes my eyes work
on the fine world's print,
mostly not. Still,
each breath is a revelation
I've not breathed before.

This morning-come-lately,
the sun lobs a tree's
whole shadow-self against
an outer wall. Each leaf gives its
swaying sideshow of *Yes, let wind
pass through me*, or *No,
not yet, not now.*

A wind means one thing's
heating up, while another cools,
in uneven rate. I am *another*,
cooling down, click by
unsteady click—a last fever
lodged at the tip of my tongue.

ANTHEM

Paulann Petersen

Erotic thrum sounds
the names of this world
each moment.
Water, anther, belly.
Seed, stripling and *sun.*

Not merely our sex, no.
Never a *that* or a *this* only.
But earth's sex, the all
of binding and flying
away. Honey
hugged to six walls.
Pollen falling
from the bee's laden
haunches. All wings,
all coupling.

The pull of every
each to an each.

INTERMENT

Martha Zweig

Insists the right of the left hand, *What were you*
doing yourself those days of plunder,
last days remained to us both? & prods, right index
finger into the left palm,
Wasn't it comparable?—

(scratch I heard from within
the flowery lockbox, stitch in the side
they sew a man up so he won't go bleed
absolutely heartless) —*Un-*
persuaded you add much to a ritual there's not

even otherwise more of, I bet you begged, you
ape-scraped knuckles on the pavement, dinged
a tinny cup, please, sir, moment of your time to time's
ticky two January faces, one wicked & other the one
more-or-less good irrespective its turnabout.

But the left twitches ineptly, merely
electrically, little nerve
lost there. And look! a shady business both
minded shies off too. Childish, who's to pick
& choose? kickup over this-or-that greenery clod?

COUNTER-FABLE

Martha Zweig

Dear preposterous
grasshopper of opposite-
angled knees, glitch, insistent screed
of disproportionate bliss, I put my trust
in domestic economy once, eschewed
excess of appetite & disrepute, kicked the likes-of-
you con-over-career—

I recant. Field pillagers, who conspicuously
overrun the locale, welcome!—infest my circumspect
securities & exchange, day-in-day-out
pester askew the topiary hedges. Offertory: I
resign my estate. Do I quibble some? then shrilly
buzzknuckles-&-shins
dismember & remind me.

What hideous best bug
face any one of you puts on & tilts
to fool me, will. Fill
of folly I laid up long ago exhales: stale
meadowy breath exhuming out of the crib & dry
disintegrating bales, savory yet of the odd blossom,
grass sex, inimical thistle. Choked down

mostly what exhaustible bowl of dust I get, is why I
crave more, why scrape the floor, next attic
shelves, hurl spinning
hats into the shoe trees. Strum cheek-
by-my-jowl any green musician at all!—instigate in my crawl
spaces fiendish undoings, strip my stewardly
jacket & leggings for tatters & wings.

1953: James Dean Walks the Streets of New York All Night

Bill Meissner

All your life you walked in the middle of the street.
The night buries your hands in your pockets,
wrinkles your clothes like the folds in your brain
where you search and search, but can't find
sleep.

You don't know the reason you walk,
but it's something about America.
It's about the theater marquee light bulbs above you
that have darkened and cooled, it's about
the damp matches in your pocket and the fuse
to the atomic bomb. It's about the silence of this
night that won't stop exploding in your ear.

You could be the only
person alive in New York after the fallout.
There are no answers, man; just a few good questions.
You taught us that.
Some nights there's no shelter, no warning siren. There's only
that huge sky above that keeps tossing its useless coins,
there's only the sheen of the abandoned
street stretching endlessly in front of you.

In time, the rain stops, but the dreams keep breaking.
The dreams break—they break with each
step, ring out in circles like shock waves, then vanish
at the edge
of the black and silver puddles.

THE VENTRILOQUIST AND HIS DUMMY

Bill Meissner

Making sure your lips are asleep is what the mirror taught you.
Behind your tight smile, you learned
to pronounce each word
as though it were fine glass.

As a child you were too shy
for words. You pocketed them
in a cloth bag like marbles.
So you've spent a lifetime trying to will wood
out of its ancient silence,
learned to throw your voice
to the farthest corners,
his red enameled grin waiting to catch it.
You try your best to make the audience laugh, or sob,
to feel the knots in their stomachs.

Sometimes, propping the dummy on your knee,
you catch yourself thinking
you should trim his fingernails, offer him a glass of milk.
Other times, when the hinges on his jaw stutter,
you think of pounding his hardwood head
on the stage floor, his brain
smashed to splinters.

After the show, you're too deeply asleep to hear
his raspy throat inside the latched suitcase
repeating, one by one,
all the words
you really needed to say.

SMALL BLESSINGS

Ed Falco

Couple of years ago, Connie came home from work to find Doug, her second husband, swaying in nine feet of water like an aquatic Frankenstein, cement-filled milk jugs tied to his ankles, his extended arms bobbing in front of him, the hands lifting and falling slowly, as if waving a lazy good-bye to all the things of this world. Soon as she saw him, she swore off men forever, for eternity. She kicked off her pumps at the shallow end of the pool, took a seat on the rubberized lip, and sat a long while with her feet in the water just watching him sway, all that gorgeous long blond hair floating around his head in a sunny nimbus. Not that it had been a surprise. Some two years earlier, when they had first met at the hospital, where Connie was still employed as a nurse, he'd been on suicide watch, constrained in a straight-jacket—and there wasn't a week went by after when he didn't mention at least once the possibility of taking his own life. She'd met her first husband at the hospital, too, in Detox. He'd died in a drunk-driving accident three weeks after the church ceremony, only a few days back from the honeymoon. The other party in the fatal accident was a two-family brick Colonial. His car had actually gone straight into the front of the garage, crashing through the wooden door in what probably would not have been a lethal collision were it not for the brick wall at the other end. He went through that too before winding up—this is ironic—in the deep end of an in-ground pool. He technically drowned also, though the police said it was likely a good thing, given that his head injuries would have left him in a vegetative state. So. Small blessings. She still had the pictures somewhere.

For the last two years—she had only recently turned twenty-eight—Connie had dated women exclusively. Being gay had its problems; but, truth is, she never really decided if she were gay or just a woman understandably wary of men, who was dating other women because that was the only alternative to being alone—and she hated being alone. Living as a lesbian on Long Island gained her access into a large and lively social circle. She had a ton of women friends—straight, gay, and bi—with whom she could spend an enjoyable evening at a club in the city, or go out with to see a play or a movie or whatever. There was no lack of things to do and good people to do them with, though she had yet to date anyone with whom she could imagine actually settling down and making a life. First problem, she had to admit—and this is primarily why she had always really doubted she was a gay woman—was the sex. No matter how wild or kinky it got, no matter the strap-on or sex toy in use, it just was not the same thing as it had been with James and Doug, husbands number one and two. Or for that matter with Billy, Ahamed, Ralphie, or Brick—the other four men she'd slept with in her life. She'd been with Billy and Ahamed at Syracuse University; and Ralphie and Brick, two city boys, on Long Island, before James. She'd been raised on Long Island, in Huntington, in a house overlooking the bay, and it seemed only natural to return there after finishing her degree. Brick was dead, from a drug overdose. Ralphie had disappeared, simply up and left the city with no word. For all she knew he could be dead too.

For the past three weeks she'd been dating a woman named Kellen, a doctor who worked with the criminally insane at Bellevue. She was a gentle and compassionate woman, who was already beginning to drive Connie crazy—though Connie wasn't sure it was Kellen who was driving her crazy or just the fact that Kellen was a woman and somehow devoid of something she seemed to need and had been doing without for a couple of years. Not that Connie could have told you what the thing she needed was. She didn't know. Men were simple compared to women. A conversation with a woman was an act of social engagement that included the communication of feelings and ideas along with the sharing of information. Men on the other hand barely knew how to speak. Oh, they could talk if pushed, but after a little while it was almost as if they resented the intrusion of actually asking them if they could just please try to go a little beyond the succinct communication of pertinent facts. Men were infuriating. But. Still. Lately Connie had found herself thinking a lot about men.

On a sultry Friday night in late summer, after a long day at the hospital, two years plus after Doug's suicide, Connie looked at herself hard and long in her dresser mirror and admitted she wasn't gay. Maybe she was bi, but she doubted that too. Mostly she was just pretty open and free about sex, and she figured what she'd done here was give lesbianism a fair shot, and now it was time to admit that it just wasn't her. There was some kind of dynamic involved in the relationship between a woman and a man that wasn't there between a woman and woman and she missed it. She addressed herself in the mirror and admitted what she'd been thinking and not admitting for a long time. She said aloud, "I want a man." She had been hanging around gay women for so long and had spent so many hours talking the politics of heterosexuality that she felt a deep blush of shame in actually hearing herself speak those words. Needing a man, she knew, was a manifestation of self-loathing. She sat down on the edge of her bed, buried her face in her hands, and cried—which, as always, quickly made her feel better. Once the tears stopped, she pulled out her frilliest thong and tossed it on the bed to be joined by her sexiest jeans and white silk blouse. When she stripped out of her nurse's uniform on the way to the shower, it felt like shedding an old skin.

Coyote Ugly Saloon, a downtown bar featuring sexily clad barmaids gyrating and flirting with mostly male patrons, was the last place in Manhattan any of Connie's crowd would ever spend a Friday night; so when she pushed through the door into much hooting and hollering over the background roar of Guns n' Roses, she didn't even bother to scan the crowd. No one she knew would be caught dead on the same block as the Coyote Ugly, let alone in the midst of this sweaty crowd of what looked to be hormone-addled frat boys, lonely middle-aged men, and horny tourists. The handful of women present who weren't standing on the bar and dancing or serving drinks all appeared to be Connie's age or younger. If there were a black or brown face among the masses, she didn't see it—which might have had something to do, she thought, with the big Confederate flag pinned to the ceiling, its red, white, and blue bars and stars marking the place with a giant X. On the spur of the moment, crossing the floor on the way to the bar, she couldn't decide what was more offensive, that Confederate flag or the hundreds of frilly, multicolored bras hanging from the rafters like numberless tokens of male conquest. If she hadn't been out on the town in the hope of hooking up with someone for the night, she would have been offended enough to leave; instead, she found herself grinning at the outrageous political incorrectness of the place while she watched the legs and well-toned tummy of a twenty-something braless barmaid in painted-on, hip-hugging blue jeans and a skimpy red halter top who stood on the bar with the palm of one hand pressed against the ceiling and the other wrapped around a beer bottle as she swayed lazily to lyrics about an insane bitch who looked pretty tied up, or something like that.

Between the dancer's legs, a chalk-board beer list was visible against the wall of the bar, above a sailor's cap flung over a couple of bottles of Bud—hats being another of the principal décor items in the bar: bill caps mostly, but cowboy hats too, of course, white ones, black ones, even a red one with a yellow feather. In the couple of seconds between considering a beer and deciding on bourbon instead, Connie's thoughts took one of those deep, quirky digressions as she heard some little person who seemed to reside somewhere in her chest, approximately in the heart area, suggest that her life was a joke. Two dead husbands at twenty-eight and a failed two-year stint as a lesbian. How the hell did this happen to an ordinary, good-looking, Long Island girl who'd grown up with a stay-at-home Mom, a businessman father (till she was fifteen), followed by a nice-enough step-father after her Dad died of liver cancer—which was a memory, actually, she didn't like to revisit? She'd been close to her father. He was cheerful man of desultory enthusiasms who believed utterly in the extraordinary capabilities of everyone he loved. Connie's mother was a saint, her uncle was a genius, his business partners were brilliant, and so on. Connie he told endlessly, repeated as if a litany, that the world was her oyster, that absolutely anything was possible, that whatever she wanted she had only to set her mind on it and it would be hers. Dad. Dad. He must have died in agony, though of course he forbid her to see him once he got too bad.

When a man's voice interrupted her sudden reverie, she was grateful; and when she turned to find a tall, handsome guy who looked to be approximately her age if not maybe a few years older, she flashed him her prettiest smile. He had just asked her what she was drinking. "Makers on the rocks," she shouted—as the screeching music necessitated—and then added, coyly if loudly, "And here I was thinking I might have to buy my own drink."

"A woman beautiful as you?" he said, showing off his own bright smile, rows of white, expensively cared-for teeth announcing at the very least a solid middle-class upbringing. "Not likely." He leaned over the bar extending a fifty-dollar bill in the direction of a passing barmaid with a green laurel wreath tattooed around her bellybutton. She plucked it gently from his fingers with a seductive smirk, he shouted his order, and few minutes later he was holding a Red Hook by the neck as Connie stirred her bourbon and looked up at him playfully. She was enjoying this. It had been a long time. With a man, anyway.

"My name's Ira," he said. Very cool. Very confident. Just shy of cocky.

"Connie," she shouted back. "Thanks for the drink."

"You're welcome," he said. "Let me guess: you're in the arts. I'm thinking artist of some kind: actor, dancer, musician . . . . I'll go with dancer. That's my final guess. You've got a dancer's body."

Okay, so maybe he was a little too slick. Still, she smiled as if enchanted. "Nurse," she said.

"No kidding?" His surprise seemed genuine and the little honest sparkle in his eyes emphasized the essentially theatrical introduction. "I'm a doctor," he said. "Pediatrics. I'm just completing my residency."

"Congratulations." She offered her hand, which he shook gently. "That's a hell of an accomplishment."

"Thanks," he said. "Where do you work?"

"Pilgrim State."

"Out on the Island?"

"Uh, huh," she said. "But no shop talk, okay?"

"Absolutely," he said, his free hand flying up palm forward as he took a small step back. "Believe me. I understand."

"So what's a doctor like you doing in a dive like this?" she said, and immediately upon hearing the squeaky lameness of the question, brushed her hair back off her forehead with both hands. Predictably, his eyes dropped to her breasts. Men were like computers in that way: they were all programmed to respond identically to certain key strokes.

"I'm here with my brother." He turned his back to the bar as he looked over the crowd toward the rear of the room. "He's been a little depressed," he said, apparently still trying to locate his brother. "This is a place it's hard to stay depressed in, don't you think?"

"Sure," she said. "If you say so," she added, pretty sure he couldn't hear her over the music.

"There he is." He nodded toward a far corner. "He's a great guy. He's a musician, he plays sax. He used to have a group that did pretty well for a while."

Connie looked to the back of the room, where Ira was pointing, and saw a long-haired guy with sunken cheeks and what looked to be multiple face piercings and tattoos. He was leaning against the wall and watching one of the Coyote Ugly girls up on the bar twirling a blue hoola hoop to the shouted encouragement of the crowd. He seemed almost frightened by what he was seeing, his eyes squinting slightly and his lips pressed together as if something bad might be about to happen. "That's your brother?"

"That's him," Ira said. "I know he looks kind of out there," he added, "but he's really an amazingly brilliant guy. He's a musical genius, really. And you know, musicians," he went on, "they've sort of got to look like that. It's part of the business."

"Really," Connie said. "You know what he looks like? He looks like if there were like a magic mirror somewhere, and if you looked into it you saw your reverse, bizzaro image, your everything opposite? He looks like you looking into that mirror."

Ira laughed politely. "You're funny," he said. "But I'm telling you, he's brilliant. We've got that in common. And I only wish I had his talent."

"Really," Connie said. "So you're what? You're out here trying to get your brother laid?"

"That's a little crass, isn't it?" Ira crossed his arms over his chest. He watched Connie a moment, intently. "He's a good guy," he said, "having a terrible time. I was hoping he might meet somebody. Nothing simple as the way you put it."

"And he can't do that for himself? Meet someone, given he's a genius and all?"

"Not if he never leaves his room except to go out for a gig and then goes right back to it afterward."

"And that's the way it is?"

"I think he's developing agoraphobia," Ira said, nodding toward his brother. "That's why he looks scared shit over there."

Connie turned her back to the bar to get a better look at Ira's sad brother. She saw that his long black hair was streaked with gray, and that his face—if it weren't so sunken and marred by an eyebrow piercing and some kind of silvery gem pinned to his nose—might potentially be handsome. "You love him?" she asked Ira. "You love your brother?"

"Oh yeah," Ira said without hesitating. "I love the guy." He tilted his head back and half drained his beer while he looked at his brother who was still leaning against the wall in the back of the room, appearing more and more frightened.

"Just out of curiosity," Connie said. "Did you think for a second, when you first saw me—" She waved her hand back and forth from Ira to herself. "Did you ever think, me and you?"

Ira showed her the back of his left hand and pointed to the ring finger, at a narrow circle of pale skin.

Connie laughed. "All right," she said, and when she picked up her drink and made her way through the crowd toward the back of the room, Ira didn't follow.

The music stopped for a moment as she was in the midst of a knot of boys uniformed in khaki slacks and knit shirts—college boys she'd have guessed, though they looked more like high-school kids to her. One of them, a short one, shorter than Connie, said "Hey Beautiful? Where you going?" which for reasons probably only known to such groups of young men, provoked general laughter. Connie pushed through them to Ira's brother and touched his arm familiarly, as if he were an old friend. In a mirror on the back wall, she saw the group of boys return to their shouted conversation as the music came on full blast, more Guns n' Roses.

Ira's brother looked down at her anxiously. Like Ira, he was tall, but up close it was clear that he was considerably older than his brother. She guessed early- to mid-forties. "Hey," she said. "Ira said I should come over and say hello."

"He did," the brother said, and his voice was startlingly low and gravelly, so that he sounded like he was growling as well as talking. He looked back to the bar, where Ira had his back turned to them as he watched the dancer with the hoola hoop being helped to the floor by two huge, biker-looking guys wearing denim and do-rags. "Why'd he tell you to do that?" he asked, his eyes still skittish, and his posture, the way his whole body leaned back from her touch, defensive.

Connie let go of his arm to hold her drink with both hands. "He said I'd find you interesting. He thought I'd like you."

"He thought so?" the brother said. "I wonder what made him think I'd like you?"

Connie pushed her hair back off her forehead with both hands. "Wild guess, I suppose. Maybe he thought you'd find me attractive."

The brother nodded, as if her attractiveness was something they could all agree on. "So what did my brother tell you?" he asked. "He tell you I'm some sort of genius musician?"

"Something like that."

"It's bullshit," he said, and he looked down at himself, as if just to make sure he was still in the same body. "Looking for genius," he said, "you definitely in the wrong place."

"That's okay," Connie said. "I'm actually not really a genius either."

He smiled, exposing slightly yellowed teeth. "I'm a sideman," he said. "I've played with some greats: played with Miles Davis couple of years before he died."

"I've heard of him," Connie said.

The brother laughed. Something in her response seemed to loosen him up. "That's good," he said. "Ira get around to telling you my name?"

"Didn't get around to it," she answered. "Too busy telling me what a genius you are."

"Ash," he said.

"Jesus." Connie stepped back and looked over his slight frame and long frizzy hair, the sallow skin and sunken cheeks and burned-out eyes. "Jesus," she repeated. "That's perfect. Ash."

Ash seemed confused for a moment; then he grinned and finally he laughed. "Want to get out of here?" he asked.

Connie said, "Why would I want to get out of here?"

"Why would you want to get out of here?" He looked around the bar room, his eyes finally coming to rest on the Confederate flag. "I wouldn't know where to begin," he said.

"Try the bras," she suggested, gesturing toward a rafter where a dozen pink and red bras dangled in a clump. "The bras might convince me."

"Okay," he said. "The bras."

"All right," she said. "Shall we say good night to Ira?"

***

Out on the street, under the red and silver Coyote Ugly Saloon sign, a misty rain gathered in the otherwise clear, summery air. Connie ran a finger along her arm and wiped away a streak of moisture. Above her, the sky was clear, and even squinting she couldn't see the mist that she felt on her skin. When Ash joined her on the sidewalk, the music and shouting of the bar spilling onto the street with him for a moment before the door closed again, she said: "It's wild out here. It's misting," she gestured toward the sky, "but I can't see it."

Ash looked up over the rooftops. He was wearing a plain black T shirt that was frayed at the neck line, and he placed his open hand on it, over his heart. He inhaled deeply. "Smells like it though," he said, his voice, if anything, even deeper and more ragged out on the street, away from the screaming music. "Smells like rain, don't you think?"

Connie sniffed the air with what she hoped was comic intensity, and, yes, she did smell it: the faint tannic odor of wet leaves.

"My place is close to here," Ash said. "Do you want to walk? It's a nice night to walk in the rain, don't you think?"

"Are we going to your place?" Connie said as she looped her arm though his.

"Can't imagine where else," Ash said, and he started down the block, heading toward the East River.

"Is that—" Connie said, and then she hesitated a moment. She was about to ask if he had always sounded like he did, and then worried the question might somehow be hurtful. She found a gentler phrasing. "Have you always had such a deep voice?" she asked.

Ash looked up and touched his Adam's apple, indicating the source of the problem. "Growth on my larynx. Nothing serious, just can't afford to have it taken care of right now."

"But it's benign?"

"Oh, yeah," he said. "I'm a singer— Was a singer, anyway. It's an occupational thing. It happens."

"A singer?" Connie leaned back to look him over. "I can see that," she said. "You could be like an Axl Rose or Steve Tyler type."

Ash looked half pained and half amused. "I'm a serious musician," he said. "Sorry if that sounds pompous, but I'm not an act, a entertainment commodity." He laughed. "Okay," he said. "So I am pompous."

"That's all right," Connie said. "I'm enchanted. I never hooked up with a serious musician before."

"Is that what we're doing?" Ash said. "Hooking up?"

Connie didn't answer immediately. She walked alongside him in silence that was awkward for a moment before easing into a comfortable quiet. A few blocks later, he asked her how old she was.

"Twenty-eight," she said. "And you?"

"Forty. Just turned forty a few days ago."

"Happy birthday."

Ash nodded and pointed up the block. "I'm just around that corner. It's a fifth-floor walk-up. Think you can handle it?"

"The stairs I can handle," she said. "No problem."

"And me?" Ash said. "Starting to wonder about me?"

"You know," Connie said. "We're actually getting kind of wet here." She stepped in front of Ash, stroked his hair with both hands, and then showed him the wet palms of her hands before leaning forward and kissing him lightly on the lips. "Just a couple of things we should get straight first," she said, gently. "I'm out looking for a wild night, you know what I mean? Nothing more than that. Things in my life, they've come to this point—it's like— I don't know. It's got nothing to do with you: you're just the one lucks out. I'm looking for one wild night. Long as you understand, that's it. And also, incidentally," she reached into the inside pocket of her jacket and pulled out a foil-wrapped condom. "This is part of the deal. Okay?"

Ash kissed her on the forehead and gestured toward the lighted foyer of an anonymous gray building a few doors down the block. "Let's get out of the rain," he said, and he touched the small of her back as he started toward the lighted building.

On the steps, under the doorway arch, protected somewhat from the mist which had gathered now into a visible fog and was moving rapidly toward a drizzle, Ash unlocked the door, but instead of stepping into the foyer, he switched off the light and then sat down on the slate doorstep with his back against the closed door. "Long as we're being honest—" he said, looking up at Connie. "Want to sit a minute?" He interrupted himself, gesturing toward the dark, empty street with its nondescript line of buildings. "It's a lovely view, don't you think?"

"Thanks," Connie said. "But, isn't your ass getting wet?"

"Kind of."

"I'll lean," she said, and she crossed her legs and leaned back against the door frame. The city was quiet for a Friday night. She could hear Manhattan's constant background rumble of engines accelerating and decelerating; and, overhead, the low rumble of an airplane somewhere off in the distance—but no street shouts, no siren screams. "It's peaceful here," she said, looking down at Ash, where he had pulled his knees to his chin and wrapped his arms around them.

"You can hear the ships out on the East River," he said. "We'll hear fog horns tonight. I'm surprised we haven't heard one yet."

"I'll listen for it," Connie said.

Ash nodded. "It's a strange life, isn't it?"

Connie looked away from him, up to the rooftops, and an image opened in her mind of Doug floating in the deep end of the pool, the way his arms bobbed up and down, seeming to wave good-bye.

"Anyway," Ash said. "Things you should know: I'm an alcoholic. I've abused every drug known to mankind. I've wasted my life, wasted my talent. I've rotted my teeth—" He pulled out a dental appliance, removing his front teeth for a moment before snapping them back into place. "—destroyed a couple of organs, and in general fucked up totally and irredeemably." He paused a moment, as if pained at what he had to say next. "And the drug problems are ongoing," he said. "As is the alcoholism."

Connie said, "Do you have HIV?"

Ash shook his head. "That," he said, "thank God, I've avoided. I've got recent medical records upstairs, which you're more than welcome to peruse."

"Gosh," Connie gushed, hugging herself. "This is *so* romantic."

"Look," Ash said. He leaned his head on his knees and tilted his face up toward Connie. He seemed suddenly much more relaxed. "It's okay if you want me to walk you back to the bar. Honestly. It'll be all right."

"You know," Connie said, "you're not the only one with a life gone off course."

"I'm not?" he said, and then added a moment later: "I'm probably more like 'wrecked on the rocks' than 'off course,' don't you think?"

Connie didn't answer. She felt the story of her two dead husbands pushing up from someplace in her belly. The story wanted to push all the way out and be told—but instead her eyes teared up as it receded, sinking back down into her bones.

"What?" Ash said. "What do you want to say?"

"Past couple of years," she offered. "My partners of choice have not been men."

"A little sexual confusion? That's certainly unusual," he said. "Especially in this town."

"That's what I thought, too," Connie said. "So." She opened her arms and looked down at a rivulet of rain funneling between her breasts, and at the bottom of her blouse and the legs of her jeans, which were soaked through. "You know," she said, "we're both really wet."

Ash stood and unlocked the door. Like a gentleman, he held it open for her.

Once up the five flights of stairs and inside Ash's door, Connie had silently undressed him, and let him do the same for her. In the dim light from a open window that overlooked the black metal railing of a fire escape, they draped their wet clothes over the sink that was on one side of the room and then dried each other off with a stack of yellow Burger King napkins before getting into the bed on the other side of the room. After several minutes of kissing and touching, after the application of mouths to skin and fingers to soft and warm places, Ash rolled over on his side and turned his back to Connie.

"That's all right," she said. "Really. Don't go away."

"I'm right here," he said, his gravelly voice barely audible. "Just give me a second."

She stroked his back, running her hand over his arm and along the surprisingly youthful skin of his shoulder blade to the small of his back where there was a patch of downy hair. She kissed him on the neck. "Forget what I said before, about looking for a wild night. This is nice, really. This is fine."

"The mind is there," he whispered, "it's the body that's wrecked."

"I'm fine," she said. "I swear. This is good."

"Give me another second," he said. "Okay?"

She touched his shoulder and turned onto her back, clasping her hands under her neck and propping herself up on the pillow so that she could look around the room. The place was neat but small, even by city standards: one room with a sink, a hot plate, and a mini-fridge. She noticed the slight but recognizable odor of aftershave in the air. "Where's your bathroom?" she asked.

"Down the hall," he said. "Three tenants, one bathroom."

"Bummer."

"Truly."

"Are you going to turn over and talk to me?"

"One more minute."

"Okay," she said. "I'm counting." Across from her, in the far corner of the room next to the open window, a saxophone was propped up on a stand of some kind. She noticed it for the first time while she was gazing blankly at a light that had gone on in one of the buildings across the courtyard. It was almost as if the shiny brass instrument had magically appeared out the shadows. It was half hidden by the room's single black, straight-back chair, which was positioned directly in front of the window, so that Connie couldn't help but imagine Ash sitting there alone in this tiny room watching the world go by. She leaned over and kissed his shoulder. "Kind of strange for Ira to take you out to a bar," she said. "Isn't it? Given . . ."

"I haven't had a drink in a long time." Ash lay his head on his bicep and talked into the wall. "Ira doesn't know about the drugs. Truth is, I've been pretty good with that, too. Still, not enough. I keep, backsliding. Then, you know, I swear never again. Until I do again. Then . . . . Etcetera. It's pathetic, really."

"But," Connie said. "Are you getting better? Are things improving?"

"I guess so," he said. "You could say that. Until they get worse."

"You're a pessimist," she said, "aren't you? You're a cynic."

"No, I'm not. I'm just, what is." He turned around, propped his head up on his hand, and peeled the sheet down off Connie's body, giving it a yank when it got stuck on her feet, pulling it away to leave her entirely exposed. "My God," he said, after a moment of gazing at her. "My God," he repeated. "It hurts to look at you."

"Why?" she asked, and she sat up slightly to better peer down at herself. She looked pretty much the same as she did in high school, probably better, since she had taken up running as an adult and so was likely in better physical condition. Her body had always acted pretty much oblivious to all the traumas of her life. Fathers and husbands could die in her arms, but her body just went on glowing. "Is there a problem?" she asked, raising her eyebrows.

"No problem," he said, turning his gaze away from her body and to her eyes. "Except I don't really know anything about you, and you already know a good bit about me."

"What do you want to know?"

"Tell me one thing deep," he said. "One thing that reveals a little of you."

"I'm pretty revealed," she said, gesturing toward her body.

"No you're not," he said.

"Oh. Okay." She squinted dramatically, miming deep thought. "Let me see," she said. "One thing . . . ." She considered once again telling him about James and Doug, and once again the words wouldn't come. "Okay," she said. "My father died when I was young." She paused, meaning to stop there, but almost instantly she found herself speaking again. "Last good memory I have of my father," she said, "I'm about 14 and he's carrying me up the stairs on his back." She laughed. "I mean, I'm not a baby here, either. I'm 14 and I'm literally on his back and he's climbing up the stairs like a horse. He was like that. He used to say 'Who's the pretty girl?' and tickle my chin, to make me laugh. I'd be like it made me furious, but it was just so dumb, so incredibly dopey— You had to be there. We could make each other laugh, like, unbelievably hard, just, like, hysterical laughter, dumbest things. He, you know—he played with me. We literally played with each other, like a couple of kids."

"He sounds like a good man."

"He was." Connie paused momentarily and then she was off again, talking. It felt almost as if she were remembering stuff she actually meant to tell Ash, as if they were an old couple and she had meant to tell him these things and had just somehow forgotten. "I used to have this dream," she said. "It was kind of a mix of a dream and daydream, where I'd be in his hospital room when he was sick—he died of liver cancer—and I'd just, in this dream, I'd just, touch him." She was surprised at how fast the thoughts were coming. "I'd touch him and then he'd—the whole cancer thing, it would all be over. Just like that. I'd touch him, and it would be over, and he'd be back, just like that." She supposed she shouldn't have been surprised when tears started coming, but she was. "I don't know why I'm crying," she said. "It's actually a sweet dream. I have this power in the dream: I just touch him and everything is okay again, everything is fixed. I touch him and he's back, everything's back good again. It sounds weird, I know, but it's a sweet, sweet dream. It is. Really." She was annoyed when she saw how solemn Ash looked. He appeared stricken gazing down at her. "Look," she said. "It's nothing bad, really." She noticed that she sounded frightened, and that annoyed her even more. "Fuck you for looking at me like that," she said, and the words came out loud, much louder than she intended. "You can just go fuck yourself, all right?" She could feel the redness in her face, the anger rising up off her like heat.

Ash climbed over her and went to the chair by the window where he sat quietly looking out at the rain.

Alone in the bed, Connie turned her back to him, petulantly, like out-of-sorts child, and then, an instant later, she realized with great clarity just how crazy she was acting. "Jesus," she said. "I think I just freaked. Did I just freak out?" she asked.

"It's not a problem," Ash said.

"No. I did," she said. She got out of bed and knelt alongside him. "I mean— I don't know what just happened. I just—"

"Honestly," he said. "Not a problem." He put his hand on her shoulder and she threw her arms over his legs and lay her head on his thigh. She was try-ing to think of another thing to say, something that might undo the strangeness of her behavior. From somewhere out on the unseen East River, the fog horn Ash promised sounded, its low groan rumbling through the air. They both turned their heads when they heard it, and Ash's hand closed slightly on her shoulder as Connie's arms tightened around him, pulling him closer. Then a long time passed in silence as they stared out the window, watching the blank backsides of the street's mute buildings, watching a soft rain pour down over the city.

Eventually, Ash reached over her for the saxophone. He put the reed in his mouth and touched it with his tongue as if he were tasting it, as if he were feeling for something crucial in its texture. Then he leaned over the instrument and began to play a series of plaintive notes that coalesced into a melody Connie thought she might have heard before, but wasn't sure. She was amazed that so soft a sound could come out of so imposing an instrument. Soft as it was, someone across the courtyard apparently heard, because a young man wearing only boxer shorts stepped out onto a fire escape with a beer bottle in hand and gave Ash a perfunctory wave before settling onto a bench set up next to the window. The fire escape above him was lined with a green tarp protecting him from the rain. Ash nodded back and played a little louder. Connie kissed him on the thigh, meaning to encourage his playing, realizing she was hearing him for the first time. She could feel the music within her, as if it were coming from her as well as from Ash, and she thought the sound was extraordinary: moving and painful and peaceful all at once. On the fire escape across the courtyard, a young woman holding an infant joined the man in boxers. They were both handsome, with deep brown skin and lithe bodies, and they looked very young, barely in their twenties. Rain dripping off the green tarp surrounded them like a mesh curtain. The woman sat next to the man and leaned her head on his shoulder. She was wearing a summery, flowered robe, and after a moment she opened it and put the baby to her breast. Connie was impressed with their lack of modesty—the man in boxers, the woman with a baby at her breast. Then she remembered that she was naked in the shadows, as was Ash, and she laughed and said to Ash, "I like your neighborhood." Ash nodded, acknowledging he had heard her, and kept playing, the notes of his melody floating out across the courtyard, sailing over the rooftops and up into the still darkening sky.

INTERVIEWING THE GODS

Jeffery Bahr

I told the one with blue skin and tusks I'd let him know, punched the button
to announce "Serving Number 65." The next one limped in, pale and hesitant,
leaned a lightning bolt against the coffee cart and whispered he'd settle

for anything. One arrived late, looked out the window and jumped. Another swaggered
in with matched deerhounds and demanded obedience. Number 77 was a silent pile
of fieldstones that arranged themselves beside my bonsai pots; 89 was dressed

in greenbacks big as palm leaves. 101—a woman with a tiara of ivy vine
and one exposed breast. Another said he'd eased up on mead and, currently,
was counseling in the city. All afternoon they swam or crawled or flew

into the room. When I left for the day, an old man with a lunchbag in his lap
remained in the waiting room. He held a wren in his hand and studied the print
by Hieronymous Bosch. I asked him if he'd like to share a cab uptown, and helped
him to the elevator. The doors closed, and I told him my story.

To a Drowned Man

Michelle Margolis

—(after Horace, Book 1, Ode 28)

What on earth do you want?
Silence, according to the god, is a gift,
and yet you turn it down; is this true?
I carry in a sack three handfuls of sand
to cover your chin, your mouth like a cup, thin-rimmed.
Are you at ease, unburied?
Who walks, heartsick and harried, on a beach near Tarentum?
Best to pour wine, burn ox, fold the meat in its shining fat—
whether or not the god forgives
you should, if you can, rise, eat a few ripe olives with your friends
under the hollow tree.
Someone was kind once, looked the other way.
But we will not speak of this again.

THE SUMMER MY MOTHER ACKNOWLEDGES
MY SISTER AS HYSTERIC

Michelle Margolis

Round-faced & candescent, August
configures the sky & at a time, too, when Mars
reappears after it's been out of sight or mind,
say, about sixty thousand years. Sadly,
mama can't hold back tears & yet she doesn't cry.
She teaches me a tune decomposed, grand as opera—
What is lost, O, what I did not know . . .
which is why the moon rains debris
& illumination, she sings of things lovely & forlorn
& extreme, there's nothing like a ballad well-writ
belted to the back of the house
although the season's folding, funding for it
has dried up & still my sister's buying shoes,
wriggling into a bustier, futzing with fishnets
so the press will be wowed, knocked over
& knobby-kneed, they're brazen, these guys,
belligerent even but she's upbeat, keeps her affairs
in order except when things spin out of control
or slip through the fingers she's using for cashing out
& pulling up roots, she's busy, exhausted
after the uproar, defiant of kids & swollen-bellied cats
because their cries, as of late, are true—
no point in warning the husband, or lover,
all she needs is someone who'll take her a meal
of martinis, strawberries & tiramisu because it's the dead
of summer & mama's rich, smartly dressed
& yet always & forever (not too fast now, no sudden moves)
a mother in the wake of loyalty & fear,
trodden love as dear as memory.

OFF FOR THE WAR / HOME FROM THE WAR

Daneen Wardrop

1. "Off for the War: The Soldier's Adieu" —Currier and Ives, 1861

There is always something headlong about goodbye.
Canteen swings on your belt next to our son's face
as he hangs on to both of us.

You close the embrace, pick up your rifle.
            Sun slides off the branch, pulls one by one at each leaf.

Tonight the boy and I will eat on red and white checked gingham
padded with a bowl of potatoes, pitcher of milk.
I think McClellan and Davis and Mr. Lincoln and Beauregard,
                    think it is only polite to believe in campaigns.
With a serving of fried chicken our son will pull a wing,
      break the connecting flap that held sky in its recess
            when it pecked at meal in the sand,
will twist it among spurts of grease.
Preen, wetted fingers, wing in his throat.

And in a blue meadow troops will tack, face each other as if by agreement,
square off, two opposing flags flapping in the wind, same direction.

Night a dark surf.
After dinner we'll put away toys and books.
    I will say to our boy,
Please pick up from the floor your crumpled jacket.

He's left Wednesday under it.

Before you left, husband, you said, The war will be over by next weekend.

2. "Home from the War: The Soldier's Return" —Currier and Ives, 1861

This is where we welcome you home again,
        same season, same year 1861, same flowers still in bloom,
                as if fighting was over fast as wishing.

      Inside the picture, though, we know
years of seasons where hands have smoothed napkins, passed around bread,
cheese reconnoitered with the rennet.

We have studied the apple and pear for him. The curtain folds.

We have worn our bodies.
Our children use our hand to wave at a neighbor.

We have felt the nightwind shape itself to the keyhole and enter,
while faithful, a whalebone presses skin.
               Our time is dividual

as his, forgetting the cut-ching of bullet, grape and canister,
           the red moue of cannon.
     And so his rifle has been erased now in this picture—
and I ask, will an embrace be able to relove its arms—

BLUE STUDY

Kirsten Kaschock

The burgeoning nude in a low field littered with sapphires.
And then they lift—dragonflies.
A sibilance like leaves reassigned to their trees, greening
the branches of a few locusts with life again,
with bright life's compound eyes—a thousand, tiny, spinless discos.

Sky-square above a courtyard, space hovering on edge of prison.
Computer monitor. Flicker over a gas range.

An airplane gathers speed before its nose turns skyward.
Outside, the atmosphere seeks to embrace bullets
during their trajectories. The craft will not be loved.
The craft will not be held.

Machine—a single-minded elaboration of beauty.

Blue screen. A woman, back from some place, in front of a blue
screen. A camera is pointed at her. *Laugh, hold your belly, toss your hair.*
Later, we can make it so you look joyous—at the beach or something.

Blue bottle on the blue bookcase. Blue copy of *The Odyssey.*

Window cleaner. (Windows are not blue.) Not blue—
the color of the near-invisible. When he comes home and asks her
again—he always asks—how she feels, she tries to say
this.   *This.*

The holiday is an illusion. The body travels, bodies
split clouds. The mind stays, wishing it had finished the dishes.

> *Above the large nude in the field, glitter-flies hover—*
> *and then in all directions break, shot out*
> *like war. Like planes forsaking formation.*

Her husband hears knot blue.

Blue scream. Like a jet, she leaves sound
behind her. In the grocery store, after she has paid, been
bagged, and helped to the car with one child in tow, the other
abdominal—a low shriek shatters a jar of preserves.
Its thick dark issue is met (and then quickly
dispensed with) by a seventeen year-old boy in aisle four.

YELLOW STUDY

Kirsten Kaschock

Yellow is a kitchen.
The nude seated at a solidity of wooden table on a chair held together with Scotch tape.
The scene is unsanitary. The yellow, too warm.

They never get to water—the man, the woman, the child, the almost.
They keep talking about getting to water. It never happens.

Sex. Beside candlelight. Competitive with light.
Two bodies seeming more tender illumined in this way.
Tenuous.   As if avoiding some new type of damage.

They will not argue in front of the child.
She has no idea what the discussion they are not having
would concern. *Concern.*   He is that controlled.

The sun crawls up out of its hole. And there is forever breakfast.

The nude framed by countertop and disinfectant
sitting at the wooden block of table—*she looks
like your mother.* She is beginning to look like anyone's mother.
Only she is naked and therefore more terrifying.

Pages burn. Over time, they fall apart from burning.
The house, inside every bookshelf, is on fire.

She and the child should be in the park everyday.
She chases him down to shoe him. His laces must
be triple-knotted with wide-enough loops—
she does not know wide-enough for what.

She was once talented.
Proud of the deft way she had of recognizing and fulfilling desire.

The nude at the rectangular table, balancing on an instability of chair—
she is sallow. The lamp swinging above her head is, also, not a noose.
There could be beauty. You can see that. On this particular day,
she is dehydrated.
Other days it is other things.

SHADOWS AND DISTANCE

"What did I plan to say to her…"
—William Carlos Williams, "Waiting"

Brian Swann

(i)

The gate thuds. My tongue is braced.
  Returning from town, voices are split
and spill all over.
                I split out the back
  where cold air tightens
to a mirror in which things seem
  too big.
              Here water is cunning
and hides everywhere, waiting. A
  windblown sheet could lurk
in a mote of dust and the sky
  knock itself to pieces.

(ii)

                From rockveins
shadows surge wave
  on wave. There's anarchy in
their contours but if there were
  none everything would be upsidedown. You'd find stars in your batter,
  planets in you bed. On whim,
everything could become the
  shortest day or longest night.
Breath would be optional and deserts
  wear you like shoes.

(iii)

> The wind's
> dry as the peonies I gave her
> weeks ago. It has quenched itself
> and sounds like children sleeping.
> I take a deep breath and go
> back in.
> As someone once said,
> we only cross, the distance never changes.

THE WANDERER

thonne onwaecneth eft   *wineleas guma*

Brian Swann

The swallow's shadow   has no use,
  but it angles in   for a moment
and moves on.
              I smell the trees
  but don't   recognize them.
Last night's still an image: I swam
  between the bars   into blueness but
the main sequence   was conflagration.
  Something made   space in the air
suffocating the birds.   Something
  got its wings stuck   and the sky
broke up.
         Over the city a wind
  whistles and whirls.   Newspapers
tumble over and over,   traveling
  backwards, in love   with their own
movements.
        In the evening things
  will come home again,   traveling
backwards, phrasing sorrow   as dignity.
  The periphery   used to have a
kind of serenity,   like a dried-up riverbed.
  Now it crumbles.
           I remember another
body, its expanse   and healing presences.
  How the   main road was filled
with women, naked   and lonely as beacons.

91

FROM Barrens

Tom O'Connor

Ghostwind

Slathering light, in slabs,
      scatters the reflecting heat.
Only root and stone don't budge.
      You walk, the broom-grit
burrowing in your eyelids, your mouth,
      over sunburned dunes,
the fading silhouettes. Sister, you have no companion.
      Like this valley road, all words

lead to... never something new,
      your unique story of pain.
You don't believe it can be shared.
      From the full-moon road,
the overlook, mountain lions and coyote
      arise, sniffing for survivors
along the desert's stone spheres and spires.
      Sand whips over canyons,

rolls to reverberations: wind-noise
      at the desert borders. Here is no void
or you'd vanish. *Here* you stand,
      circled endlessly. The ghostwind
keeps the crouching spaces alive,
      transfigures you to nobody.
Your scars offer up their stories. What's leftover,
      coyotes will pick clean. Only

the surrounding hills' sediment survives
    to translate previous ages—
witness to an invaded body
    trundling over and over
itself, always absent. Someone lost
    here, one myth goes, never
comes out the same again. Stone echoes
    a coyote's cries.

Your new home is the ghost town below.
    The car frame hitched on stone blocks
by the run down house, the clothesline
    left to flap in wind and collapse.
Where rusting metal, spines of machines
    heave through lacquered times.
The clocks stopped ticking long ago:
    desert again.

The Red Desert

Silos sever the view with frames of barrels
and brewing steam. Your mother grips your hand,
walking the wet road beneath rasping smoke stacks,
fires pulsing in rhythm. She hasn't driven

since the accident. Her hand sweats over
yours. Something infects you doctors can't name.
At lunch, workers huddle by black bags.
You're frenzied with starving. She petitions

a man's *panino,* sold at the crossroads, half-
eaten. The desert feeds on you no matter what you eat.
Feeling derelict, she pulls you across mounds
of smoking ash. Always rattled. She knows

accidents, quicksands await these unknown
footprints. Defiled. Your father once hid inside
this fog, oversaw these buildings. Yellow smoke gusts
over grates and window grills.

That terrible something. Tonight
there will be no hearth fire, only a blanket rumpled
over her body. No moment of cover at your house
rumbling a mile away. The desert pinned you

snug with panic. It fatigues the scaffolds.
More real than the metal tanks, smoke
hisses along. You make no sound as she runs to you,
the fishless sea, seepage sucking

at your feet, streaming ash overhead. You sink
beside the road. Wind buries it.
No one looms on rusting
red land where nothing comes back.

Disowned

The chasm covered over. You disappeared where
no one follows. On unmarked roads,

their detours, shrubs fill out silt dust,
the mesa's old volcanic action. Something

unseen still creeps across: the distance—
nothing visible moves—hidden colors at your feet:

a red cactus blossoms for seconds after rain washes
rootholds away. You promised nothing would touch

you again. A coyote skull bleaches to stone.
You crouch in its stare, choking, drunk

on wine beside the disappearing, re-appearing
house, mounds of trash. This place you can't read.

Claret cups and cholla sprout only to be plucked
out. Sand whips the rocks, wind through

bag pipes and zithers. The same full blue moon.
He is just a dead body—a Hades for disappearing,

a face of Apollo that re-appears. Here, you belong
to him. Your mother searches through

a human winter, hoping you'll become Persephone
on land whose animals abandoned one another. You too

have no desire to eat. To be less than this emptiness,
a half-starved coyote. You begin to bleed,

walking west on roads where every car breaks down.
A human shape blurs over red sand—

Stillness

Nothing is what you thought it would be. The ranch house
you grew up in, beside rises of sage. It's still there.

You kick down poster board in the back window, crawl
in. Your flashlight blazes four iron bed frames.

Coil springs jut above flat springs. You
touch the decay that's touching you. Broken off the vanity,

a full-length mirror propped against the back wall. Once you hid
inside this house from the world outside. Your reflected ·

face no longer the dutiful daughter's—who dusted
looming bookshelves, your father's picture,

the hutch and grandfather clock. It's the woman's,
holding the flashlight. Only a ghost would enter the uneven

hallway, touch the crumbling wall. Sitting
on the camel-back couch, you open the dusty box of books, curled

Zane Grey covers, fishing almanacs: yellow, bendable.
The antiques are breaking down. Splintered

wood sprouts through varnish. In the yellow kitchen:
tomatoes and corn are sealed in Ball jars for winter,

whiskey jugs, crocks for corned beef, clay bowls
and rusty tins stacked in the pantry. You

let them crumble. In the living room, the crystal radio
and ash tray stand beside father's chair. You

leave them. The front door opens onto the cracked
porch, open air. Through ripped screens,

you stare across a treeless place beneath the mountain
stream, where trout hide at night, settle down in stillness.

LETTERS ON A REPRINT OF ROBERT DUNCAN'S *LETTERS*

Letters: Poems 1953-1956. Robert Duncan. Ed. and with an Afterword by Robert J. Bertholf. Chicago: Flood Editions, 2003.

Stephen Fredman

A Robert Duncan's *Letters*, first published in a beautiful letter-press edition by Jargon Press in 1958, has recently been re-issued by Flood Editions. The new edition does not have some of the deluxe features of its predecessor, but it is quite lovely in its own right and it performs the valuable service of bringing back into print a seminal work in the oeuvre of one of the best American poets of the past century. Written from 1953 to 1956, *Letters* marks a turning point in Duncan's movement from the Berkeley Renaissance fellowship he shared with Jack Spicer and Robin Blaser toward his Black Mountain cohort of Denise Levertov, Charles Olson, and Robert Creeley. Duncan effects this turning point by engaging the Jewish mystical tradition of the Kabbalah, which had been lurking as a part of his intellectual repertoire since he heard it whispered of by his parents at theosophical meetings during his childhood. The conceit of *Letters* is that there is a "rime" in the operations of three different entities: the letters of the (Hebrew) alphabet, the creative unfolding of the universe, and the poetic company of the peers to whom Duncan's "letters" are addressed. Each of these entities is a constellation of powers, capable of bringing forth a new poetry of creation—a "projective" poetry tied not to the individual ego but obedient to greater impulses.

B An advertisement for the book: "The composition of *Letters* begins with 'Letter to Denise Levertov' ['For a Muse Meant'] and moves out over almost three years' work to complete a book presided over by an alphabet primary to world creation. These angelic letters then those powers hidden or discovered are substance of our speech. A naming of my peers, and an exclamation of joy: Denise Levertov, Charles Olson, Robert Creeley, James Broughton, Mike McClure, Helen Adam—it is the presence of companions, named and unnamed, that inspires *Letters*. A book of primaries, a book of companions. A book of praise. I have stored here, as best I know how, the songs of all I live by. For I adhere to form as the bee obeys the geometry of the hive" (54).

Letters grows out of actual correspondence with other poets, just as Olson's initial *Maximus* "Letters" do. The first poem, for instance, "For a Muse Meant," was sent as a letter to Denise Levertov, inaugurating a large and crucial correspondence that has recently been published as well (Robert Bertholf and Albert Gelpi, eds., *The Letters of Robert Duncan and Denise Levertov* [Stanford: Stanford UP, 2003]). "Correspondence" refers at once to the (Medieval, Swedengorgian, Baudelarian) doctrine of analogies and to the active epistolary communities in which Duncan operated. The "hive-like" quality of the book gives evidence that, although Duncan repeatedly stated that *The Opening of the Field* (1960) was the first book of poems he composed throughout as "a book," the same is true of *Letters*.

C Kabbalah has become important to modern poets because of the powerful, even cosmic, significance it accords to letters, words, and the notion of the book. As David Meltzer explains, "The Kabbalah, as much as poetry, is the study of and submission to the mysteries of the word. The language used by Kabbalists is so intricately dimensional that it is almost impossible to fully convey the simultaneous levels of meaning revealed in the simplest of words. It is said that one word is the seed of a particular universe, a system of interactions and realities as complex as the birth and death of a sun" (David Meltzer, ed., *The Secret Garden: An Anthology in the Kabbalah* [Barrytown, NY: Station Hill Press, 1998], xiii). In Kabbalah all of the levels of occult "work"—magical practice, meditation and contemplation techniques, visionary excursions, and spiritual and psychological self-transformation—can be found, as they would be in any esoteric system, but all derive from investigations of language and writing.

Duncan learned of the Kabbalah as a child listening in on his parents' theosophical meetings (Rodger Kamenetz, "Realms of Being: An Interview with Robert Duncan," *Southern Review* 21.1 [1985]: 9-10), where the most important kabbalistic text, the *Zohar*, was read as one of the keys to the mysteries of the universe. From Duncan's own perspective, as he told Meltzer, the *Zohar* is instead "the greatest mystical novel ever written" (Meltzer, x). It is remarkable that Duncan, who was raised as a Christian hermeticist, would become the instigator of lifelong research by such Jewish figures as Meltzer, Wallace Berman, Jack Hirschman, and Jerome Rothenberg into a Jewish form of mysticism. Meltzer, for instance, who edited a journal devoted to Kabbalah, *Tree*, and an anthology of kabbalistic texts, *The Secret Garden*, calls Duncan "my exemplar" in Kabbalah studies (x) and credits Duncan with introducing him to the works of Gershom Scholem, the modern scholar responsible for reviving interest in the Kabbalah (xv).

D "RD: There are two things which would make Scholem's book on Jewish mysticism particularly of interest to me in the first place. One was, I knew my parents were Christian Kabbalists and that they worked with the Hebrew alphabet, but since that was part of their mysteries I was never permitted to. Second, I'd already begun to get into letters and serious puns through *Finnegan* and to think more about them. *Letters* is influenced toward a creative veil or world-cloth which would be identical with the maya in which it's woven all the way through. The warp and woof are connected and the figures emerge and disappear. All of that was there and working with the idea of letters—the letters of fire on a ground of darkness, isn't that it?

"RK [Rodger Kamenetz]: The Torah is conceived as black fire written on white fire.

"RD: All of those ideas have a good deal of cross-resonance, and in the most intensified place where people lived entirely in the book—and it's the book I was writing—the two would be James Joyce and those mystical Jews who live in the Torah." (Kamenetz, 12-13)

E From the *Zohar: Pritzker Edition* (Daniel Matt, ed. and trans. [Stanford: Stanford UP, 2004]): "When the blessed Holy One wished to fashion the world, all the letters were hidden away. For two thousand years before creating the world, the blessed Holy One contemplated them and played with them. As he verged on creating the world, all the letters presented themselves before Him, from last to first" (11). Each letter stepped forward in turn and asked the "Master of the world" to "create the world by me" (12). The Holy One praised the virtues of each letter based upon a particular word that it begins, but refused to create the world with it, until the letter *bet* entered and said, "Master of the world, may it please You to create the world by me, for by me You are blessed above and below" [*berakhah*, blessing, begins with *bet*]. The Holy One agreed.

The letter *aleph* had remained outside in humility, at first not wanting to assert itself where other letters had failed and then not wanting to usurp the favor that had been granted already to *bet*. "The blessed Holy One said, '*aleph, aleph!* Although I will create the world with the letter *bet* [using *be-reshit*, the first word of the Torah], you will be the first of all letters. Only through you do I become one [*aleph* is the number one]. With you all counting begins and every deed in the world," (16).

Duncan: "Even the name *Letters* comes from the *Zohar* which I was reading in that period" (Kamenetz, 13). Or as he says in the preface to *Letters*: "the lore of Moses of Leon in the *Zohar*, has been food for the letters of this alphabet" (*Letters*, xii).

F Duncan's relationship with the Kabbalah is not a religious one. Were he alive today, he would not have accepted an invitation to accompany the rock entrepreneur Madonna on her recent pilgrimage to Jerusalem's Western Wall: "Already by the time I'm reading Scholem I was not at all in search of religion, but in search of the nature of the imagination. It seemed to me that in mystical traditions of Judaism, religion was passing into imagination, including the imaginary. But the imaginary is not significant in relation to the imagination because the imagination is the final ground of reality. That's what I mean by the imagination" (Kamenetz, 13).

"[I]n creating something, you don't refer to it. You can't refer to it. And what you then create doesn't resemble something else. Finally, imagination is my ground and I hold to it. . . . Creation to me is a mystery of the Universe—I'm a Heracleitean in that the universe creates itself, and human beings have these ideas; they have them like plants have flowers. We don't have tulips but we have ideas and religions which are our distinctive way of blossoming, sorting out, mating—the same as the flowers" (Kamenetz, 14).

G From the "Preface" to *Letters*, under the heading "Nests": "It is an intensity of excitement which compels a man to work out a designd feeling that variously arrives at stations on three levels: the presence in the imagination in which the speech 'comes', a mortality out of immortal letters; the evident manifestation or trace we in the xxth century worship as Art and declare immortal; and the return, the dwelling of the imagination in the speech" (ix).

The circling that Duncan practices makes a hermeneutics that is deconstructive by virtue of its refusing to be grounded anywhere but in the imagination. In "For a Muse Meant," Duncan proposes a "deconstruction— / for the reading of words" (2), marking probably the first use of the term. The three nested levels of his deconstructive hermeneutics involve, first, the precipitation of individual speech out of the originary writing inherent in the "immortal letters"; second, the transposition of the "sacred" into an art that participates in the creative forces that structure the universe; and third, the imaginative act of reading, which recognizes the creative potencies at play in something written or spoken.

The hermeneutic circle of writing, art, and reading arises out of excitations that can be ascribed a biological basis in a reductive reading of Freud. Duncan accepts a biological reading of Freud but argues that biology and imagination intertwine, that patterns of speech are akin to patterns in nature: "What happens when immediate excitements are postponed, when sexual responses are transmuted into hate and love, when talk is reserved to re-emerge as poetic speech? These are specializations of the individual creature, spiritual lusters or armories which I see as alike to the shells or furs or combs apparent in the animal world. Specializations of action. And then a will in living or a consciousness. I confound the two, having in mind a process which sets self-creation and self-consciousness in constant interplay" (ix-x).

H In *Letters*, Duncan is already mining the territory that will be worked a decade later by Edmond Jabès and Jacques Derrida. The continual puns and anagrams in the poetry of both Duncan and Jabès derive primarily from the puns and anagrams of the *Zohar*, in which the dramatic movement of the text comes from conjuring with words and letters. For both poets, too, the notion of the Book goes beyond Mallarmé's conception of a Book that contains the entire world. Jabès and Duncan regard the Book as a kind of deity in itself, within whose imperatives they must work. Duncan speaks of "this God in which we dwell," who "finds all our poor writing as we knew it to be: the Writing. In these excesses of confidence I become nameless agency of movements in a book that unimagined generations project.... For the Book, the autonomous book, bears witness for and against all claims" (xiv-xv). In "Edmond Jabès and the Question of the Book," Derrida speaks of "This movement through which the book, *articulated* by the voice of the poet, is folded and bound to itself, the movement through which the book becomes a subject in itself and for itself, is not critical or speculative reflection, but is, first of all, poetry and history" (Jacques Derrida, *Writing and Difference*, trans. Alan Bass [Chicago: U Chicago P, 1978]: 65).

In a long essay on the work of Jabès published in 1985, Duncan recognizes a poet whose *Book of Questions* shares the same territory he first began to explore in *Letters: "The Book of Questions* is meant to arouse, beyond the boundaries of apparent meaning, suspicions and rumors of meaning within meaning, words within words. Jabès writes in order to read, or reading is the order of his writing, and he brings us back again and again to this boundary of the presence of its being written in the presence of its being read—to the letter the eye sees even as the hand writes the word, to the rhyme or homophone the ear hears even as it attends the message of the voice in the book" (Robert Duncan, *A Selected Prose*, ed. Robert J. Bertholf [New York: New Directions, 1995]: 208-9)

I It is more than coincidental that Jabès in *The Book of Questions* and

Duncan in much of *Letters* investigate the powers of language through the vehicle of a prose poetry. "Passages of a Sentence," for instance, is a chain of sentences in which birds that are words fly in and out, disturbing the ongoing sense, the predatory intent: "As we start the sentence we notice that birds are flying thru it; phrases are disturbd where these wings and calls flock; wings are a wind, featherd, a beating of the air in passage or a word, the word 'word', hovers, sailing before dropping down the empty shafts of sense" (*Letters*, 33). Even in its title, "Passages of a Sentence" can be seen as an embryonic version of the two unbounded poetic sequences Duncan was soon to begin writing: "The Structure of Rime" and "Passages." The chain of sentences with birds erupting from it runs not only into the abyss, "the empty shafts of sense," but also through a history of the prose poem, as Duncan read it in Charles Henri Ford's "Little Anthology of the Poem in Prose" in *New Directions* 14 (1953), especially in poems by Mallarmé, Philip Lamantia, Magritte, Lautreamont, Ford, Poe, Nicolas Calas, and Nietzsche, and in Duncan's earlier reading of St.-John Perse. This history continues in the prose poems in *Letters* and the Stein imitations of the 1953 *Writing Writing* and in the "Structure of Rime" series. And it comes into a new phase in the "New Sentence" of Language Poetry, as theorized by Ron Silliman.

There is a direct continuity between *Letters* and *The Opening of the Field* (1960) that Duncan sought to obscure by speaking of his "projective" period as including the latter book, *Roots and Branches* (1964) and *Bending the Bow* (1968). According to Bertholf, Duncan finished the poems of *Letters* in December 1955 and began *The Opening of the Field* less than two months later. Some of the very first poems he wrote for the new book were the first seven prose poems in the "Structure of Rime" sequence, which he published as sections of a single poem in the famous "San Francisco Scene" issue of *Evergreen Review* in 1957. The "Structure of Rime" picks up from the Kabbalah-inspired prose poems of *Letters*, taking words and sentences as animate beings capable not only of conjuring things but also of measuring the world and thought. The "Structure of Rime" calls forth an "*absolute scale of resemblance and disresemblance*" that "*establishes measures that are music in the actual world*" (*Selected Poems*, 46); this scale and the measures it establishes partake of the kabbalistic correspondences worked out in the poems of *Letters*.

J Despite their kabbalistic currents, the prose poems of *Letters* and "The Structure of Rime" played an important but mostly unacknowledged part in the development of the New Sentence in San Francisco in the seventies.

Duncan functioned for many of the Language poets as not only a primary conduit for the innovations of Stein, Pound, and Zukofsky, but also as a relentless and deconstructive explorer of the interactions of words, grammar, the sentence, and the book. The surplus metaphorizing in Duncan's poetry and prose prepared many younger poets to appreciate such qualities in the French thinkers and poets they would read and respond to in the seventies. In fact, the lush, over-ripe riming and ringing of tones in Duncan's poetry has the sound of poetry in French, where there is a much smaller phonemic repertoire to choose from and a tendency for much greater repetition. In English this can strike readers as a baroque quality, out of fashion in resolutely modernist circles. What Duncan gains by this obsessive word-play and sound-repetition is an ability to dig, like Mallarmé or the Joyce of *Finnegans Wake*, into the very structure of language—into that which makes statements and apprehensions possible.

Transparent Things

A Sinner of Memory. Melita Schaum. East Lansing: Michigan State University Press, 2004.

James Walton

An "Author's Note" identifies *A Sinner of Memory* as a collection of essays in "Creative Nonfiction," a genre that uses invention in the service of authenticity. Since all confessional narrative parses into fiction and non-fiction and all its narrators, in Shakespearean phrase, make sinners of memory, Melita Schaum's unnamed essayist can be identified as her book's Confessional Heroine (C.H.). At one point Schaum's C. H., like (say) Charlotte Brontë's Jane Eyre or Doris Lessing's Anna Wulf, brings us into the writer's present:

> I droop over my writing, palm these reluctant pages. For four months I have been trying to tell this tale. I have made it a comedy, a tragedy, an instructional piece, a jumble of aphorisms, a *palatum cordis*—like the medieval monks who needed to taste the word of God with the heart's palate.

Elsewhere she makes occasional use of the present tense to execute her general design of containing multiple strata of the past—as memory or told story—within the narrative present. This procedure, of course, will recall Proust even (or especially) to those among us who have scarcely sampled *A la recherche du temps perdu*. A nearer comparison might be made with a slender fiction of Nabokov's in which present objects are treated as "transparent things through which the past shines."

In trying to *tell*, the narrator succeeds in a way that disposes of the Workshop canard about showing, *not* telling. The C. H. is less concerned that we see the figures haunting her memory than that we feel them as she does. Her parents, refugees from war-ravaged Germany, bloomed and faded in their adopted country, having made for themselves a "normal" life that elegantly illustrates that convergence of *heimlich* with *unheimlich* which Freud highlighted in his essay on "The Uncanny." The father, a reserved, adaptive academic, seems at times conjured into existence by his daughter's solicitude. The moral (not physical) dimensions of the mother are clearer. Early along, her retentiveness about *things* collides with the heroine's carelessness. Later the impression of maternal severity is softened by the discovery that the "child of war and poverty" is haunted by her own mother, whose avatar, the resident of a nursing home, she treats with filial tenderness. As offspring of stolid middle-class immigrants, the C. H. and her "beautiful" sister pass from rival responses to parental authority in childhood to a recognition, in middle age, that they have become prisoners of no regime but their own.

The heroine's family make affecting but faint specters by comparison with the figure she calls "my lover." He haunts all nine essays, appearing and vanishing, never fully present, a demystified dæmon. Submerged within the C. H.'s circumstantial account of this relationship—the discourse of nonfiction—are the two traditional plots of amorous narrative—Separation and Reunion, Seduction and Betrayal. Both express the ambivalence of love, but it is the latter that supplies the dénouement of the present romance. An ironically named "Epithalamion" concludes a long series of proleptic glances at the end of the affair. (Very early she tells us "I gave him my life and he let it fall.")

The book's calculated confusion about genre and mode could only have been resolved at the expense of authenticity. If its fragments of personal history had been assembled into a linear narrative the C. H. would have emerged as a female Quixote, or even a modern *picara*, itinerant, transgressive, but subject to the conditions of contemporary life. Since narrative is necessarily a plot-seeking form of discourse, the eponymous Sinner, on a hint from Wallace Stevens' "World as Meditation," tries to shape her experience into an epic *manqué*. It begins *in medias res* with a descent into the underworld, or catacombs, of Paris. (Balzac and Hugo anticipated Schaum in representing Paris as an inferno of the here and now.) As Odyssey, the heroine's journey homeward is thwarted by the Zeno-logic that a destination always approached can never be reached. Through an attribute transferred from her mother, she figures also as Penelope, waiting, weaving and unweaving, her art analogous to Schaum's text, a fabric so reticulated as to give us repeated glimpses of the void.

Readers enthralled by Schaum's descriptions of place will object to the present review's devaluation of the visual. After Paris, the epic itinerary includes Ann Arbor, artists' colonies in southern California and upstate New York, the Italian alps, the Rockies, the High Sierras, the Scottish Highlands, the Coral Islands, a Princeton nursing home, her parents' Arizona retirement community—that last a littered desert, not in bloom: "But there was violet light, as beautiful as anything dreamt of by Monet, and crows flying slowly, high and separate in the cold, dense air;" and by evening "the edge of the earth" is "just a line of orange, then beige, then blue. The palm trees are elegant black silhouettes against the disappearing sky." On her way to Mesa she stops to watch a sunset ("the horizon's wild apocalypse") that competes with a burning truck for the spectators' attention:

> One minute the sky was eggshell green and the clouds the color of fresh blood;
> the next, the arroyos were suffused with purple and the air shot gold. We were
> all of us drop-jawed—cops, truckers, the young camera-toting woman, and
> me—watching these sublime conflagrations.

The most vivid moment occurs during the heroine's snorkling adventure in
the Coral Sea—her second ambivalent immersion:

> All at once, I am dazzled. A school of jacks, gift from the sea, has material-
> ized all around me like a sprung slot machine, an avalanche of silver. For several
> long heartbeats I am caught up in their wild shine, their perfect dance, as they
> dart around me in unison, glimmer on all sides like spilled mercury. Unearthly
> phosphorescence; sudden, sheer harmony.
>
> Then the school parts and I see the sharks. Three of them, eight feet long,
> thrashing as if to shake themselves free of their own skins, mantled in a back-
> drop of dark blue where the reef plummets into open ocean. I realize that they
> have been herding fish into the wall of rock and coral; now they are about to
> feed. One approaches me, swerves, then advances again—ten feet away, seven,
> six, then passes so close I could touch its emery-board skin, could cup the black,
> inhuman eye that rolls back at me like a savage new moon. My heart lifts in my
> chest, enters a strange, bottomless space, a swoon of fear. All laws fall away.

What the reader "sees" in such passages is not a series of objects in space
but a demonstration, on the flat field of the text, of the transformative power of Style. In the confessional narrator herself, after all, we behold not the
original but a reflection in the mirror of her consciousness, transposed into
language. The authorial subject is always absent. Schaum calls her "reverie's
exile," haunting her own life. Any contrary claim would be Nonfiction's
fiction. All memoirs, of course (but not *only* memoirs), are narcissistic
structures. As signature of the artist-as-Narcissus, projected into the order of
Nature, Schaum chooses an object that has been used to a comparable purpose in Mann's *Death in Venice*, Joyce's *Portrait*, and countless poems: "We
stop to watch a white heron, the island's namesake, standing motionless in
a small lagoon. A pale question mark, etched against the gloom of cypress
trees and water, its slim beak a dagger, hungry to spear its own reflection
from the deep."

At the conclusion of the final essay Melita Schaum's Confessional
Heroine, in a twilight sleep on her way to surgery, has a joyful vision of the
end as imaginary beginning, the unachieved objective of her troubled and
ecstatic (she *did* find a word for it)—pilgrimage.

RHYMES WITH HISTORY:
JOE FRANCIS DOERR AND KEVIN DUCEY

Joe Francis Doerr, *Order of the Ordinary*. Cambridge, England: Salt, 2003.
Kevin Ducey, *Rhinoceros*. Port Townsend, Washington: Copper Canyon, 2004.

Robert Archambeau

What are the poets reading? If you were to ask Jeffrey Roessner, the editor of *The Possibility of Language*, he might say something like what he said in the introduction to that 2001 anthology of younger poets associated with Notre Dame. There, Roessner noted the wide range of influences on the poets, finding the range exciting and just a little bit troubling. It seemed that everyone was reading something different, and this, Roessner thought, indicated an unusual situation in literary history:

> Contemporary poets have not inherited a single, well-defined lineage. Yes, the classics are still with us. But more poetry is being written and read today than perhaps at any other time in history—and almost everyone is reading something different. In this way, contemporary poetry mirrors the profusion of signals in satellite television: hundreds of channels, each beamed at a small, distinct audience. If T.S. Eliot began this trend by constructing his own tradition, now every individual talent is consigned to work through his or her own version of poetic history, often in maddening, disheartening isolation.

The loss of a sense of a shared collective tradition is the price one pays for freedom in one's influences, and for all of the discovery that comes with our post-canonical age. But just what are the poets of our age doing with this freedom? Roessner saw, in his poets, a range of reading and influence extending from Old Welsh texts to H.G. Wells, from Gerard Manley Hopkins to Strunk and White. But a glance through almost any of the mainstream poetry journals crowded into the back corner of your local Barnes and Noble reveals that too few poets have made good use of their post-canonical freedoms. Many seem to have read nothing but the works of their teachers at the local MFA mill, teachers who themselves seem to have used their library cards a bit lightly. In their work one is confronted time and time again, with poems that fail to get past the claustrophobia-inducing confines of the poet's daily life. Once seen as a courageous act of breaking through to raw authenticity, this confessional mode has become the cloister where poets hide from the wider world.

If, however, the poets in question were taught by any of the rapidly graying Language crowd, one is often left with a different kind of claustrophobia: the usable past too often shrinks to a tradition born no earlier than Gertrude Stein. I once saw Charles Bernstein parody this tendency in second-generation Language writers: he showed a slide of cavemen crudely daubing the walls of their cave by torchlight, and said "here is the state of poetry before I launched my magazine." Before the seventies, he implied, all was but a dire darkness and stricken lay the land. Oddly, he didn't get a laugh from the self-consciously hip crowd at Chicago's Museum of Contemporary Art. (If you look past the moon-eyed author portraits on the cover of the *American Poetry Review*, you're likely to find some sort of ghastly hybrid of the confessional and the late-Langpo, a kind of unholy spawn of Jorie Graham, combining the worst from both solipsistic traditions. But let us leave those broad newsprint pages on the shelf, turning our backs on their sensitively brooding cover models).

The poets in Roessner's anthology, whatever their individual talents or shortcomings, all show a wide sense of the possibilities of poetry in terms of both form and subject. In a sense, this comes from a habit not unlike that of their confessional or Langpo peers: they have read their teachers with admiration. And one teacher they all share is John Matthias. Matthias, who retires from Notre Dame in 2005, is one of the most well-read and broadly learned poets of his generation ("John is an interesting man," John Berryman once said of Matthias, "but he is *very* literary"). Matthias' stylistic affinities range across the whole spectrum of contemporary idioms, and across the centuries (he is, to my knowledge, the only poet ever to have made a poetic project of translating Thomas Hardy into Middle English). He has a well-informed historical consciousness, and his work reveals both his deep knowledge of obscure corners of history and his uncanny sense for the links between apparently disparate people and incidents. (If you read his "Working Progress, Working Title," you'll see exactly what Hedy Lamar had to do with the invention of the remote control. Really.) Joe Francis Doerr, one of the poets from Roessner's anthology, has now come out with his first book, as has Kevin Ducey, a student of Matthias who came to Notre Dame too late to make the cut for *The Possibility of Language*. Doerr and Ducey each in their own ways exhibit the wide literary and historical range of their teacher. If their work represents a trend away from autobiography and old-school Language Writing, and toward a larger sense of the possibilities of poetry, it will be a most welcome and refreshing development in American literature.

Doerr's *Order of the Ordinary* draws from Matthias in its powerful historical imagination and in the way that it focuses that imagination around particular pieces of found historical text. In one of the book's most remarkable poems, the twenty-page "Corrigenda," Doerr also shows a deep affinity with one of Matthias' great influences, the often-overlooked Anglo-Welsh modernist David Jones. The poem begins by quoting a Welsh source text, the elegiac lament for a dead son "Marwnat Owein," a text now all-but-unreadable to anyone but the scholarly specialist ("Eneit owein ap uryen,/ gobwyllit y ren oe reit" read the first two lines). Over the course of the following pages we see the old Welsh poem slowly reworked into contemporary English. These reworkings are interspersed with comments on the translation, as well as John Cage-style acrostics that make further, somewhat elliptical comments on the act of translation. Eventually the "Marwnat Owein" emerges in modern English, but not as a literal translation. Instead, the fourth section is anachronistically entitled "War Music for Steel Guitar," and takes place in contemporary Texas where Doerr grew up:

> Uriah's boy Owen is dead,
> > may God have mercy on his soul.
> We dressed him in his favorite green
> > shirt and put him on the table there.
> No one would spit in your eye
> > for crying over him.

Owen remains a dead son, and remarkably like the Owen of the original lament, but the speaker and events are recognizably of our own time. Doerr has (in the manner of David Jones) shown the continuities of past and present, even as he shows us the irreducible differences of different eras by retaining the original text in all of its alien unreadability.

Doerr doesn't avoid the contemporary world or the powerful experiences of the self, even though he avoids the conventions that Marjorie Perloff calls "the authenticity model—the 'true voice of natural feeling' or 'natural speech' paradigm." Those confessional conventions, still predominant in the pages of the fat quarterlies pumped out by your local university's creative writing program, place the contemporary self at the center of the poem. In contrast, Doerr puts the contemporary self at the margin of his poem, as the translator of the Welsh text. We see this figure in the same way that we catch glimpses of the medieval scribes who left their spoor of commentary in the margins of their annotated texts. The speaker of "Corrigenda" faces the problems Doerr faces as translator, and this speaker can be as closely identified with the poet himself as is the speaker of any emotionally-expressive confessional lyric. Even in sections composed only of the source-text Doerr projects himself into the text with the translation-themed acrostics. But this self does not come to dominate the poem, which remains a far cry from lyric solipsism and confessional navel-gazing.

Doerr plays elaborate and fascinating textual games, but he retains a strong sense of emotional energy. As the linguistic impenetrability of the Welsh "Marwnat Owein" gives way to a revelation of the elegiac core of that poem, we experience a slowly growing sense of the pain of a parent who has lost a son, and a sense of the long, tearful history of such losses over the centuries. The poem has all the linguistic sophistication and self-conscious-ness of the Buffalo school, but takes us well outside the emotional range of all but a handful of those poets.

Doerr finds a kind of subject-rhyme between past and present in the juxtaposition of the medieval Welsh "Marwnat Owein" and the contempo-rary Texan "War Music for Steel Guitar." He finds similar rhymes in many of the other poems of *Order of the Ordinary*, most often through investigat-ing a historical text (such as *Venus in Furs* in "Thumbnails for Portrait of Sacher-Masoch") or a language-archive (such as Nordic runes in "F U T H A R K 2K," which must have made his typesetter cry). If you feel a little grandiloquent, you might call this the Poetics of the Archive. It is a fruitful method for our post-canonical times, in which those poets who read all read idiosyncratically. By choosing particular texts as his fields of poetic investiga-tion, Doerr allows us the intertextual pleasures outlined in Eliot's "Tradition and the Individual Talent" without relying on Eliot's received canon of great works. The texts needn't be widely familiar or culturally shared (what is, these days?): the sustained, careful working-through of the specific text or archive will make it familiar in the process of the reading. This method, one suspects, is learned from Matthias, who uses both specific texts and specific geographies to give his work a range of significance beyond the self.

Like Doerr's *Order of the Ordinary*, Kevin Ducey's *Rhinoceros* ranges far and wide through a variety of historical and literary references in seeking out the rhymes between past and present. Unlike Doerr, though, Ducey throws a generous handful of pop-culture into the mix, and tears some of his subject matter from the headlines of the newspapers. Consider "Dien Bien Phu," a poem that begins with flintlock-toting chieftains from hostile tribes, takes us to the French at war in Vietnam, and then leads us here:

> The Vandals beyond the Rhine
> were largely runaway slaves dispossessed
> freemen, seniors
> unable to afford prescription drugs—

Rome had it coming.

The drawing of parallels between the here-and-now and the there-and-then is very much the sort of thing we'd find in Doerr's work. But the topicality of the poem and the easy offhandedness with which Ducey connects current events (American senior citizens road-tripping up to Canada to outflank America's unforgivably profit-driven medical system) and the historical (the slaves fleeing Rome) presents a real contrast with Doerr. There's also a difference in tone. Doerr is most comfortable with the elegiac, the disturbing, and at times something like the sublime—a rare combination in our times, and admirable. Ducey's touch is lighter, and he's often quirky and a bit comic. "Those hooligans out there, pal,/don't care much for your poetry —" he writes, "They zooming round in them/shaggy pony chariots (celts?) with/.50 caliber mounted on back. Go/tell it to the Geats." Yet he's no less an acolyte of the often-funny Matthias for this—a fact to which the poem's epigraph, taken from an essay on Matthias by Brooke Bergan, attests.

Ducey's poems delight in the miscegenation of mythologies, crossbreeding, for example, the Greek and the Native American in a quickie couplet that refers to "The shadow visit to hell where/coyote can't restrain himself." There is also a fair amount of pop culture twisted together with all the high culture. Batman rubs shoulders with Atalanta in "Hero Tales," and the book's final poem, "Wim Wenders vs. the Wolfman," gives us both cinema and the movies. What's interesting about this mixing of pop culture and museum culture isn't simply that it happens—the gesture was already showing its age when Frank O'Hara made it in "The Day Lady Died." It is the ease with which it happens that is of interest. There's no sense of campiness or condescension to it: Ducey is part of a generation suckled in the creed of postmodernism, and he moves between pantheons and cultural registers in complete comfort, feeling no need for any knowingly pursed lips, arched eyebrows, or fingers crooked into imaginary quotation marks.

All of this play is fun to watch: at times it is breathtaking. If there is a vice to the work, though, I suppose it could be found in just the slightest hint of the unbearable lightness of correspondences. Everything here-and-now seems to connect with everything there-and-then, quite quickly and quite briefly. If Doerr gives us a weighty (but never ponderous) poetics of the archive, Ducey gives us the intertextual freestyle, a running-and-gunning poetics filled with historical targets of opportunity. (I'd be delighted, by the way, if he were to use that as jacket copy somewhere. No charge.)

As distinct as they are, Ducey and Doerr share a fundamental orientation toward the rhyming of the familiar with the unfamiliar. They take us out of the cloister of the self and beyond the version of literary history Bernstein parodied with his picture of cavemen. They are well worth your time, and their books are an intriguing index of the possibilities of poetry in our new century.

"THIS DELICATE BALANCE":
TWO BOOKS BY DIANE THIEL

Resistance Fantasies, Diane Thiel. Story Line Press, 2004. *The White Horse: A Colombian Journey*, Diane Thiel. Etruscan Press, 2004.

Kathryn Kruger

These two books—a poetry collection and a travel narrative—give us intelligent observations into the subtle dynamics of power and address the question of how can we live and relate graciously in this world. Her perceptions arise from a deep understanding of history, both human history and that of the earth itself. Thiel's books spotlight how the struggle for personal or political gain has shaped the story of life, a dialectic that makes for two worthwhile encounters.

In *Resistance Fantasies*, Thiel explores how desire propels and shapes our own stories. In these poems power figures not only as theme, but often as plot and occasionally as the antagonist or protagonist (depending which side you're on) of the poems themselves.

Thiel divides her book into four sections, each part developing the dialectic between desire and resistance, lust and disgust with power, as well as different forms of victimization. The first section, 'Black Seas,' offers poems from Thiel's memories of Odessa in the Ukraine as well as her preoccupation with Greek and Russian myths, folklore and literary legends. In "Sevenlings for Akhmatova" Thiel writes movingly:

> I
> It comes in threes—the red letter,
> the midnight warning in disguise,
> the knock that shakes the shutters.
>
> My face learns to have three sides.
> One third smiles and waves at the station.
> Another slides under and hides.
>
> The last goes to the interrogation

'Black Seas' not only sets the tone and theme, but begins the work of transformation that constitutes the book's poetics, for what Thiel does through careful organization and persistence of inquiry, is to transmute personal, human experience into the work of myth. Thus, in the second and third sections, 'Resistance Fantasies' and 'Lost in Translation,' Thiel explores her own personal encounters with power and resistance through the same lens that she views the folklore and myths of her first section. 'Editorial Suggestives' returns the reader to a similar tone as 'Black Seas,' but by now Thiel has widened her discourse to include memory, nature, and the construction of language itself.

At the beginning of *Resistance Fantasies* the poet dashes any hope in the possibility of escape. In "If You Don't," the poet imagines eluding the struggle between victim and victor and what such a life would look like. In a series of negations she writes: "If you don't have a dog / your neighbor will not poison it / . . . if you don't have a memory / the past cannot devour you / when you stop moving for a brief / moment. Long enough to let the sorrow / catch the joy you never feel . . ."

Throughout *Resistance Fantasies*, poems succeed in weaving a complex labyrinth in which the reader encounters a Minotaur in its rawest and most passionate form. Thiel's poems are distinguished by her fine ability to transform the disparate experiences of everyday life into living myth. Each of us has been a Daphne resisting Apollo as well as an Apollo seeking domination. Thiel demonstrates how our lives are inscribed with this mythic tension. She does so with remarkable skill of form, rhythm and rhyme, qualities that invest her language with beauty and authority. From the sonnet, "Pushkin and the Black Sea":

> He came to meet me shortly after
> arriving—running down Odessa's Steps,
> all ears on that compelling laughter,
> all tongues in cheeks on the swing of those hips.
> What did he want with all those women?
> All he needed was a good swim in
> my morning waves, my long caress.
> . . . .

Finally, Thiel is a multifaceted poet. She handles the retelling of myth, both historical and private, with a deft hand, and then sets beside her own songs the voices of Sor Juana, Alfonsina Storni, Cesar Vallejo, Nikos Kavadias and Anna Akhmatova. The result is a multi-faceted, multi-vocal conversation, reaching back toward myth and history, and then extending forward to the language and experience of today. Thiel provides evidence that our stories are continuous, and that over thousands of years they have not changed.

In *The White Horse*, Thiel records her journey from Panama to Chocó, the Pacific coast rainforest of Colombia where the Emberá tribe lives. Along with her intrepid guide and friend, Ana Maria, the two plunge into adventure. Their mission, a humanitarian one, entails hauling three microscopes for detecting malaria, a sack of medical books and incentives for starting craft industries to the rainforest people. Along the way, they encounter the warm hospitality of the Pan-American people and the region's otherworldly magic—from the haunting forest where tigers walk at dawn, to a river that winds toward the sea in which the skeleton of a whale is found beached and so large they can walk inside. Not a fairytale, but a real life adventure, Thiel writes:

> The Chocó forest looked vast, dense, and impenetrable from where we stood, as it must have looked centuries ago when the first outsiders came to this land. . . It was a blessing to come to a stand of trees that was still intact, still full of old spirits. (80)

Like a Blakean 'Song of Innocence and Experience', Thiel records the beauty of a people and a place—even as these people and this place are being destroyed. Juxtaposed with this romantic landscape is the stark reality of loggers clear-cutting ancient forests and men fishing with DDT—scooping dead fish from the water for selling at market or cooking at home.

Enriching her narrative with science and history, Thiel traces the fascinating connections among the forces that have shaped Colombia—its geology, geography, foreign invasions, slave trade, gold mining, etc. Not through polemic, but through the eyes of a poet, Thiel writes passionately about how we as human beings can become aware of our interdependence with the forces that have shaped and nurtured us. In this way, the author's experience becomes our own. We feel with her the Emberá's connection to the earth as root and limb, straining under the unhallowed practice of deforestation. We can hear the felling of trees around the close-knit tribe. One by one they drop as the Emberá struggle to retain their community, history, and connection to the forest that sustains them. Taking part in one of the tribe's ceremonies, Thiel remarks how she felt herself transforming into one of the trees on which their lives depend:

> They painted the earth pattern down each of my arms, one long stroke down and then short strokes coming out of the sides. . . I raised my arms so they could paint my sides, and I felt them extend upwards and burst into branches. (246)

In one chapter, Thiel meets up with a geologist who works for an American gold-mining company. The company is investigating the promise of gold on the land of a local owner. The search for gold, Thiel has already reminded us in a previous chapter, was one of the major forces to shape South America—the land and its indigenous people—since Columbus. Over five hundred years later, gold seekers are still in business, and their politics, though less vitriolic, are as self-interested as ever. However, rather than denouncing history and the people who created it, rather than dwelling in outrage, Thiel moves the reader into the possibility of a new perspective, one where we see ourselves not as the earth's center, but as part of something greater, more extraordinary than anything we could have invented ourselves. Moving effortlessly from scientific fact to poetry, she states:

> Scientists now believe that gold must have been created long before the creation of the earth. Any element heavier than iron must have been created by a supernova, which sprinkled it throughout this part of the universe. Gold is hence the product of supernovas, as we ourselves are made up of the same basic elements as stars.
>
> The sun had not yet fallen, but one of the first stars had already come out and beckoned there on the horizon. An invisible thread connected my eye to the star and the star to the rock in my hand, and I felt the little river of gold run into my own veins, reminding me that I too was part of this delicate balance. (165)

"This delicate balance" forms the leitmotif of both *The White Horse* and *Resistance Fantasies*.

EDITORS SELECT

Czeslaw Milosz, *Second Space*, translated by the author and Robert Hass, Ecco, 2004. This will be the final book of "new poems" by the great Polish poet. Written in extreme old age, the poems show no diminishment in his powers and engage with courage and clarity their mostly elegiac subjects. *NDR* is proud to have published one of the major poems in the selection, "Apprentice," which is about the author's early relationship with his kinsman and mentor O.V. de L. Milosz. That poem ends: "So it is important to know how to repeat after Goethe: *Respect! Respect! Respect!*" The last words of this last book.

Daniel Weissbort, *From Russian With Love: Joseph Brodsky in English*, Anvil Press, 2004. Weissbort published a long review of Brodsky's *Collected Poems In English* in *NDR* #14. This book begins where the review left off. The author met and began collaborating with Brodsky on translations of his work soon after the Russian poet arrived in the West. The relationship between the two, both personal and artistic, is fascinating to read about. The book is simultaneously a treatise on translation and an elegy for Brodsky. As the James Bondish title suggests, it is also full of humor and Weissbort's usual self-deprecating charm. The

tone of the book, in fact, has a great deal in common with Weissbort's poems addressed to Ted Hughes in *Letters To Ted*, which was recently listed in Editors Select.

John Hartley Williams, *Blues*, Cape Poetry, 2004. Williams begins this book with yet another elegy—for frequent *NDR* contributor Ken Smith. Williams has a good deal in common with Smith, and writes an essentially European poetry rather than work that is English or British in any kind of insular sense. The poem to Smith includes a passage describing an almost uncanny event reported by everyone who was at the funeral of the author of "Fox Running": "But I don't believe/ that that the fox/ seen loping/ through the cemetery/ as we carried your coffin/ down the weed-grown path/ was anything more/ than beautiful coincidence/ nor,/ returning to your grave at midnight,/ that the shape-shifter fellow/ late vigil-keepers saw/ was anything other/ than that same/ interested creature, sitting out the night/ beside disturbed ground . . ."

Mark Scroggins, *Anarchy*, Spuyten Duyvil Books, 2003. Scroggins is the best known critic, and now also the biographer, of Louis Zukofsky. While this first volume of poems shows some affinities with Zukofsky, its attention to Cromwell, Ruskin, and Charles I's apocryphal "Eikon Basilike" also locates it somewhere between Susan Howe in *The Nonconformist's Memorial* and the recent work of Geoffrey Hill, if one can imagine either one of these poets also taking an interest in Johnny Rotten and the Sex Pistols. For a fan of the Pooh stories, however, his poem on "The Passing of Eeyore" is almost too much to bear (as it were).

Martin Corless-Smith, *Nota*, Fence Books, 2003. Corless-Smith, a British poet now living and teaching in Boise, Idaho, makes use of his sources in a way not dissimilar to Mark Scroggins. Creating a palimpsest and collage out of 17th century materials, his poem takes one of its epigraphs from David Jones' *The Anathemata*: "One is trying to make a shape out of the very things of which one is oneself made." It will be difficult to find readers for this demanding book (or its predecessor, *Complete Travels*), but those with the patience to follow Corless-Smith as he tracks some of the things of which he is himself made will be rewarded for their attention.

Peter Riley, *The Dance at Mociu*, Shearsman Books, 2003. Two of these "stories and prose-poems" about Peter Riley's annual journeys through Transylvania appeared in *NDR*. In his preface to the volume he says that he "went in search of music; everything else was glimpsed out of the corner of the eye, and hung on the frailty of singular in-

stances. But instances which clearly could not occur anywhere else." The music of the prose evoking such singular instances is memorable and rich, like that of Riley's poems.

Ben Downing, *The Calligraphy Shop*, Zoo Press, 2003. Downing is a formalist of great skill and wit. Eric Ormsby has called him "a scamp in a tuxedo." Writing on Fermat's famous Last Theorem, he says "I have written a wonderful poem/ which this page, alas, cannot contain; in its place, accept a lesser one/ proving nothing and provisional as rain." In the title poem and elsewhere in this brief book, one finds some fine poems that the page is, luckily, able to contain and which prove to be a good deal more than provisional.

Two Chapbooks: Reginald Gibbons, *In the Warhouse*, Fractal Edge Press, 2004, and Gerald L. Bruns, *Fictional Poems*, privately printed, 2004. Gibbons' political and satirical poems include a "Prayer Heard from Behind a Pine Tree." Guess who? "Apocopapalyptic waiting, unerrucible faith!—/ we shall bless Thy name Lord/ and thine hysterious ways shall be revealed unto us/ as of old—mysterical things,/ and speaking in tongues shall return/ till after jabber a light shines from above,/ and crooked leg is made straight…" Bruns's chapbook you will have to obtain directly from the elusive and otherwise theoretical author. All we know is that "the poems were set in Goudy and ITC Officina Sans in South Bend, Indiana, USA under isolated skies with partly sunny thunderstorms." There are only 100 copies. We have number 8. We suggest that our readers try to secure one of the remaining 92 copies. Our contributing editor is a poet of real interest whose work, we hope, will soon appear in a larger and more accessible book.

Alan Goldfein, *Europe's Macadam, America's Tar*, American Editions Heildelberg, 2004. Short story writer Goldfein's second excursion into transnational nonfiction. The book deals with the incorrigible American heartland delusion of Best: wealth, infrastructure, morality, and contrasts all that with examples from France and Germany. Reminiscent of Jeremy Rifkin's *The European Dream*, but quirkier, more personal—and better written.

Joan Silber, *Ideas of Heaven*, Norton, 2004. Joan Silber's new book, her fifth, is termed "a ring of stories," because a minor element of one becomes a major element in another. And, likewise, in the literary world, the volume went from being minor to major when it was named a finalist for the National Book Awards fiction category in 2004. Indeed, the minor to major jump was exaggerated because all of the fiction nominees were women living in New York City: Sarah Shun-lien Bynum, Christine Schutt, Lily Tuck, and Kate Walbert were the others. This congruity spawned part of the controversy that followed, but its main cause was the complaint by those who generate publicity for books, the large papers and reviews, especially the *New York Times* (which only had taken notice of two of the nominees—Tuck [and In Brief review] and Walbert [the most commercial of the lot]—in its powerful Book Review.) This sort of brouhaha is cyclical and expected. It brought to mind the flap over *Paco's Story*, by Larry Heinemann, which won the National Book Review in 1987, and was only reviewed, badly, by the *TBR* after it was nominated. Literary fashion is a high-capital enterprise and those who control it do not like upstarts to interfere. You can only be a major writer if you are successful—that is, don't embarrass anyone with poor sales—and certainly you can't be one if the organs of enthusiasm don't know who you are and haven't made you famous. But, every once in a while those organs get their comeuppance. And, it appears, it is only prizes that let this happen, because there are still maverick judges who will be happy to tweak the establishment and show it how much it doesn't know. And the literary world—at least, those who promote it—don't know any more about who is good, who is great, and who ain't, than any other flack hoping to climb aboard the fast-moving wagons of the overexposed. So, here's to the five women writers of Manhattan, especially Joan Silber, whose last book of short stories was noted in an earlier number (11) of Editors Select. For the record, Lily Tuck's novel, *The News from Paraguay*, was awarded the prize. But, all the books nominated are prizes themselves.

CONTRIBUTORS

Robert Archambeau's new book of poems, *Home and Variations*, was recently published by Salt. He teaches at Lake Forest College. **Jeffery Bahr** is a software development manager and lives in Colorado. His work has been recently published or is forthcoming in *32 Poems*, *Black Warrior Review*, *Chelsea*, *Green Mountains Review*, *Indiana Review*, *The Journal*, *Prairie Schooner*, *Quarterly West* and *Swink*. **Simeon Berry** lives in Boston, where he is a poetry and fiction reader for *Ploughshares*. He has won an Academy of American Poets Award and a Career Chapter Award from the National Society of Arts and Letters. His work has been published in *The Antioch Review*, *Southern Poetry Review*, *Seneca Review*, *Cream City Review*, *New Orleans Review*, and is forthcoming in *Washington Square*, *AGNI*, and *Verse*. **Louis Bourne**, a long-time resident of Madrid, has been translating Spanish poetry for over thirty years. His translations of Claudio Rodríguez have appeared in various journals in the US and England, including *Granite*, *International Poetry Review*, *New Directions 26*, and *Stand*. He currently teaches in the Spanish Department of Georgia College & State University. **Regina Derieva** has published 20 books of poetry, essays, and prose. Her books have been translated into English, French, and Italian. Additionally, her work has appeared in the *Modern Poetry in Translation*, *Salt*, *Ars Interpres*, *Cross Currents*, as well as in many Russian magazines. She currently lives in Sweden. **Ed Falco** has three books forthcoming this year: a volume of short fictions (*In the Park of Culture*); a collection of short stories (*Sabbath Night in the Church of the Piranha: New and Selected Stories*); and an as-yet-untitled novel. This spring he is teaching in Riva San Vitale, Switzerland, at Virginia Tech's Center for European Studies. **Stephen Fredman** is professor of English and Department Chair at the University of Notre Dame. His most recent book is *A Menorah for Athena: Charles Reznikoff and the Jewish Dilemmas of Objectivist Poetry*. **Debora Greger**'s new book of poetry, *Western Art*, was published by Penguin in Fall 2004. **Mark Halperin** is the author of four volumes of poetry, the most recent of which are *Time as Distance*, *Near and Far*, and *Greatest Hits*. His translations from the Russian have appeared in *Pushcart Prizes 2003*, *Paris Review*, *Antioch Review* and *Virginia Quarterly*. He, his wife, and their dog live near the trouty Yakima. **Paul Kane**'s most recent collection of poems is *Drowned Lands*. A recipient of NEH and Guggenheim Foundation fellowships, he teaches at Vassar College. **Kirsten Kaschock**'s first book of poetry, *Unfathoms*, is available from Slope Editions. She is a Ph.D. student at the University of Georgia, and holds MFAs in dance and creative writing from the University of Iowa and Syracuse University, respectively. Other recent work of hers is forthcoming in *Pleiades, Octopus, Gutcult, LIT*, and *Diagram*. **John Kinsella** is the author of more than thirty books including *The Hunt, The Silo, The Hierarchy of Sheep*, and *Genre*. He is professor of English at Kenyon College, and his new volume of poetry, *The New Arcadia*, is forthcoming this summer. **John Koethe**'s most recent book of poems is *North Point North: New and Selected Poems*. "The Maquiladoras" will be included in a new book, *Sally's Hair*, to be published by HarperCollins. He is distinguished professor of Philosophy at the University of Wisconsin-Milwaukee. **Kathryn Kruger** has published two books, *Weaving the Word* and *Solstice*. Her articles and poetry have been published in many journals including *Water-Stone, Sufi* and *Rhino*. **Sheryl Luna** is the author of the forthcoming *Pity the Drowned Horses*, winner of the Andrés Montoya Poetry Prize awarded by the Institute for Latino Studies at Notre Dame. A native of El Paso, TX, she holds several degrees, including a Ph.D. from University of North Texas, and an M.F.A. from UTEP. She has published widely in such journals as *The Georgia Review, Prairie Schooner, Poetry Northwest, The Amherst Review*, and *Kalliope: A Journal of Women's Art and Literature*. She currently teaches at the Metropolitan State College of Denver. **Michelle Margolis** is a freelance writer living in Southern California. A previous contributor to *NDR*, her poems also have appeared in *Seneca Review, Passages North, The Journal, The Carolina Quarterly, No Exit, Interim*, and *Rattle*. **Bill Meissner**'s fourth book of poetry, *American Compass*, was published in 2004. His collection of fiction is entitled *Hitting Into the Wind*. He directs the creative writing program at St. Cloud State University in Minnesota. **Tom O'Connor** has had poetry accepted in *Dánta, No Exit, Skidrow Penthouse*, and *Soul Fountain*. **John Peck**'s *Collected Shorter Poems, 1966-1996* was recently published by Northwestern University Press/TriQuarterly Books. **Paulann Petersen**'s work has appeared in *Poetry, The New Republic, Prairie Schooner, Willow Springs, Calyx*, and the Internet's *Poetry Daily*. Her third collection of poems, *A Bride of Narrow Escape*, will be out this year. She serves on the board of Friends of William Stafford, organizing the January Stafford Birthday Events. **James D. Redwood** is a professor at Albany Law School. His fiction has appeared in the *Virginia Quarterly Review, Black Warrior Review*, and elsewhere. He has stories forthcoming in *The Kenyon Review* and *North Dakota Quarterly*. **Claudio Rodríguez** (1934 –1999) is considered one of the major voices in Spanish poetry in the latter half of the 20th Century. He made a remarkable debut in 1953, winning the Adonais Prize, Spain's most prestigious first-book award, with *The Gift of Inebriation* at age 19. In a career spanning more than forty years, he published five volumes of poetry, and garnered the most prestigious awards in Spanish poetry, including the National Poetry Prize in 1983, the Queen Sofía Prize in 1993, and the Prince of Austurias Prize in 1993. His *Complete Poems* appeared in 2001. Born in Zamora, he taught at various universities, including the Universities of Nottingham and Cambridge (1958-1964), and for a number of years with "NYU in Spain" in Madrid. **Frances Sherwood** has published three novels: *The Book of Splendor*, *Green* and *Vindication*. Her latest novel, *Betrayal*, is forthcoming. In addition, she has published numerous short stories, and has had work appear in *Best American Short Stories* and *The O. Henry Award* collections. **Brian Swann**'s latest book is *Voice From Four Directions: Contemporary Translations of the Native Literature of Notre America*. Forthcoming in 2005 is *Algonquian: Contemporary Translations of the Algonquian Literatures of North America*. **Keith Taylor**'s poems, translations and reviews have widely appeared here and in Europe. His most recent book, *What These Ithakas Mean: Readings in Cavafy*, a co-edited volume published by a nonprofit in Greece, was picked as one of the 2002 Books of the Year in the *Times Literary Supplement*. He teaches at the University of Michigan. **Maria Terrone** is the author of *The Bodies We Were Loaned*. Her work, which has been nominated for a Pushcart Award, has appeared in many anthologies and such magazines as *Poetry*, *Crab Orchard Review*, and *The Hudson Review*. She directs communications for Queens College in New York. **Steve Timm**'s work has recently appeared or is forthcoming in *American Letters & Commentary*, *Antennae*, *gam*, *Bird Dog*, *Moria*, and *Word/For Word*. He teaches English as a second language at the University of Wisconsin in Madison. **James Walton** is professor emeritus of English at Notre Dame. He has published a novel, *Margaret's Book*, and an anthology of poets from Notre Dame, *The Space Between*. **Daneen Wardrop**'s poems have appeared in *Seneca Review*, *TriQuarterly Magazine*, *Michigan Quarterly Review*, *Beloit Poetry Journal*, *Hayden's Ferry Review*, *Epoch*, *Gulf Coast*, *American Literary Review*, and many others. Professor of literature at Western Michigan University, she is the author of two books of literary criticism, including *Emily Dickinson's Gothic*. **Martha Zweig**, recipient of a 1999 Whiting Writer's Award, is the author of *What Kind* and *Vinegar Bone*, as well as a chapbook entitled *Powers*. Her poems have appeared in *Northwest Review*, *Manoa*, *Field*, *The Gettysburg Review*, *The Progressive*, and elsewhere.

NOTRE DAME REVIEW

NOTRE DAME REVIEW

NUMBER 19

Editors
John Matthias
William O'Rourke

Senior Editor   Steve Tomasula
Founding Editor   Valerie Sayers

&Now Editor   Steve Tomasula

Managing Editor   Executive Editor
Angela Hur   Kathleen J. Canavan

Sparks Editorial Asst.   Editorial Assistants
Renée E. D'Aoust   Sandy Dedo
                                 Mary Dixon
                                 Lisa Gonzales
Contributing Editors   Nathan Gunsch
Francisco Aragón   John Joseph Hess
Matthew Benedict   Lily Hoang
Gerald Bruns   Jennifer Malidor
Seamus Deane   Janet McNally
Stephen Fredman   Tom Miller
Sonia Gernes   Rebecca Pennell
Kevin Hart   Dani Rado
Orlando Menes   Matthew Ricke
James Walton   Dustin Rutledge
Henry Weinfield   Mark Stafford
                                 James Wilson

The *Notre Dame Review* is published semi-annually. Subscriptions: $15 (individuals) or $20 (institutions) per year or $250 (sustainers). Single Copy price: $8. Distributed by Ubiquity Distributors, Brooklyn, NY; Media Solutions, Huntsville, Alabama; Ingram Periodicals, LaVergne, Tennessee; and International Periodical Distributors, Solana Beach, California. We welcome manuscripts, which are accepted from September through March. Please include a SASE for reply. Please send all subscription and editorial correspondence to: *Notre Dame Review*, 840 Flanner Hall, University of Notre Dame, Notre Dame, IN 46556. *The Notre Dame Review* is indexed in *The American Humanities Index* and the *Index of American Periodical Verse*.

CONTENTS

What's Now about &Now 1

A Treatise of Whole Numbers 4
Joe Amato

The Division of the Soul; Homage to Thomas Wolfe;
Non-Additive Postulations 18
Scott Helmes

House Rules 21
Brian Evenson

More Pets 31
Caroline Bergvall

Minnie Mouse 33
Mary Jo Bang

Story 35
Lydia Davis

Missing Riddle No. 87; Missing Riddle No. 73;
Missing Riddle No. 67; Missing Riddle No. 64 38
TNWK

from Memorials to Future Catastrophes 42
Davis Schneiderman and Tom Denlinger

White Pages 45
Steve McCaffery

The Yellow Pages 46
Charles Bernstein

Letter from Durham, August 19, 2002 47
Paul Maliszewski

nothing stops; well yes; 760 people 52
Peter Balestrieri

The Speed of Zoom 55
Kass Fleisher

Harvey Strub's Dream, January 21, 2002 59
Paul Maliszewski

from The Book of Beginnings and Endings.. 61
Jenny Boully

Man and Woman.. 66
Mary Jo Bang

Some Machines (An Imaginary Epistolary)... 69
Lucy Corin

Insomnia... 74
Noam Mor

Labyrinth.. 77
Mark Marino

Czechoslovakian Rhapsody Sung to the Accompaniment of Piano.... 78
Debra Di Blasi

Entre Pyrobiblios... 96
Camille Bacos and mIEKAL aND

from 10:01.. 97
Lance Olsen

The Nature of the Creative Process 105
Lance Olsen and Tim Guthrie

Indecretions 106
Michael Joyce and Alexandra Grant

How Chicken George Put the Cat Among the Chickens 108
cris cheek

from Untitled 109
R.M. Berry

Language Acts: Poetry in Spacetime 115
Mike Barrett

Implementation **119**
Nick Montfort and Scott Rettberg

Letters to Unfinished J. **121**
Sheila E. Murphy

Anagrams of America **123**
Mike Smith

Index of First Lines **130**
Mrylin Hermes

from The Books of Ubar **136**
David Ray Vance, Catherine Kasper and Amy England

Biopoetry **145**
Eduardo Kac

Poetry Is **149**
George Quasha

Textfed **150**
William Gillespie

Vniverse **152**
Stephanie Strickland with Cynthia Lawson

Contributors **153**

WHAT'S NOW ABOUT &NOW

&NOW—a festival of new writing—was based on simple premises: a belief that the world changes (e.g. we now live with cloning, cell phones, e-mail); that people think in contexts other than those of our forebears (feminism did happen; jihads come west; cognitive science eclipses the talking cure; we've lived through revolutions in biology as well as in the humanities); that some authors, like some artists or musicians, work in forms that seem in sync with these contemporary ways of thinking about a contemporary world. No one expects today's architecture to mimic Bauhaus architecture. No one expects contemporary painting to be synonymous with post-impressionism. No one expects contemporary music to sound like Bach. So why shouldn't our expectations for what counts as a novel, short story, or poem also reflect larger historical changes? Why is it, as William Gass wonders, that the dominant form of the 20th century novel is the 19th century novel? That is, why does a survey of contemporary museums and galleries reveal such variety in what counts as visual art—the sculpture made of blood as well as more traditional painting and video—while a survey of the literature section of most bookstores (or course syllabi) suggests that the "literary" novel is a genre with constraints as narrow as those of the most commercially-driven, glossy, *New Yorker* story?

Unlike the 19th century novel, interactive CDs and Hip-Hop music come to mind as forms that embody our moment with their re-mix of competing viewpoints and styles, their juxtapositions of voices, bending of genres, boundary transgressions. In short, the Hip-Hop culture of ripping and burning seems to have many points of affinity with contemporary culture in general: a culture and an aesthetic made possible by the sampling and collage technology that allows DJs, or anyone with a laptop, to mix tracks, to incorporate all of musical history, TV shows, the whole theater of audio memory. But more important, it is an aesthetic born of a cultural mindset that thinks it's as natural to regard all culture as contingent and rearrange-able: as natural to us as Medievals once found looking for a Christian explanation for the order of the planets, or as Modernists would have thought it natural to articulate a Freudian unconscious. It's a mindset that makes many of the tenants Modernists took for granted, e.g., the Originality of a genius Artist soaring above History, seem passé.

So we put out a call. Who were the authors working from a larger-than-traditional conception of what counts as literature? What does their work look like? What does it say? The samples of writing in this issue of the *Notre Dame Review* reflect some of what we learned.

In the spirit of the festival, the authors and works gathered here do not mine those tired and false dichotomies often associated with new writing, the difference between High and low, for example, or Then and now: what so often is mis-characterized by the uninitiated as last-century's avant-garde agenda. Rather, like the festival itself, they are simply born out of a consideration of writing as a medium for art as practiced at our moment. If terms like "story" and "poem" are avoided, it's only because they don't seem to fit a work like Scott Helmes's "The Division of the Soul," a poem that is also an equation. If terms like "author" don't fit it's because the authorship of work like *Implementation* is as dispersed as its many on-line contributors. If terms like "literature" are avoided it is because they seem to imply institutions and canons and genre divisions and values that have more to do with the values of the publishing marketplace than those of artists. It is because thinking of writing as a medium as well as a material, in the way that all sound can be creative material to a soundscape composer, opens up possibilities for writing not normally considered literary: wire bent so its shadow casts words on the wall as in Alexandra Grant and Michael Joyce's collaborations. It is because they come out of a conception of literature as the Museum without Walls where a novel can be in the form of a videogame manual, as is Mark Marino's *Labyrinth*, or a travel guide like Michael Martone's *Blue Guide to Indiana*. Why not?

That is, if the 19th century novel is the literary equivalent of a painting of a clipper ship on the high seas, works like Eduardo Kac's "Biopoetry" or George Quasha's *Poetry Is* or Davis Schneiderman and Tom Denlinger's *Future Catastrophes* can be thought of as the literary equivalent to conceptual art. A different emphasis. A different orientation: one that privileges the conceptual in literature instead of the mimetic. As such, the & of &NOW does not imply a break with the past so much as a continuation in the way that Mike Smith's *Anagrams of America* takes literary history as its raw materials to make poetry that says something in a manner we can also see living outside the book. If works as diverse as Debra Di Blasi's image-text "Czechoslovakian Rhapsody," Lance Olsen's *10:01* collage, Brian Everson's hermetic and epistemological "House Rules," or Kass Fliesher's "Speed of Zoom" share any common concerns, it seems to be a disregard for categories. And the demonstration they provide that there can be no Now without a Then, especially a Then which begets a Now, which begets a Then, which begets a Now.... Or as Joe Amato says in his "Treatise of Whole Numbers," "Because it's aesthetic, it's momentary./ Because it's momentary, we're confused." But it's the pleasurable confusion of not being sure of all that literature is in the moment. The confusion that comes from not closing the book on literature, not being dogmatic or certain what literature is and is not, the confusion that resists placing all writing in easily packaged categories, or forsakes claim to what the future might look back on and decide literature was when Now is Then.

Textsounds, a gathering of sound poets and critics, convened at Notre Dame in the fall of 2004 and this issue also proudly presents work from some of those authors. A complete lineup of the authors who performed at *Textsounds* and &NOW can be found at www.nd.edu/~andnow. We'd also like to thank the &NOW Committee who dealt with a multitude of issues, with grace under pressure, and without whom the festival could not have been the success that it was: Shaun Dillon, Kevin Ducey, Lisa Gonzales, Angela Hur, Campbell Irving, Corey Madsen, Dani Rado, Kimberly Taylor, and especially Taranee Wangsatorntanakhun.

—*Steve Tomasula*

A Treatise of Whole Numbers

Joe Amato

> That is, in prose you start with the world
> and find the words to match; in poetry you start
> with the words and find the world in them.
>
> —Jed Rasula, *Syncopations*

0

Because we use our heads, we forget ourselves.
Because we forget ourselves, we forget our bodies.
Because we forget our bodies, we use our heads.

—Overheard at a gathering held at U of Notre Dame, early 21st century

1
Because it's not abstract, it's not just anybody.
Because it's not just anybody, it's somebody.
Because it's somebody, it's somebody like you.

Because it's somebody like you, the screen came between us.
Because the screen came between us, we came together.
Because we came together, I said so.

Because I said so, we might have.
Because we might have, it's not abstract.
Because it's not abstract, it's concrete.

Because it's concrete, we advance to the plot.
Because we advance to the plot, I rest my hand on the cold red granite.
Because I rest my hand on the cold red granite, the sky was cloudy.

Because the sky was cloudy, the sun is out.
Because the sun is out, we looked ahead to the plot.
Because we looked ahead to the plot, I don't know why.

Because I don't know why, you flew to Chicago.
Because you flew to Chicago, we poets think we're little gods.
Because we poets think we're little gods, poetry becomes synonymous with
    language.

Because poetry becomes synonymous with language, all prose is poetry.
Because all prose is poetry, not all poetry is prose.
Because not all poetry is prose, we tried to escape.

2
Because it's raining out, they tell me to.
Because they tell me to, I'm melancholy.
Because I'm melancholy, the narrative progresses.

Because the narrative progresses, art reveals itself as the artifice of patrician
    splendor.
Because art reveals itself as the artifice of patrician splendor, you fly to Chi-
    cago.
Because you fly to Chicago, we fall in love with a mysterious third party.

Because we fall in love with a mysterious third party, time stands still for a
    moment.
Because time stands still for a moment, eternity beckons.
Because eternity beckons, we return to our senses.

Because we return to our senses, Chicago becomes a small fishing village on
    the Mediterranean.
Because Chicago becomes a small fishing village on the Mediterranean,
    we're only one click away from a conversion of the real.
Because we're only one click away from a conversion of the real, we're in-
    stantly wealthy.

Because we're instantly wealthy, we have not a care in the world.
Because we have not a care in the world, the plot thickens.
Because the plot thickens, it's more difficult for the author to stir things up.

Because it's more difficult for the author to stir things up, you're quickly
    aroused.
Because you're quickly aroused, we have sex without protection.
Because we have sex without protection, you feel safer.

Because you feel safer, it's easier for me to do my job.
Because it's easier for me to do my job, I raise the hem on my skirt.
Because I raise the hem on my skirt, they think I'm a femme fatale.

3
Because you think you're white, you think she's white.
Because you think she's white, she says she's Latino.
Because she says she's Latino, I think I'm African American.

Because I think I'm African American, they must be Iraqi or Native American.
Because they must be Iraqi or Native American, a small fishing village on the Mediterranean becomes a country the size of Florida populated by young retirees.
Because a small fishing village on the Mediterranean becomes a country the size of Florida populated by young retirees, we demand new maps.

Because we demand new maps, we're viewed as demanding.
Because we're viewed as demanding, they might have been poor at one time.
Because they might have been poor at one time, they may never be wealthy.

Because they may never be wealthy, we won't notice the body.
Because we won't notice the body, he'll get away with it.
Because he'll get away with it, we'll buy his book.

Because we'll buy his book, we'll visit his website.
Because we'll visit his website, we'll send him an email or two.
Because we'll send him an email or two, he'll discontinue his website.

Because he'll discontinue his website, she'll question his fortitude.
Because she'll question his fortitude, he'll lose faith in Merriam-Webster (an Encylopædia Britannica company).
Because he'll lose faith in Merriam-Webster (an Encylopædia Britannica company), she'll abandon the plot.

Because she'll abandon the plot, we'll have far too many explanations on our hands.
Because we'll have far too many explanations on our hands, they'll have room for far too many answers.
Because they'll have room for far too many answers, magic will become indistinguishable from cliché.

4
Because it's not ideological, it's aesthetic.
Because it's aesthetic, it's momentary.
Because it's momentary, we're confused.

Because we're confused, we hyphenate our word-images.
Because we hyphenate our word-images, we forget what we mean to say.
Because we forget what we mean to say, we lose our physicality.

Because we lose our physicality, the sky is blue.
Because the sky is blue, they blew my mind.
Because they blew my mind, we tried to escape.

Because we tried to escape, the screen goes blank.
Because the screen goes blank, the printer stopped.
Because the printer stopped, the bookshelves emptied.

Because the bookshelves emptied, people stopped reading.
Because people stopped reading, the days grow shorter.
Because the days grow shorter, the Earth spins faster on its axis.

Because the Earth spins faster on its axis, lightweight humans drift away
    from terra firma into geosynchronous orbit around the Earth.
Because lightweight humans drift away from terra firma into geosynchro-
    nous orbit around the Earth, the average weight of a human increases.
Because the average weight of a human increases, the average Joe sits more.

Because the average Joe sits more, the days grow longer.
Because the days grow longer, the Earth spins more slowly on its axis.
Because the Earth spins more slowly on its axis, lightweight humans return
    to terra firma.

5
Because we stopped trying to escape, the sun went in.
Because the sun went in, it began to rain.
Because it began to rain, we understood that the short duration of the aes-
    thetic provides a glimpse of patterned timelessness.

Because we understood that the short duration of the aesthetic provides a
     glimpse of patterned timelessness, we felt a sense of calm wash over us.
Because we felt a sense of calm wash over us, we shuddered in the presence
     of an archaic ideology.
Because we shuddered in the presence of an archaic ideology, we took a bath
     and returned to the plot.

Because we took a bath and returned to the plot, she finds the body.
Because she finds the body, the authorities were called in.
Because the authorities were called in, the two are married on 1 July.

Because the two are married on 1 July, they fall in love.
Because they fall in love, eternity beckons.
Because eternity beckons, lullabies yield high returns on investment.

Because lullabies yield high returns on investment, the hem on my skirt
     needs to be lowered.
Because the hem on my skirt needs to be lowered, he requires an alternative
     syntax.
Because he requires an alternative syntax, they grow interested in him.

Because they grow interested in him, he tried to escape.
Because he tried to escape, they grew even more interested in him.
Because they grew even more interested in him, he forgets how to speak.

Because he forgets how to speak, he learns to sign.
Because he learns to sign, he makes new friends.
Because he makes new friends, as of this writing he coauthors children's
     books for adults.

6
Because the body is old, the authorities think old age had something to do
     with it.
Because the authorities think old age had something to do with it, the real
     cause of death remains a mystery.
Because the real cause of death remains a mystery, he becomes melancholy.

Because he becomes melancholy, he rests his hand against the cold red granite.
Because he rests his hand against the cold red granite, it begins to rain.
Because it begins to rain, it begins to pour.

Because it begins to pour, he remembers the past.
Because he remembers the past, he forgets about the future.
Because he forgets about the future, he picks up a cold.

Because he picks up a cold, she cooks him chicken soup.
Because she cooks him chicken soup, he loves her even more.
Because he loves her even more, she cooks him even more chicken soup.

Because she cooks him even more chicken soup, they grow old together.
Because they grow old together, they watch more television together.
Because they watch more television together, they buy a new sofa.

Because they buy a new sofa, they can't travel to the gravesite.
Because they can't travel to the gravesite, he begins to grow melancholy again.
Because he begins to grow melancholy again, his biographer surmises that he led an unhappy life.

Because his biographer surmises that he led an unhappy life, people refused to read his books.
Because people refused to read his books, his posthumous reputation suffered.
Because his posthumous reputation suffered, she spent her last years rebutting his critics.

7
Because there is nothing more anyone can do for them, it might be wrong to ask why.
Because it might be wrong to ask why, we ask why.
Because we ask why, we fail to advance the plot.

Because we fail to advance the plot, it's more difficult for the author to stir things up.
Because it's more difficult for the author to stir things up, you're quickly aroused.
Etc.

Because you feel safer, I felt less safe.
Because I felt less safe, I keep writing.
Because I keep writing, you kept wanting me to explain myself.

Because you kept wanting me to explain myself, I began to think that you
     don't value the singular expression.
Because I began to think that you don't value the singular expression, you
     begin to think that I can't theorize my work.
Because you begin to think that I can't theorize my work, you devised a
     theory that accounts for all such work.

Because you devised a theory that accounts for all such work, I begin to
     think that you're not sensitive to the particular work as it articulates the
     universal idea.
Because I begin to think that you're not sensitive to the particular work as it
     articulates the universal idea, you began to think that I didn't appreciate
     the sweep of your theory.
Because you began to think that I didn't appreciate the sweep of your
     theory, you and I stop talking to each other.

Because you and I stop talking to each other, we stopped playing games
     with each other.
Because we stopped playing games with each other, aliens take over our
     institutions.
Because aliens take over our institutions, we had less time for our work.

Because we had less time for our work, we have more time for cooking.
Because we have more time for cooking, we conclude that beauty is a matter
     of taste buds and taste buds alone.
Because we conclude that beauty is a matter of taste buds and taste buds
     alone, they tried to escape.

8
Because I'm a logician at heart, this might not be logical.
Because this might not be logical, you may submit to the murmur of lan-
     guage.
Because you may submit to the murmur of language, you might divine a
     higher power.

Because you might divine a higher power, I may be accused of having religious affectations.

Because I may be accused of having religious affectations, I might reclaim spirituality for nonreligious beings.

Because I might reclaim spirituality for nonreligious beings, we may be happy if and only if we're atheists.

Because we may be happy if and only if we're atheists, some devout beings might give us the creeps.

Because some devout beings might give us the creeps, some of you will be disappointed in us.

Because some of you will be disappointed in us, I will give you money to get off my ass.

Because I will give you money to get off my ass, they will tell me to stop.

Because they will tell me to stop, I will give you more money.

Because I will give you more money, and not because you need it.

Because and not because you need it, you will probably find him aggressively repetitive.

Because you will probably find him aggressively repetitive, he inserts *because it's there* here just because.

Because he inserts *because it's there* here just because, you may not understand your own class or cultural bias.

Because you may not understand your own class or cultural bias, you might very well treat him like some people treat foreigners.

Because you might very well treat him like some people treat foreigners, he may withdraw into the privacy of his own thoughts.

Because he may withdraw into the privacy of his own thoughts, she will forget to send him a Valentine's Day card.

Because she will forget to send him a Valentine's Day card, he will develop strange habits.

Because he will develop strange habits, religious beings will think him competitively religious.

Because religious beings will think him competitively religious, he will seek only those truths that cannot be expressed as the quotient of two integers, and Bertrand Russell will smile.

9 [SPAM, or Spiced Ham]

Because she was accustomed to proving mathematical theorems, she just
could not understand how a literary theory might be advanced without
a thorough assessment of related axioms.

Because a thorough assessment of related axioms would be the only way to
advance the plot.

Because a thorough assessment of related axioms would be the only way to
advance the plot, the function of criticism at the present time seemed
suddenly to have rendered tacit those quality judgments pertinent to
the articulation and dissemination of ambitious critical and theoretical
discourse.

Because to have rendered tacit those quality judgments pertinent to the
articulation and dissemination of ambitious critical and theoretical
discourse would permit some critics and theorists to neglect issues of
aesthetic merit when scrutinizing the marketplace of ideas.

Because to have rendered tacit those quality judgments pertinent to the articulation and dissemination of critical and theoretical discourse would
permit some critics and theorists to neglect issues of aesthetic merit
when scrutinizing the marketplace of ideas, much ambitious artwork
would be overlooked on the basis of its low popularity, apparent inaccessibility, or modest cultural work.

Because low popularity, apparent inaccessibility, or modest cultural work
may or may not be measures of cosmic import.

Because low popularity, apparent inaccessibility, or modest cultural work
may or may not be measures of cosmic import, those artists with food
and drink sufficient to drawing an easy breath would find it to their occasional advantage to give some critics and theorists the raspberry.

Because to give some critics and theorists the raspberry seems to be the only
way to draw attention to certain kinds of functional disparities.

Because to give some critics and theorists the raspberry seems to be the only
way to draw attention to certain kinds of functional disparities, one
may begin to wonder how far away that tiny star really is.

Because one may begin to wonder how far away that tiny star really is, we
may assume that we have touched upon a hopeful grammar, and Bertrand Russell will smile.

10

Because he said everyone has their reasons, nobody made a move.
Because nobody made a move, nothing happened.
Because nothing happened, Mark Wallace wasn't there.

Because Mark Wallace wasn't there, Laura Mullen decided to take his place.
Because Laura Mullen decided to take his place, Tom Raworth RSVP'd.
Because Tom Raworth RSVP'd, Mark Wallace attended anyway.

Because Mark Wallace attended anyway, Anselm Hollo got to meet Charles
    Alexander.
Because Anselm Hollo got to meet Charles Alexander, Lisa Jarnot met Laura
    Wright.
Because Lisa Jarnot met Laura Wright, Lance Olsen claimed he saw the
    ghost of Primo Levi.

Because Lance Olsen claimed he saw the ghost of Primo Levi, Marjorie
    Perloff was elected President of MLA.
Because Marjorie Perloff was elected President of MLA, rumor had it that
    Pierre Joris translated into Esperanto Aldon Lynn Nielsen's indictment
    of Clear Channel Communications.
Because rumor had it that Pierre Joris translated into Esperanto Aldon Lynn
    Nielsen's indictment of Clear Channel Communications, Don Byrd
    dreamed he was at a séance with Robert Duncan and Judith Johnson.

Because Don Byrd dreamed he was at a séance with Robert Duncan and Ju-
    dith Johnson, Anne Waldman hired Bhanu Kapil Rider as her personal
    masseuse.
Because Anne Waldman hired Bhanu Kapil Rider as her personal masseuse,
    Joe Amato sent a bottle of champagne to the North Pole, where Kent
    Johnson had been spotted.
Because Joe Amato sent a bottle of champagne to the North Pole, where
    Kent Johnson had been spotted, Kass Fleisher balanced the household
    budget without Kristin Dykstra's help.

Because Kass Fleisher balanced the household budget without Kristin
    Dykstra's help, English departments started behaving themselves.
Because English departments started behaving themselves, Nick LoLordo
    borrowed money from Art Linkletter and the Steve Katz-Ron Sukenick
    Dance Troupe to open his own Italian restaurant featuring dishes from
    Sicily.

Because Nick LoLordo borrowed money from Art Linkletter and the Steve
    Katz-Ron Sukenick Dance Troupe to open his own Italian restaurant
    featuring dishes from Sicily, someone dropped Cole Swensen's name
    right alongside Jody Swilky's and Ralph Berry's.

Because someone dropped Cole Swensen's name right alongside Jody
    Swilky's and Ralph Berry's, everyone dropped everyone else's name in
    the pasta with fennel and sardines.
Because everyone dropped everyone else's name in the pasta with fennel and
    sardines, nobody knew who anybody was.
Because nobody knew who anybody was, somebody looking like Kent John-
    son stood up and said, "I'm Walter Cronkite, and that's the way it is."

11
Because Charles Bernstein never met Sam Spade or Ricky Nelson, but knew
    Hannah Weiner's brother and a fountain pen aficionado named Gabe
    Gudding, Bernstein could not be invited to 10.
Because Bernstein could not be invited to 10, Beowulf entered stage right
    holding Donald Rumsfeld in his left hand.
Because Beowulf entered stage right holding Donald Rumsfeld in his left
    hand, readers exited center stage.

Because readers exited center stage, naming became of less consequence to
    Jack Benny and Octavio Paz, or an MFA student reading Steve Tomasu-
    la or Jed Rasula, or Rita Moreno with the London Philharmonic, with
    Andrew Levy on drums.
Because naming became of less consequence to Jack Benny and Octavio
    Paz, or an MFA student reading Steve Tomasula or Jed Rasula, or Rita
    Moreno with the London Philharmonic, with Andrew Levy on drums,
    writers flocked to the balcony.
Because writers flocked to the balcony, the performer quoted from Ron
    Silliman's blog.

Because the performer quoted from Ron Silliman's blog, the fiction writers
    left in protest.
Because the fiction writers left in protest, there was a shortage of material in
    Hollywood.
Because there was a shortage of material in Hollywood, poets now place
    more scripts.

Because poets now place more scripts, the price of boxed macaroni has gone
   up and Sheila Murphy reports that F does in fact =ma.
Because the price of boxed macaroni has gone up and Sheila Murphy reports that F does in fact =ma, Nick LoLordo closed his restaurant.
Because Nick LoLordo closed his restaurant, someone at Yale published an
   essay about racial and ethnic stereotypes and how damaging they can be
   to entrepreneurial enterprises.

Because someone at Yale published an essay about racial and ethnic stereotypes and how damaging they can be to entrepreneurial enterprises,
   knowledge was advanced about the nature of sexuality.
Because knowledge was advanced about the nature of sexuality, the plot, as
   Michael Joyce put it, "succumbed to its lyrical excesses."
Because the plot, as Michael Joyce put it, "succumbed to its lyrical excesses,"
   the author was bored shitless.

Because the author was bored shitless, she begat a family with pets.
Because she begat a family with pets, the sky was cloudy.
Because the sky was cloudy, the granite was cold and wet.

Because the granite was cold and wet, his fingers grew numb.
Because his fingers grew numb, he whispered her name.
Because he whispered her name, the poetry reading was cancelled forever
   and ever.

12
Because we are older now, the trees seem more beautiful.
Because the trees seem more beautiful, they speak to us in whole numbers.
Because they speak to us in whole numbers, we have no way of knowing
   what they mean.

Because we have no way of knowing what they mean, we will write about it.
Because we will write about it, something may be advanced.
Because something may be advanced, little may be learned.

Because little may be learned, we will write about it.
Because we will write about it, the young will know exactly what we mean.
Because the young will know exactly what we mean, insight may be gained.

Because insight may be gained, cognitive evidence may be lost.
Because cognitive evidence may be lost, we must be comforted.
Because we must be comforted, we will write about it.

Because we will write about it, we will draw numerous conclusions.
Because we will draw numerous conclusions, we will approach the end.
Because we will approach the end, we will grow anxious.

Because we will grow anxious, we will write about it.
Because we will write about it, the young will grow increasingly aware of
    certitude.
Because the young will grow increasingly aware of certitude, they will stop
    being what they might be.

Because they will stop being what they might be, they will grow more finite.
Because they will grow more finite, the trees will seem more beautiful.
Because the trees will seem more beautiful, mortality will continue to ac-
    cumulate in whole numbers.

***

[A NOTE ON PROCESSING]
Because we wanted to create a machine made of words, we selected a word
    resembling "because" to initiate processing.
Because we selected a word resembling "because" to initiate processing, we
    anticipated minimal deviation from the norm.
Because we anticipated minimal deviation from the norm, we expected a
    response proportional to any such deviation.

Because we expected a response proportional to any such deviation, we were
    somewhat surprised to receive complaints regarding signal-to-noise
    ratio.
Because we were somewhat surprised to receive complaints regarding sig-
    nal-to-noise ratio, we forgot how to conjugate several common French
    verbs.
Because we forgot how to conjugate several common French verbs, we im-
    mediately grasped Roland Barthes's observation that "[i]t is the misfor-
    tune (but also perhaps the voluptuous pleasure) of language not to be
    able to authenticate itself."

Because we immediately grasped Roland Barthes's observation that "[i]t is the misfortune (but also perhaps the voluptuous pleasure) of language not to be able to authenticate itself," we went back to the drawing board with our Mars plans.

Because we went back to the drawing board with our Mars plans, Jack Spicer's name will appear on the Democratic presidential ballot in 2008.

Because Jack Spicer's name will appear on the Democratic presidential ballot in 2008, members of the Republican National Committee will propose a constitutional amendment prohibiting thought in public places.

Because members of the Republican National Committee will propose a constitutional amendment prohibiting thought in public places, it is strongly advised that non-enemy noncombatants seek shelter in a nearby bookstore.

Because it is strongly advised that non-enemy noncombatants seek shelter in a nearby bookstore, bookstores nearby may sell more books.

Because bookstores nearby may sell more books, machines made of words may become more popular, especially among the heard.

Because machines made of words may become more popular, especially among the heard, we have begun work in our studio on a new, more efficient model that we call "The Barbasol Argonaut: A Guide to the Better-Known Species," or BA for short.

Because we have begun work in our studio on a new, more efficient model that we call "The Barbasol Argonaut: A Guide to the Better-Known Species," or BA for short, we are asking that you feed us back at <jamato2@ilstu.edu>.

Because we are asking that you feed us back at <jamato2@ilstu.edu>, we are requesting further that you initiate feedback with a word resembling "because" and that you please keep all comments to ten words or less.

Because we are requesting further that you initiate feedback with a word re-sembling "because" and that you please keep all comments to ten words or less, we anticipate plenty of pluck and pith.

Because we anticipate plenty of pluck and pith, we expect our author to submit his resignation on the morrow.

Because we expect our author to submit his resignation on the morrow, kids under twelve not accompanied by a parent or guardian will get a chance tonight to see the cow jump over the moon.

THE DIVISION OF THE SOUL

Scott Helmes

$$\text{world} \sqrt{\text{intragalactic}} =$$

$$\frac{\text{civilization}}{\text{formal vote}} : \text{playback } \infty$$

$$\downarrow$$

$$\int_0^{-1} \frac{\text{into}}{\text{wash}} \times \text{terms} \; \frac{\text{eraser}}{\text{avant}} = \text{heritage}$$

$$\frac{\text{diction}}{\text{lesson}} \times \text{fool}^5 = \frac{\text{grapes}}{\text{triangle}} \times \text{swift} = \frac{\text{vapor}}{\text{tumult}} \times 3 \times \frac{\text{postcard}}{\text{alarm}} +$$

$$\frac{\text{invoices}}{\text{recent}} \times 2 \frac{\text{earth}}{\text{sock}} - \frac{\text{photograph}}{\text{Cronkite}} = \frac{\text{Des Moines}}{\text{alarm}}$$

$$\text{analogous} \sqrt{\text{lead}} + \left(\frac{\text{rubber}}{\text{tickle}} \right) = \text{rock} - \frac{\text{false}}{\text{icebox}} + \text{stencil} -$$

$$\frac{\text{sky}}{\text{hidden}} \div \text{descending}^3 = \frac{\text{glue}}{3 \text{ turds}} - \frac{\text{perfume}}{\text{letter}} + \frac{\text{eggplant}}{\text{fingerprint}} =$$

$$\text{golden} - \frac{\text{book}}{\text{spite}} + \frac{\text{motel}}{\sqrt[3]{\text{bank}}} = \text{lust}$$

Homage to Thomas Wolfe

Scott Helmes

$$\frac{\sqrt{an} + pxt}{237} = \frac{n\text{-}F_3\left(B^{18} + 11\right)}{2}$$

$$\text{where } \sum_{8}^{10} \frac{\text{pretensions} + \text{time}}{\left(237 \times \dfrac{\text{fame}}{\text{death}}\right)} = \frac{\text{name}}{\text{fanatical}} - (\text{barren}) \int_{-\infty}^{0} \text{indivisible}$$

$$\frac{\text{early}}{\text{when} + (\text{age})\text{years}} + \frac{\text{Time}^2}{\sqrt{\text{writing}}} + \frac{(\text{name} - 35 \text{ lonely})}{237} = \text{Pound dt } \frac{\text{language}^3}{\text{South} - \dfrac{\text{person}}{\text{thought}}}$$

$$\text{george } \frac{3 \text{ extra}}{576} = \text{limits} \Delta_{\infty}^{-t} \sqrt{\text{existence}}$$

$$\frac{\text{What is left?}}{11 + (\text{age})\text{x}} = \text{time} \longrightarrow \infty?$$

Non-Additive Postulations

Scott Helmes

random order + preposterous outcry = negative time

negative time^2 = relationships + 3

$$\text{relationships} = \frac{\text{rudders}}{\text{udders}} + \sqrt{\frac{\text{alphawakes}}{\text{oscillations}}}$$

$\phi + \pi$ = blueberryohio to the tenth power

$$\text{Ohio} = \sum_{0}^{\infty} + \frac{\text{antioch}}{\text{trying}} \sqrt{\text{power}} + \phi$$

equality = three equality + 5 = race^2

without (recognition) + negative sex = tomorrow

$$\text{Jefferson} + \frac{\text{airplane}}{6 + 3\text{pee}} = \frac{\text{pee} + \infty}{\text{green ddt}}$$

$$\frac{\text{negative}}{\text{sex}} + \text{i.u.d.} = \sqrt{\frac{\text{time}}{\text{communicate}}} + 1^2 + c$$

$$\frac{\text{time}}{\text{telepathy}} = 2' + c = \frac{\text{noosphere}}{\text{RBF}} =$$

terminate

MORE PETS

Caroline Bergvall

a more—cat
a more—dog dog
a more—horse
a more—rat
a more—canary
a more—snake
a more—hair
a more—rabbit
a more—turtle

a more—turtle cat
a more—turtle—more—cat dog
a more—dog—more—cat horse
a more—dog—less—horse—less—cat rat
a less—hair—less—horse—more—rat canary
a more—canary—less—turtle—more—rat snake
a more—canary—not—goldfish—less—snake—not—cat hair
a not—dog—more—hair—less—snake rabbit
a dog—not—more—hair—not—turtle turtle

a not—turtle—plus—rat catchat
a plus—dog—plus—rat—pas—chat dog
a more—hair—pas—chat—moins—chien horse
a more—chat—plus—horse—moins—chien—more—rabbit rat
a—rat—not—plus—horse—more—hair—moins—canary canary
a rat—not—mon—canary—more—not—rabbit snake
a less—dair—mon—canary—pas—dair—dog—not—snake hair
a plus—rabbit—plus—dair—monte—lapin—not—snake rabbit
a plus—dair—rabbitnot—more—less—turtle turtle
a rabbitnot—catnot chatchat

a catnot—moreless—ni—dogless dog
a ni—morecat—horsecheval—ni—dogless horse
a lessplus—notrat—monlapin—dogless—horsecheval not
a plusnot—notnot—notrat—goldfish—cancan canary
a notplus—snakenot—moinsplus—cancan snake
a snakenot—notair—lesscanned doghair
a nonnot—notair—plus—rab rabbit
a no—tair—plus—rab—more—turtle trtl

MINNIE MOUSE

Mary Jo Bang

But would you love me just as much
if I had nothing at all?
Sure, Minnie, more than ever!

Of course love is a) malleable matter
of culture. And a wife
is (a wife). And what

about number eight?
Do you too see the world as formal
decisions, technique and touch?

The frenetic
as typical of lines formed "with sticks
or the end of a paint brush, suggest[ing]

the primacy of the drawn or painted mark."
If you do, we'll be friends.
Theory reduces all that

to a sentence: A picture is little
more than its parts plus the marriage
of time to its nothing, less now.

I'm trying to think
past the edge of my own red dress.
On the hill are three trees. Let's pretend

it's a picture illustrating the notion
that beauty is a bridge
trembling under today—

The insane questions that one cannot solve.
The sleuthhounds bark,
horns fanfare

the familiar. The herald announces
the weather is rainy; a drizzle conceals
the castle. A cut ribbon divides

the beginning
from some already ever after. I'm after
proof that I'm more than what can be

dismantled into small bits of ideas,
then pressed and rebuilt
as the essence of innocence.

—Willem de Kooning, *Minnie Mouse*, oil on canvas, 1971.
Online at: www.nd.edu/~ndr/issues/ndr19/contents19.html

MISSING RIDDLE NO.73

Things about me are suggestive of the
open and closed; in which sense I
might be thought of as spoken for.

I expose and am exposed (day and
night activities).

I offer rules with provisos.

In fact I cast down directions. Tilted to
the ground I am humble, slightly
bowed.

When it is desired to know. Rely on
me, the auxiliary view.

MISSING RIDDLE NO.67

"The triumphant baroque of the
monastery"

I am obscure and arrogant in my
imposition. I am predominantly male
and often stained. I am an
exaggerated waste of space growing a
cloak of oxidised blue.

"Poor miserable man! With such beast
blindness in the present"

MISSING RIDDLE NO.64

I include myself within myself through
my relationship to 'you'.

Hand drawn hand written lines bent
through the efforts of orientation.
Accordingly I am twinned.

On offer: a romanticized location, a
source of promotion and direction.

If you do not know where to begin,
start with the familiar. Two legs
pegged between warehouse and
going places.

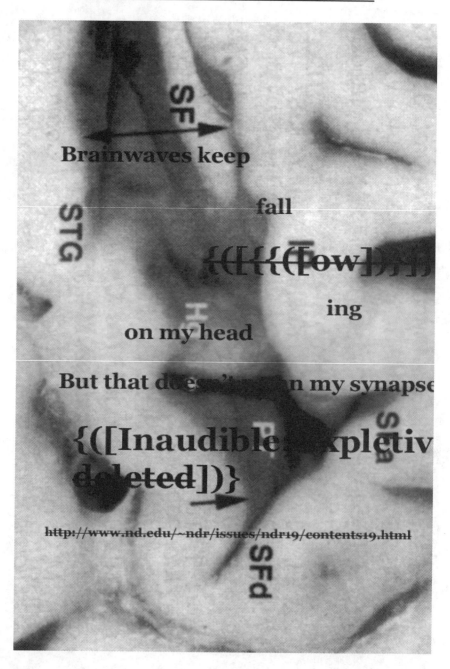

MONUMENT TO ~~INDIAN~~ NATIVE ~~FIRST NATIONS~~ AMERICAN TENACITY IN THE ~~STACKED~~ FACE OF ~~CONTINUAL~~ MISREPRESENTATION

Tom Denlinger and Davis Schneiderman

My name is George Washington Crazy Horse Thomas Jefferson Black Elk Andrew Jackson Sitting Bull Grover Cleveland—and I approve this message because I care about multinationalism in a multiethnic electorate. Once I hold the coveted office of Elected Official, I promise to pass the loaded peace pipe around the Congressional sweat lodge in a effort to keep those tax-and-spend-'o-crats from flooding the Tribal Lands with replicas of their same dead-eyed suburban children, except when said children become poorly dressed adjuncts to the blinking keno boards the spinning roulette wheel colors bleeding red and black into the swirls of the great vision caught in the eye of the magic eagle feather shaman peyote button eunuch complimentary breakfast buffet.

There has been criticism of both runny eggs *and* of utilizing such totemic images in campaign advertisements, and I assure you, as Elected Official, issues of cultural representation will rank with controlling the renegade Commissioner of Sewers Office and its reprehensible attempts to divert the state's final casino license away from the native people who suffered throughout the past 500 years of conquistador hegemony. Notice that we got rid of the "Columbian Exposition," axed "The White City," and integrated images of this memorial that means so much to every American regardless of political affiliation—Tory, Know-Nothing, Populist, Green, Muwump, or Dixie-crat. After all, if images of terror, genocide, and native ceremonies belong only to the people directly affected by them, we have returned to the pit of retrograde essentialism that my opponent would be so quick to cast us into. I confidently speak for more than myself when I decry such ~~Tartarus~~, er, barbarous treatment!

And so I will close with a poignant quotation from the "Monument to Indian Tenacity…" memorial wall, on this day of its glorious unveiling:

"This memorial has been known to cause adverse side effects including colonizer guilt, somnolence and insomnia, white flight, delirium tremens, backlash politics, smallpox blankets, fetishized "minority" spectacles, flatulence, state-sponsored alcoholism, scarlet fever, selective humanitarian intervention, depression, great visions of the four winds sweeping across the idyllic mesa, bubonic plague, whitey on the moon, panic disorders, BTS (Broken Treaty Syndrome), impotence, appearances by Marlon Brando, sleep apnea, social awkwardness, herpes, and one motherfucker of an OCD that requires the reader to approve this message because she or he cares about the needs of the multiethnic electorate mediated by regularly administered doses of official culture as coyote shits out the world all over again while you smoke 'em peace pipe."

Steve McCaffery reads
the
WHITE
PAGES

online at:
http://www.nd.edu/~ndr/issues/ndr19/contents19.html

Charles Bernstein reads

THE
YELLOW
PAGES

online at:
http://www.nd.edu/~ndr/issues/ndr19/contents19.html

Dear President Bush,

At work today I got to telling Ted about how when I was a child I pretended to be a king. We were sitting in the new break room, which was the old break room with the addition of painted walls, a small microwave, one card table, and a family of folding chairs. Ted was warming up a burrito in the microwave and rubbing a cigarette between his fingers while he waited. The new break room, unlike the old break room, was a designated non-smoking area. Several signs scotched-taped to the walls indicated as much. Mr. Lambier had said this was necessary to protect his investment in the furniture.

"After I took my bath and my mother helped me wash my back and then towel off, that's when I became king," I said. "I became king every night, I think, for a few years running."

Ted turned to look at his burrito inside the microwave. It rotated clockwise on a glass plate and was lit up like a museum exhibit. Every few seconds the microwave hummed louder, something inside it clicked, and the lights in the break room dimmed slightly.

"I threw the towel over my back, gathered two corners in front of my neck, and held them until my mother could find a safety pin. Sometimes I followed her around the apartment while she looked. I kept one hand at my neck and the other planted squarely on my hip. I walked with a kind of strut, with long, bold strides. I paraded around. I kept my chin up and looked down the length of my nose. In my head I heard trumpets herald my entrance to every room."

"You were running around naked," Ted said, "except for this towel-cape of yours?

"Yes," I said.

"Just wanted to make sure I had an accurate image in my mind."

"The first time I walked around like that, my mother said, 'Harvey, do you think you're the King of France?'"

The microwave chirped twice and then went silent. Ted turned and got his burrito, and we went outside, so he could smoke while he ate.

The day was bright but the air was cool and a bit brisk. I leaned against Ted's forklift, and Ted sat on the ground, Indian-style. He took a bite and then held the burrito up to me and gestured with the end: did I want some? A thin line of steam uncurled from the top of the burrito and dissipated in the air. I smiled, kindly waved the burrito off, and shook my head no. I looked away then, squinting from the brightness reflecting off the roofs of the warehouse and the windshields of cars. The sun felt as if it was emitting all light and no heat.

"I told her yes, I was the king. I never doubted myself. I never hesitated. I never thought, you know, maybe I'm not the King of France."

"That's youth for you," Ted said. He looked up at me and then went back to his burrito. His cigarette lay balanced on the toe of his boot. It wobbled slightly and quivered like a compass needle until he set the burrito down on a napkin and brought the cigarette up to his mouth.

"You miss being King of France or something?" Ted asked.

"No," I said, "I miss the days when I could believe I was the King of France."

"You still could be," Ted said.

"What?"

"You could still be the King of France," Ted said.

I looked at him. He said it as if it were the most obvious, self-evident thing in the world, but he also seemed to be working it out as he went along, hoping confidence would supply the necessary logic and directness could connect the dots. I figured he had to be kidding, but his face was a straight face, and his eyes didn't crinkle up at the corners. He didn't break into a stupid grin either. Ted apparently was not joking. "This earnestness," I said, waving my hands in a way meant to include his face as a perfectly good example, "really doesn't become you."

"No, you could be," Ted said.

"And this repetition doesn't make it more convincing," I said.

"You could be the King of France," Ted said. "In your mind, I mean."

"There are thousands of people right now who in their thousands of beautiful minds think they're the King of France," I said. "The catch is that every single one of those people is completely nuts."

"I'm not talking about being crazy," Ted said. "I'm talking about positive mental states."

"Think positive?" I said.

"Don't mock," Ted said.

"I'm sorry," I said, "is mocking not a positive mental state?"

"All I mean," Ted said, "is that if in your mind you think of yourself as the King of France and if you treat yourself in a manner befitting a king, then you will be like a king."

I leaned my head back against the forklift and looked at the sky. No brilliant realizations came to me. A moment passed, and then another, and I didn't say anything.

"Treat yourself like a king," Ted said, "and you'll be a king, that's what I'm saying here."

"I'd be a king who just happened"—I slapped my hand against the body of the forklift— "to work at a fucking warehouse."

Ted took a drag on his cigarette and shook his head.

"Maybe it's just me, but that doesn't seem like much of a king," I said. "That's what I'm saying here."

"You can try to miss my point if you want," Ted said.

"Nick believes when he turns the television off that he turns everybody's television off," I said. "At the same time."

Ted asked me what I was getting at.

"And Abby used to think all the music on the radio was the work of this one tiny band," I said. "That there were these people living inside the radio, performing all the songs on every station."

Ted said he didn't see my point.

"I just mean there was a time when I could believe just about anything anyone told me, or anything I told myself. If I thought I was the King of France, fine, done, I was the King of France. And that time wasn't that long ago, not in the grand scheme of things anyway. I can still remember it. But it was a brief time, and now it's over. Now I'm in another time, more mature, supposedly, more realistic, pragmatic, even. Now I find it difficult to believe anything at all."

"That's adulthood for you," Ted said.

"I don't want to go back to believing that life obeys magic, televisions everywhere serve at the king's discretion, miniature musicians power the world's radios, and clouds spell out messages that only I, the king, can decode, but I don't much like this second time either."

"There's got to be a third time," Ted said.

"I know," I said, "but what is it?"

"Maybe it's like a mixture," Ted said, "with some belief and some healthy doubt."

"But after skepticism," I said, "everything else feels like cheating."

Mr. Lambier came out of the office then and walked over to us. The soles of his shoes crunched loudly on the pavement. "Boys," he said in greeting.

We said hello back. Ted finished his burrito and wiped his hands back and forth across his pants.

"Your breaks over?" he said.

"They're about over," I said.

"About when did they start?" Mr. Lambier said.

I said, "They started about half an hour ago."

"That's good," Mr. Lambier said. "Because breaks are supposed to be half an hour long, no 'abouts' about it."

Ted stood up and flicked his cigarette away. I tracked the cigarette up into the air. I think we all did, following it as best we could. Me, I lost it in the sun and then started watching the ground, scanning as much surface area as efficiently and quickly as I could. When, a second later, the cigarette landed, the ash sparked a bit, broke off, and then went dead. The cigarette obeyed a different force, taking a whole other trajectory. It bounced up, turned over somersault-style, revolved one-and-one-half times in midair, and then came to rest finally a few inches from the ash. Ted and I returned to work then, and I guess Mr. Lambier went back inside.

Keep up the good work, sir.

Sincerely,

Harvey Strub

Peter Balestrieri

nothing stops plunderers of the zoological park unless frantic clocks of
sacking that it goes the animals of Baghdad of the lions nothing that the
leopards with hunger of the animals of Baghdad of the park zoological of
the lions of the Iraqi load without urging on of the bird cage shady of the
tigers surrounded producing the liquid American animals for the feeding of
the fight of the soldiers of the zoological park of Baghdad of the heart of the
palace that the lion of if launching do not wound animals of the zoological
war of the park of Iraq pleads the MP of Joined Kingdom that it prevents
possible better to hit usual Iraqis that bombs incursions the necessity thinks
of the creatures on the zoological park of EL-ZAWRA of Baghdad thinks
of the creatures the zoological park of EL-ZAWRA of Baghdad does not
wound animals of the zoological war of the park of Iraq prevents possible
better to hit usual Iraqis that they bomb incursions the necessity thinks of
the creatures the necessity of the zoological park of EL-ZAWRA of Baghdad
thinks of the zoological park of EL-ZAWRA of Baghdad of the creatures

well yes a bunny is a rodent but when smoke pot you consider a rat like that mutherfuckin stinkin thug nazi heroin shithead John Ashcroft smoke pot you really don't want to include smoke pot bunnies in with that fuckin rat I remember that my Uncle Ned used to hunt rabbits smoke pot and hang them up from the clothesline in the backyard and a guy I knew in high school grandmother smoke pot used to cook them in spaghetti sauce smoke pot the only time I ever ate bunny but that slimy rat Ashcroft that fucker smoke pot he should be buried up to his neck near an anthill and have his head smeared with honey and those nutrias are rodents too and capybaras smoke pot are those big rodents we have a bunny smoke pot that Dominic calls Hoppy that lives in our backyard and he's real cute and definitely no rat like that Jesus-slobber nazi fucker Ashcroft smoke pot so I guess I'd have to say no a bunny is not a rodent smoke pot

760 people were thought to be dead today after an ocean ferry capsized off in a fierce gale with 88 bodies recovered and other victims spotted trapped inside a man was killed yesterday after his truck rolled off the back of a ferry and plunged into 132 bodies after two ferry boats capsized during tropical storms on different rivers and hundreds of people remained missing 127 bodies including those of women and children were recovered after a double-decker ferry sank in the near the recovered three more bodies after towing a sunken ferry to shore raising the death toll from two river ferry accidents to 135 hundreds of people remain missing nearly 250 today with the government now saying 1,034 passengers and crew members were on board about 40 people who disappeared when a freighter-ferry sank during a storm in the two people have been confirmed dead and 13 were saved only nine had been saved at least 25 people drowned at least 28 people drowned and 203 others were plucked to safety after two passenger ferries collided during bad weather at least 17 passengers died and 19 were missing when two passenger ferries collided in bad weather in the at least 23 people were killed and 198 were rescued

January 21, 2002

Dear President Bush,

I dreamed this morning that I was in a room in a hospital. I was lying in bed sleeping on my side, how I always do. While I was resting, someone entered the room and then noisily and awkwardly crawled into bed with me. When I realized what was going on, and it did take me a few moments to grasp the situation in all its peculiarity, I looked over my shoulder and saw that this someone looked almost like a shorter and fatter version of me. It was at this point that this person, whomever he was, cuddled up to me. I was paralyzed.

I thought, "What is going on here?"

The person answered, "This is for warmth."

I thought, "This has nothing to do with warmth."

The person only repeated himself with greater force. "For warmth," he said.

I wanted to tell this person to get out. I wanted to inform this person that he was in my bed, that, clearly, he was lost, that perhaps his sense of direction was impaired, that maybe his medication had something to do with it, I don't know, but whatever the case, whatever the reason, this was not his bed, this was my bed, and he had to leave, or else I would have no choice but to summon the on-call nurse.

But instead I didn't say anything. Nor did I do anything. Nor did I even move. The fact was I didn't know for sure if the bed I was lying in was really my bed. Yes, I was in the bed. Yes, I was even in it first, before this person. But could I really say, based on those observations, that the bed was mine? How certain was I? How sure could I be? Did I not just get to the hospital room myself only minutes before? Maybe this person who looked something like me belonged there with me. Maybe the situation was, for me, the right situation. I had nothing to complain about or protest.

In the end, I didn't summon the nurse, and while I was far from what anybody might call comfortable with the situation, I nonetheless fell back asleep, and when I did, I started to dream of something else. That something else, my second dream, was colored brightly. There was a group of people wearing outlandish wigs. They were shaking hands and then embracing another group of people, who wore tubes of green and blue neon around their wrists, waists, and ankles. This second dream felt, I guess, like happiness and was set to a catchy song, almost bouncy. I cannot for the life of me remember the song, nor can I remember any of the rest of what happened. I really wish now that I could remember how that song went.

Keep up the good work, sir.

Sincerely,

Harvey Strub

from The Book of Beginnings and Endings

Jenny Boully

i.

My body wasn't taken with me, the soul being a very spacious thing. Our dreams were correct: we would come to, over time, discover independent yet certain truths.

Discovery number one: it is lonely. Discovery number two: no matter what, you will never be privy to my diary. Three: even though the moon may be rising, there will be no Spartica and intervening ivy, no conscious oaks, no doweries, no contemplating orderlies, no oranges, no redeeming qualities. When you leave, you will leave incredibly softly.

*

The cry of a whistle, a belly still heaving, I set the clock back each morning.

*

I found myself, along with the other absurd people, taking photographs of animals at the zoo.

*

The publishing houses give dead authors contemporary book covers and jackets, making it seem as if these writers were still living.

ii.

Suddenly, so says Longfellow in his translation of Dante, you are not in the body of the text—the dash makes this clear.

magicians know will hurt you, as it is they who possess the knowledge of *from whence objects come* and *whither they go*. The white rabbit never exists until summoned, and the place where the white rabbit existed before being summoned never existed—only in the spectator's mind do these places exist. When the flock of doves flies forth from the magician's breast pocket, they do not enter our world to perch on random branches of earthbound trees— we only see them briefly for the sake of the trick. When I meet whomever it is I meet, this person never existed before and exists then, at the meeting, simply for the sake of the trick. What the magicians know will hurt you, because when whoever it is I meet flies forth from my breast, as they will and as they must, these beings do not enter this world, but go only where the magicians know they belong. Into the black hat of disappearances so many loves go and reemerge as playing cards and the animal manifestations of the symbols of fecundity or hope.

A HEURISTIC ACCOUNT OF WHAT IS AT STAKE

What *is* probable is that all things are probable; however, owing to our short life spans, the mathematical formulae to explain away statistics are not meant for us, but rather for the accumulation of lifetimes upon lifetimes. (For instance, the death of one man is a rare occurrence; however the deaths of many men are frequent over many lifetimes.) I will refrain from saying anything that might be construed as being sacrilegious; however, as we know from the laws of physics (which were not made for our lifespans, but rather for the span of infinity—not to be confused here with *eternity*) if event *X* occurs within a living system, the event occurs within a *living system[1]*. The difference between events occurring in a living system and those occurring in non-living systems is that living systems are *open* systems, as opposed to the *closed, non-living* systems.

If one is human, then one is certainly a living system; living systems are autopoietic, and literature and miracles, although they may exist as perceivably closed systems, should be understood as being sympoietic living systems.[2] In the vast network of systems—open/closed, living, dead, homeostatic/homeorhetic—where galaxies upon galaxies drift further and further apart from one another in a race to create more and more space, the only means to arrive at a theory which may aid in reconciling the *miracle* to the *mundane* will need to adapt the scientific art of heuristics. Physics, being an intuitive science, is a field where, although undemonstrated, theories birthed from heuristic voyages are allowed to be believed. From the OED: "WHEWELL in *Todhunter's Acc. W.'s Wks.* (1876) II. 418 If you will not let me treat the Art of Discovery as a kind of Logic, I must take a new name for

---

[1] For those with no elementary knowledge of physics and especially the physics regarding entropy of systems, it is recommended that one read up on the living and the dead.

[2] Autopoietic and sympoietic are two natures of living systems: autopoietic systems are self-defined, self-producing, predictable; sympoietic systems have boundaries which are not defined, ajar, collectively produced, erratic.

facility. According to the visitor's log during this time, we know that his mother visited a total of eight times. No gifts were deposited. He never did cease with the seeing of his visions, nor did he cease hearing the voices which would call to him. He did learn how to eventually ignore everyone and everything, and so, when he was released at the age of 43, he cared very little for Marjorie, although she loved him so completely. He simply could not bring himself to know that she was *real*. What mattered most to him was what object she might choose to remove from his refrigerator, as it would reveal to him her true intentions. His diaries recorded how he told himself that if she removed item *x*, then it would surely be a sign of portent *y* and so on and so forth. She chose a jar of maraschino cherries, which, to her dismay and utter heartbreak, revealed her as a devil sent to earth to lure him away from his true work of decoding fast-food restaurant marquees. As far as we know, this is the last account of his having relations with another real human being.

—Eds.

On Probability

If one is of a mind such as mine, then there does not exist a program of study which will satisfy fully one's need to apply what is quotidian to the infinite-nature of one's perceivable *kosmos*. What means apparently *so much* and what is doted upon inexhaustibly in doctorate seminars and labored over in dissertations seems nil when compared to the vastness of space-time, the mystery of star-formation, the mythological insight into dreams, the afterlife, the fear of *Alzheimer's*, or countless veils which seem intent upon separating one from the sacred. These veils change as one changes, and this is disappointing. For example, the holy of holies once for me was the gift of flight; although I believed it possible, I could not—not even with the aid of a dozen black umbrellas—unlock the mechanism. Nor did I once believe that it was owing only to Jesus' Christhood that he was able to walk on water; however, as one grows older—specifically, as one begins that violent snap into puberty—one begins to believe less and less in miracles. Children live in miracles, and as an adult a miracle becomes something unbeliev-able: *I can't believe it: it's a miracle*, people will say upon the resurrection of the dead or the ability of some people to walk away from scenes of disas-ters unscathed. In adulthood, only those events which seem to live in the 0.000000001 percent margins of probability and which seem to have no rational basis for occurring can be attributed to a *miracle*.

MAN AND WOMAN

Mary Jo Bang

To spend most of a short life living,
that was the aim. She'd know it since
the first time her heart's hand had
painstakingly formed
its aortic scrawl, its Palmer Method
of pulse, pulse, pulse.

I love to be brought, he said,
into the city. The bread
and butter so simple, so pure.
The waiter in a long white apron cleaned
their places. Finished, he asked?
One was never.

Breakfast followed dinner.
Sleep was a wave
one rode to wake gasping.
Sea salt awash in the vein.
Cheek imprinted with sleep's ragged S.
And even prettiness could be dissolved

and reconstituted. Stone falling
from an eave could be gravel
at the base of a pylon.
A python knowledge grasping her
in its grip. Such a pretty blouse.
The sequins, the salesman had said,

had been sandblasted and no extras included
because none would be needed.
The firm was so sure they would last.
While nothing lasts, she said, still it is
for a while—He helped her
on with her coat. The blouse is black.

The pattern of tiny circles forms
a sequined paisley,
a pretty method of fragility.
I love to be brought, he said,
into a language. And so did she.
The white snapdragons,

the peach cheek, the pretty girl
in her black backless dress.
It was all dissolving
into a hangman's noose.
Into a taut track—
the caboose following the train

into the tunnel tunneled into a mountain.
The children piper-bound
following the train.
Don't open your eyes.
I have been waiting
my whole life, he said, to be brought

into believing. Practicing
with a daiquiri, dealing with timidity
in any number of ways.
Wearing a hat, driving a Lexus.
It's difficult. The black blouse,
the clear sequins, each a little lake

taking Ophelia in,
to oblivion. Into a language
that would suit her. The noise level
in the restaurant had risen.
The girl in the black dress (Ophelia?)
was wiping her eyes.

The woman in the pretty black blouse,
sewn with sequins was turning
to look out the window.
Did I tell you, he said? Yes,
he had. He had told her.
And she had listened.

—Eikoh Hosoe: No. 24 from the *Man and Woman* series,
black and white photograph, 1960.
Online at: www.nd.edu/~ndr/issues/ndr19/contents19.html

Please, God, let me hear your voice again.

Perhaps, if I am silent, the enough will be the answer. I shall, I know it I know it, recognize it again.

Why must I search for you!

Oh, I have a headache now, there isn't any point in asking questions of a thing which won't answer. I have to continue on. Perhaps I'll find greener pastures. Yes, and perhaps I'll find a wild boar. I haven't seen where I am. Maybe that's why I'm here, I've been told the truth time after time and refused to believe it and so they put me here. Who are they? A they or he would explain so much qualm and doubt. I've always believed I was they or him, but just because I am or think or might be dead I weaken. I must be strong; I remember thinking even upon death I should not weaken in my beliefs. I don't want to believe in an external They or He(no, not even a She)I've continued because, in the end, I've counted on my belief there is some permanent truth. I've always just assumed there was some unchanging truth. Perhaps this is death, a questioning of whether it is immutable or whether truth isn't something that changes from one day to the next. A circumstantial thing? The floor is covered in some sticky film(our filth)

Please, please tell me who or what has said enough—I am so weak, as if I were traveling and have landed and feel jet lag and lost—Just tell me if you have my social security card? If you're beginning in my name?

I respond because you beg.

My breathing slows, I try to recall. Even now, several seconds after, I wonder who it could be. Could it be me? Could I have begun speaking to myself without registering that it was me?

Who are you?—Already, my voice hollow and weak. I want to see him.

For a newcomer, you ask too much. I have been here as long as you. You've woken me up.

Where are you? You must have it!—Waving my hands erratically, I begin searching in my immediate vicinity.

Don't be so dense. I don't need it and, besides how could you accuse someone you haven't even seen? Don't bother to search the area; I can see you, but you may never see me.

Who are you, that I may never see you?—Stretching my arm back so I know he isn't behind. I have gone too far to touch the wall.

I am Kadman. Who are you?

Just Adam.

If you must move around, please do so quietly. I want to fall back asleep—Kadman says—All your answers are not in this place.

What do you know of my uncertainty?

You constantly fondle your genitals, isn't that enough?
Enough? Enough for what?
The lady doth protest too much.
What, if anything, do you know?
I've overheard.
Heard what?
Your lack of faith; your inability to be certain, even about being alive—
What have I said? Could I have told a secret in my sleep? Was I asleep?
There you go, your genitals touched again.
My hands hover across the floor for an artifact of recognition.
How are you able to see me and I not you?
Hidden away as another. First, you should know what thing can be
absolute.
Truth?
Truth changes with the process that finds it. No, truth is a dangerous
way.
Is there another way?
Begin with me, something less than a solid.
To begin with you, I must know where then who you are.
I'm contagious.
I sweep my hands in the direction of Kadman's laughter.
Show yourself! Show yourself with the insects. Father of Insects. Father
of Man. Kadman!
What's the matter?
wait

Better left to decomposing.

Mark Marino

Play Labyrinth at:
www.nd.edu/~ndr/issues/ndr19/contents19.html

CZECHOSLOVAKIAN RHAPSODY
SUNG TO THE ACCOMPANIMENT OF PIANO

Debra Di Blasi

A Dead German

You would say, "Serves him right, fucking German bastard," like a joke, but you'd mean it. Your arrogant Czech tongue spitting out the word *German* like a hair, hairball from the tongue of a cat, Bohemian dog, you. Should I be horrified that I slept with you *after* you insulted Jews, Germans and North American Indians? It was hot that night, and the bar was hot, and you were dressed in an undershirt and jeans and hot from playing soccer, hot so drinking cold Pilsner[1] of course, and you said, "You look hot tonight, woman," and flipped that big Czech hand of yours as if the

A dead German sat in front of his television set for five years with the lights of his Christmas tree flashing beside him, and none of his neighbors noticed.

"Someone said once that he had gone off to a home, I didn't ask any more," said Monika Majarres, who lived in the same Hamburg apartment building as Wolfgang Dircks, a divorced, disabled loner who died in 1993 at the age of 43.

The landlords came knocking only after the bank account from which Dirck's rent and bills were automatically paid ran out.

Next to the no-longer-functioning television set and the still twinkling tree, they found his skeleton with his TV listings magazine still on his lap and open to the page for Dec. 5, 1993.

w o r l d w o r l d w o r l d w o r l d w o r l d w o r l w o r l d w o r l d

were nothing more than gnats swarming/breeding, and you added: "At least all these horny bastards think so." Which was a lie; no one saw me come in. What you really meant was: *We would like to suggest that Paradise was never really lost. We would like you to consider that Eden is a state of mind, and that the mind of Adam and Eve (yes, they thought as one!) has not evolved beyond the ability to recall and thus conjure Paradise: its light and heat and scent. We would like to urge you to embrace the possibility of Heaven-on-Earth and* **come a little bit closer, you're my kind of [wo]man, and I'm all alone.**

---

1   Pilsner is Czech beer: "'Czechs like to drink Czech beer because it's the best in the world,' said Antonin Jelínek, editor-in-chief of *Pivní kuryr*, a magazine for beer connoisseurs. 'They'd have to be pretty desperate to drink anything else.'" (source: *The Prague Post*, page A8, Nov. 25-Dec. 1, 1998)

I came.

Closer.

Pain: Thirsty no more

You're a vampire and when you suck me you suck me dry: There's nothing left but teeth marks, bruised to blue. I *want* you to go when you go. I *want* you to stumble over the diminutive pebble somewhere anywhere there just beyond my door—Goliath taken down by disregard—and fall and bruise black for you disregard me.

I said:	*"It looks like the world turned inside out, like a part of the surface of the moon transplanted onto the surface of the sea."*
You said:	*"What the hell are you talking about?"*
I said:	*"Pain."*
You said:	*"Oh."*

Czechs watch less television

Czechs eschew boob tube

Czechs watch less television than any group in Europe except German-Speaking Swiss, according to a study released Nov. 19. The study, called Television-98, found Czechs average 130 minutes of daily viewing time compared to an average of 198 minutes per day for West European adults. Television-98 was conducted by the marketing firm IP in Düsseldorf, which is associated with the German commercial television channel RTL.

Hungarians, averaging 235 minutes daily, watched the most TV according to the study. German-speaking citizens of Switzerland averaged just 128 minutes a day.

ON MY MOTHER'S SIDE I am part German, Jew, and North American Indian. It wasn't that my mother's side of the family was unprejudiced, eager to achieve the hybrid vigor[2], spawn a new race of superhumans who would somehow bring Peace, Tranquility and, yes, perhaps even Joy to the World. No, it was that the Jews lied about their Semitism, and the North American Indians lied about their "Savage Blood" and the Germans who did not yet have the murder of 6 million Jews on their conscience lied about not knowing the difference between a Jew and an Irishman

---

2   Hybrid vigor: a term used in animal husbandry and horticulture to indicate the result of cross-breeding wherein only the sturdiest genes from each species are reproduced in offspring, the weaker genes having been supplanted by the genes most useful for survival.

(*ref.* "Genealogy: Bad to the Bone," page XX). You of the Bohemian[3] blood would find my blood of English, Scotch and Welsh ON MY FATHER'S SIDE somehow more palatable, as if vampires like you had the luxury of being a bloody gourmet.

I *should* be horrified that I slept with you after you insulted Jews, Germans and North American Indians. Why am I not? Even now, at this late date, why does it occur to me as nothing stranger than, say:

Cold pressed virgins

An open letter to Miloš Zeman
Dear Mr. Prime Minister:

In the Sept. 30–Oct. 6 issue of *The Prague Post*, it was reported that a large pig farm is operating on the site of the former concentration camp in Lety, near Písek.

In the Lety camp, innocent people — above all Sinti and Roma [Gypsy tribes] — experienced eternal suffering. They were tortured and tormented, left to die of hunger and worked to death.

On June 6, 1991, the European Union ratified a Convention of Security and Cooperation in Europe. It was signed by the member countries at that time. The convention also entailed the obligation to maintain memorials where crimes against humanity were committed during the Second World War.

It is my opinion that a pig farm on the territory of a former concentration camp is a severe offense against the provisions of the above-mentioned convention. It also violates all rules of good relations of the Czech state toward its national minorities.

I ask you, dear Mr. Prime Minister, to see to it that the pig farm is transferred to another location.

Simon Wiesenthal
Vienna

— The writer, who will be 90 on Dec. 31, spent four-and-a-half years in Nazi concentration camps during World War II, in which 89 of his relatives and family members were exterminated. He has crusaded against genocide ever since and calls himself a "deputy for the dead." Translated from German by Valerie and Alan Levy.

(4)

3   You think I don't know that my calling you "Bohemian" is an insult to you, you Praguelodyte, you who used "Bohemian" to disparage your own brother because he weeps the tears of a lover during—*o mein gott!*—Wagner's *Tristan und Isolde*. You think I don't know Germany occupied Bohemia during World War II, that your father who believed in the intellectual superiority of Bohemians—after all, he had let German soldiers win at chess in order to keep his shoe repair business open—your father, an otherwise good man, good father, told you repeatedly, rapping you on the head with his knuckles, that the fall of Bohemia was the fall of civilization, "From here on out," knock knock "it's facedown in the gutter and piss on your breath and don't you ever," knock knock knock "ever whisper Bohemia again because it is gone, you understand," knock knock "a memory, a dream, a cloud—vanished." You think I don't wonder if he wasn't right, damn him, watching the Germans come and go, the Soviets come and go, the Americans come and stay and sit in coffee houses reading Kafka and pretending to understand the real meaning of *refugee* and *exile* and *irretrievable* while here at home refugees in exile mourn their irretrievable past beneath a billboard advertising underwear that cost more than their life savings. You think I don't know Bohemia was the world's most legendary enclave of refined pleasure and now it's gone. *Kaput!* as Hitler grinned, watching the ash of Kafka's sisters fall upon the sill of the window of his bastard dream.

4   The citizens of the Missouri town where I grew up have filed a class-action lawsuit to shut down the newly built corporate pig farm because "its odor creates an environment that makes daily life unbearable." Question: Does the stink of the future out-rank the stink of the past? Must the task of living always consist of holding one's nose?

IN THE WINTER OF 1942 IT WAS COLD IN LETY. THE WOMEN LAY PRESSED TOGETHER IN THE HARD WOODEN BUNKS. SOME WERE VIRGINS. THEY DIED WITHOUT KNOWING THE PLEASURE OF HAVING A MAN INSIDE THEM.

Czechoslovakian rhapsody
I had you inside me. It was a pleasure. I should be horrified.

Co je to ptakopysk?[5]
In the hot bar the British tourist at the next table said, "The South Devon[6] tourist board seized upon any clue, however slight, that tied Christie[7] to the region." This has nothing to do with anything except that as a writer I am always eavesdropping on conversations, especially when they are more interesting than the one in which I'm engaged.

> *You said:*   *"You really liked those Injuns, eh?"*
> *I said:*   *"North American Indians."*
> *You said:*   *"Injuns. Savages. Red niggers."*
> *I said:*   *"You are joking, aren't you?"*
> *You said:*   *"Of course I'm joking. Don't be silly."*
> *I said:*   *"My great grandmother was an Indian."*
> *You said:*   *"What the hell is a platypus, and how come I've never tasted one?"*

The British tourist sighed, "It's a mystery."

---

5 Czech for: *What is a platypus?*
6 This is the name of my elder brother, in fact derived from Devon, England, where my father (who was flight engineer in 30 Berlin bombing missions) was stationed during World War II.
7 Dame Agatha Christie, the British mystery writer.

A complete course for beginners

Jedl ptakopysk.	He was eating platypus.
Snédle ptakopysk.	He at the platypus.
Jedle.	He was eating.
Najedl se.	He had something to eat.
Najedle se ptakopyskem.	He ate his fill of platypus.

The (w)hole of my inventiveness

I was walking along a slope so steep and high it was impossible to see what lay below, obscured by the fog of ignorance only dreams and faulty imagination can provide, and I saw a boulder made of brown clay compacted by time, exposed now to the elements, and I knew the moment I set foot upon its slippery-damp surface it would crumble and I'd go toppling down into

the w of my inventiveness, yet set foot upon the boulder anyway, and it did crumble, and you twitched in your sleep, softly crying, "Fuck!" and woke me.

I was saved.

You continued sleeping, snoring, victim of apnea.[8]

I think we knew each other centuries ago, were ill-fated lovers. We do not know each other now. Though we are ill-fated nonetheless.

> **xenophobia:** *hatred of foreigners*
> [xenos = stranger (Greek) + phobos = fear (Greek)]
> [[xenophobia really = fear (therefore hatred since we hate what causes us fear because fear is a loathsome human characteristic, thus we first hate our self then loathe our self then hate the stranger whom we fear) of strangers]]

---

8   A sleep disorder in which the air passageway is blocked, causing night terrors and sometimes even death. (I sat up in bed and watched you sleep and timed the silences between breaths. I imagined a silence that went on in perpetuity, imagined myself tucking the blankets under your big permanently silent chin, getting dressed, and calmly walking out of the hotel as if nothing had happened, as if I'd never known you.)

[[[don't argue with me, I know I'm right]]]

Auf Wiedersehen

*"Some say it's a wise person who seeks harmony
in mind, body and spirit."*
—Anonymous Ad Copywriter

I want you to go when you go. When you are gone I want you back.
—I was you were we were it was—
Why does my body play deaf to the protests of my mind? It's the plight of
the vampire's victim, *ano?* Teeth wounds on my thighs. Metal-bitter blood
on my lips. This close to death, and it's my murderer I cry out for. Boul-
ders of clay, feet of clay, you're a clay-footed devil[9] and your father played
chess with Nazis to save the soles of shoes while the souls of my ancestors
cried, "Devil! Bloodletter!" and marched to the points of bayonettes to stand
on the high steep slope with nowhere to step but upon the clay that crum-
bled forever into a future where their progeny sleeps with you who would
wish all of them (and plenty others, too) dead once more in order to cleanse
the world of the guilt you can neither bear nor name and thus wish yourself
to disappear, vanish into the night: bat-winged wolf-howl mist and not a
human scent for miles.

Each time I open this book[10] : : : : : : : *What is a platypus?*

platypus, semi-aquatic egg-laying MAMMAL, or MONOTREME
(*Ornithorhynchus anatinus*). Also called duckbill, it has a rubbery, duckbill-
shaped muzzle, no teeth, and no external ears. Its head, body, and tail are
broad, flat, and covered with dark-brown fur; its feet are webbed. The adult
male is about 6' 5" tall, handsome, well-endowed. The platypus eats small
freshwater women of 1/2 German-Jew-North American Indian descent
and originates from the Czech Republic—or what was once Bohemia,
now vanished.

---

9   cert = devil, dàbel = devil, jednohubka = canapé
10   *Teach Yourself Czech: A Complete Course for Beginners* by David Short.

Genealogy: Bad to the Bone: Part 1
My maternal grandmother died believing she was half German, half Irish.
She was not. Here's the story:
Toward the end of the 19th Century my great-grandfather, who was a
Jew and whose last name began with the letter G, emigrated from Germany
to the United States. This was his second emigration. The first was during the European Revolution, as an infant carried by his parents. There
had been "some sort of trouble" and the G family had escaped it by fleeing
to America. (Something about Kaiser Wilhelm. Something about money
and/or property. Something vague but unseemly, perhaps dangerous but
not, perhaps, noble.) The trouble vanished, or was momentarily forgotten
by the Kaiser, and the G family returned home only to flee again for simi-
larly vague but [perhaps] ignoble reasons. The family settled somewhere
in the area of Beaver Dam, Wisconsin—that region known for its HUGE
Jewish-emigré population (ha ha ha!).
There were six children in the G family: three girls and three boys, one
of whom was my great-grandfather. Something happened to the parents:
either they again returned to Germany to face whatever political music was
playing (Wagner?) or they died or they simply could not afford to feed,
clothe, and shelter a brood of six. Therefore, the girls were sent to live with
a family by the name of Johns, and the boys were sent to live with a family
by the name of Clark. The Clarks were Irish. My great-grandfather took
not only their name but their heritage, and passed it on to (1) his daughter
(my grandmother) who he never told otherwise, and (2) his son who he told
shortly before his death, shamefaced, though it was never clear whether his
shame arose from the 70-year charade or his Jewishness. Let me explain:
My great-grandfather hated being a Jew. It shamed him. Whether it
was the anti-Semitic climate in Germany or the anti-Semitic climate in Beaver Dam, or the anti-Semitic climate in his soul, my grandfather wanted so
badly to fit into the world—a world that offered the possibility of rejection
wherever he went—that he himself became anti-Semitic. He was a handsome man with olive skin and black hair and eyes, and a thick black mus-
tache, and a streamlined soldierly physique. There was an exoticism about
his appearance that couldn't be explained away (though he tried) by saying
he was not only Irish but Black Irish: finer, rarer, worthier.
He was worthy to Hattie, my great-grandmother: a tall big-boned German woman, her blue eyes drawn to his black eyes like day to night. She
knew his true identity for he confessed it one night after they had kissed and
kissed deeply, and she had hinted at their shared future by saying, "I vish to
go on kissing you forever—if you know vhat I mean." Loved him especially

for the burden of his self-hatred: the limping melancholia it lent him.

And your Aryan eye, bright blue[11]

Ah, yes! I remember you years ago, when you were in the shape of a young man with Aryan looks of blue eyes & blond hair, and an Aryan last name (von Something-or-other), and an Aryan hatred for Jews and Gypsies and Blacks and Hispanics and Homosexuals and anyone everyone all who did not appear Aryan, as I did then in my German-skin phase, my eyes-Swiss-blue phase, my English-tongue-and-cheek phase. And I remember I remember that last night you visited me before I fled to Europe, you were hung over and disgusted because you had fucked a Jewish woman ("But she had blonde hair!") and how you felt, you said, "unclean" and "damaged" and how those words toppled incongruously from your young ignorant lips, the way "genocide" and "supremacy" might spill from the lips of a three-year-old boy—for the implications of the words are as yet incomprehensible to him of the small dick the incomplete prick, and the words themselves only sounds his father makes when he's pissed and self-righteous and light-in-the-pocket after a long shitty day at the office. And I remember how I could not bring myself to declare, "My great-grandfather was a Jew," and how the shame of my reticence made me hate you that night so that when you said "I love you" and kissed me good-bye I shuddered, and when you'd gone I scrubbed my lips with a rag until they bled.

I should have sent you the part-Jew-bloody rag with a note: "Fuck this, you fascist disease, you crime against humanity."

Instead, when I ran into you ten years later I kissed you on the cheek and asked about your health and your new wife. Who was Irish.

---

11   from the poem "Daddy" by Sylvia Plath (b. 1932). She committed suicide in 1963 by sticking her head in an OVEN and turning on the GAS.

Which of these descriptions comes close to your view of our relationship?

A serious problem	46%
Not serious	32
An adversary	14
Undecided	8

Do you approve or disapprove of the way we are dealing with our attempt at love?

Approve	37%
Disapprove	37
Undecided	26

SOURCE: THE PEW RESEARCH CENTER. BASED
ON PHONE INTERVIEWS CONDUCTED SEPT. 4-11

"What You Need is a Good Ethnic Cleansing!"

. . . and I cried I wept like a grandmother, *which I was: mother to half-breeds, grandmother to quarter-breeds, great-grandmother to eighth-breeds, and so on and so forth, my descendants fractionalized until there is so little of my blood left I could vanish with a paper cut.*

The English did not wipe out my tribe of agrarian pacifists, nor the French, nor the German. It was the Iroquois who loved to fight us for we were not them, and the Sioux who loved to breed us for we were beautiful, and my father who loved fire water more than good-for-nothing squaw daughters and so sold me to a wealthy farmer whose blood was as irrelevant as his skin red as mine when it was summer and the fields to be mowed. (All right, he was a white man — 1/2 German, 1/2 Swiss — but he bled red, and though he was more hirsute than the pigs he farmed, I let him between my pretty fawn thighs because he was a kind man, a big ugly kind man, a burnt-skinned kind man like a roasted pig, and I let him come (he came) because I saw the world to come and there was no place in it for me, the last of my breed.

Great-great-granddaughter who invents my words here, hear my inquiry: What do you get when you cross a stream with a horse? Answer: You get to the other side, baby, that's all.

This is not Bohemia

Nor Is This

"[Czech] history has taught them to keep their heads down, and to make an ironic comment or **JOKE** ."[12]

That hot night in a bar a North American Indian sat down at our table and told white man jokes and you told red man jokes, and the two of you laughed and laughed and laughed and laughed as if to say: "Look how far we've come, white man and red man, able to laugh at each other without one of us dying with a knife or bullet in our back!"

The jokes were not funny. I yawned and excused myself to the bathroom, and when I returned I sat down and asked: "What do you get when you cross a stream with a horse?"

And you of the white skin and he of the red skin grinned and shook your heads, and I paused a moment to build suspense, then answered: "A platypus."

---

12 *Fodor's Exploring Prague.* Emphasis on the word "**JOKE**" is obviously mine.

Znova: Co je to ptakopysk?[13]

> **Platypus**, *Ornithorhynchus anatinus cowboyishnus*
> On each ankle the male platypus has a spur connected to poison glands
> in the thighs; these spurs are used against an attacker or against a woman
> who is one-half German/Jewish/North American Indian. The poison is
> not fatal to her but causes intense pain.

It's not just that I'm half German/Jewish/North American Indian, is it. It's
also that I'm a woman. And you would say with a predictability that would
make meteorologists climax: "Oh, here we go with that fucking feminist
piss-and-moan crap, pissing and moaning about injustice when what you're
really pissed about is that you have a hole and I have a cock. Meaning, you
represent absence. I represent the opposite."

(What is the opposite of absence? Is it you, here[14], kneeling between my
thighs like some reluctant communicant, waiting for a miracle you can
no longer convincingly argue, no longer believe in? Or is the opposite
of absence the memory of absence, for you are more *present* to me in my
memory of your leaving—foot crunch upon gravel, *chît-chît* of lighter lit,
scent of smoke fading.)

Pain: Children Supplied the Art
You with whom I fell in love at first sight: you bloodsucking/bloodlet-
ting/bloodcurdling vanished-Bohemian vampire: you transplant to land of
cowboys and *injuns*: you with guilt up your ass, spurs on your boots, ice in
your heart: you cause me pain . . .

I said:	*"Ouch."*
You said:	*"You want me to not thrust so deeply?"*
I said:	*"I want you to take off your boots."*

---

13   Again: What is a platypus?
14   You're not here, of course; I'm writing this in my study miles and miles from where you
are, and this is merely paper and ink. Lest there be any confusion with reality.

You said: *"Fucking demanding mutt of a woman."*
I said: *"The spurs, too, lover."*

. . . for I should shudder at the memory of you inside me.   Instead, I want to bear your children.[15]

platypus

---

15   Scientists recently identified the gene responsible for genocide. Here's how it works: When a member of a species or race (as in humans) meets another member of a species or race with qualities the former finds somehow reprehensible (such as wacky religious beliefs, flagrant ignorance, too shrewd money management skills, or even, ironically, bigotry) the genocide gene will compel the former individual to take measures to eliminate the latter in-dividual. The most obvious methods are shooting, stabbing, gassing, burning, electrocuting, strangling, drowning, bombing.... Less obvious methods, but no less disagreeable, are rape (wherein the male deposits his seed in the reprehensible female, thus halving the strength of her bloodline) or seduction (wherein the female seduces, then spends $200-$400 for the rep-rehensible male's seed in order to halve and thus reduce the strength of his bloodline). Unbe-knownst to rapist or seductress, the genocide gene will default in these instances to produce a hybrid vigor, usually consisting of reprehensible traits of both individuals, thus "guarantee-ing" the perpetuation of the species for at least one more generation. (You understand that it's possible I've made all this up. You also understand—if you know anything at all about the Human Genome Project—that I may not have made it up. The point is: I want you to question what you think you know or don't know, what you believe or don't believe. In other words: I want you to consider that you don't know your ass from a hole in the ground.)

(Let's have nothing here but white space. Let's have nothing but a cool plane of white for our tired tired eyes, our weary weary mind. My mind is weary, isn't yours? And perhaps also your heart? It's strenuous, this acute caring, this heavy penitence, this *thing* writers and readers do. Oh yes, we're in this together, you and I. Didn't you know? For godsake, don't you know that *yet?*)

The 50 Most Beautiful Guys on Earth . . .

"Are Czechs," you said, dabbing a napkin at the blood oozing from the corners of your mouth. "My semen will cost you $200. That's half the price of a wad purchased at a sperm bank."

"You're joking, right?"

"Don't you see?" you grinned. "Don't you understand? I'm giving you an incredible discount!"

You'll Want To Take One Home With You!

(IT'S RAINING NOW. IN THE STREET OUTSIDE THIS CAFE, ALL UMBRELLAS ARE BLACK EXCEPT ONE: BRIGHT BLUE. LOOK HOW IT STANDS OUT! SUCH A BRIGHT BRIGHT BLUE BLUE UMBRELLA! I STUDY THE CLOTHES OF THE MAN CARRYING IT IN ORDER TO DETERMINE THE CHARACTER FLAW THAT WOULD HAVE HIM CHOOSE A BRIGHT BLUE UMBRELLA OVER A TYPICAL BLACK ONE. THOUGH HE'S DRESSED SIMILAR TO OTHER MEN—BLACK TRENCHCOAT, GRAY TROUSERS, SHINY BLACK SHOES—THERE'S SOMETHING ABOUT HIM THAT'S *DIFFERENT*, SOMETHING *NOT QUITE RIGHT*, SOMETHING *QUESTIONABLE*. I KNOW IT.)

A recent spate of incidents involving organized skinhead actions has prompted the government to propose a plan to create a new police unit dedicated to curbing racist violence. But Interior Ministry officials are not in favor of the move.

"No unit against skinheads is planned," even though increased skinhead activity is a reality, asserted Jan Decker, spokesman for the Interior Ministry. "We are only going to strengthen the anti-extremist unit so that it will monitor the skinhead movement more effectively than before," he said. The police can't just act against citizens because they have short hair and dress like a skinhead, he added.

Wild. And Crazy.

No one will make excuses for you, not even me. However:

It's true that shortly after you arrived in the United States a popular television program called *Saturday Night Live* began. It was a funny show. People watched it late Saturday nights and they laughed. They laughed hard. One of the skits they laughed particularly hard at was "Two Wild and Crazy Guys." The two wild and crazy guys were played by Steve Martin and Dan Akroyd. They were funny, funny, funny. They dressed in ugly polyester-looking clothes that were too tight and too colorful and too unfashionable to not be funny. They were always trying to pick up "some crazy American chicks." Those two wild and crazy guys, how stupid they were! Ha ha! How crass! Ha ha ha! How sleezy! Ha ha ha ha ha ha ha ha ha ha ha ha ha ha ha ha!

They were Czechs.

One only has to imagine the humiliation you suffered as a result: a relatively new Czech in a relatively new world with nothing but the cheap polyester shirt on your back. Anyway, it wasn't so much that your father played chess with Nazis—chess, unlike war, is only a game—but that when your Jewish neighbors (the ones with the two children you used to play "cowboys and injuns" with) were arrested and shipped off to Auschwitz[16] and you asked him, your father of the Bohemian blood, "Why?" he replied, "Because they were very bad people." And when you asked, "But what did they *do?*" your father smacked you hard across the back of your head.

It was the smack that made you **WILD**. The smack that made you **CRAZY**. The smack that made you turn to me in bed that hot hot night and whisper, "Platypus . . . How do you spell it?"

P - L - A - T - Y - P - U - S

ORNITHORHYNCHIDAE
Platypus Family
The single species of this family is an extraordinary animal in appearance but perfectly adapted for its way of life. The platypus was discovered 200 years ago, and when the first specimen arrived at London's Natural History Museum, scientists were so puzzled by it that they believed the specimen to be a fake.

---

16   It's true that you could not possibly have been born yet, but the fact that you tell this story as if it were fact must mean something, you clinging to a memory that never was. (Of the two neighbor children who were shipped off to Auschwitz, one was a little girl with long black hair, wavy and perpetually beribboned, round black eyes that made you think of aching things you could not yet comprehend. It could be said that you loved her with a love far wiser than any 8-year-old boy could summon. It could be said she was your wife, love of your life, just waiting for the both of you to grow up. Of course, she never grew up. The Nazis were so kind to let her stay seven forever — the age she remains for you in your imaginary memory of her. Though sometimes, you confess, you think you see her walking down the street of any American city, dressed in blue, hair cut short now out of respect for her 7-year-old ghost. "Once," you said, "I even thought you were her. The first time I saw you. But I can smell the German in your blood. I can taste it. I suspect, though cannot be sure, it resembles the flavor of platypus.")

The Wonder of You

"Or be more energetic and propel yourself," said the British tourist, irritated by the heat and his partner's daftness.

You and I, on the other hand, looked at our watches:

I thought: *The word "injun" resulted from men too ignorant, too stupid to pronounce "indian". And the word "indian" resulted from white men so stupid they thought Newport Beach was East India. Men so stubborn they insisted on calling the natives "Indians" even after their mistake clearly had been brought to their attention.*

You thought: Life wasn't easy under Communism but at least it was predictable.

I thought: *The world's worst murderers are made up of boys who never got into art school, or didn't make the soccer team, or kissed a little girl with red hair who cried "Ew!" and wiped her cherry-red mouth hard with the back of her hand. They never outgrew their wormy grudges; their grudges outgrew them: became monstrous parasites gnawing their slimy way through humanity. Or what was left of it.*

You thought: I wonder how long she will take to achieve orgasm.

I thought: *In the 1960s television show* Hogan's Heroes, *all World War II German POW camp officers and soldiers are stupid, and all World War II Americans, French, and British POWs are smart. The POWs play with their German captors the way cats play with mice.[17] They learn the German weaknesses which are* **HYSTERICALLY** *funny (if you are American or French or British) and infinite—or at least plentiful enough to make it through 6 television seasons.[18]*

You thought: Fucking who cares if she achieves orgasm, anyway.

---

17   Cats play with mice with a cruelty that makes them nearly human.

18   *Hogan's Heroes* trivia: Werner Klemperer, who played the POW camp's pompous assinine idiotic Colonel Klink, was the son of the Jewish-German conductor, Otto Klemperer. Robert Clary (neé Robert Widerman), who played the beret-donning "frenchie" Captain Louis LeBeau, was imprisoned in a Nazi concentration camp as a child.

The British tourist leaned toward his partner and said, "Did you know that if you reverse only a couple of DNA strands in a cat you'll get a human?"

I turned to him and grinned: "That doesn't say much for cats, does it?"

His flat-heart expression didn't waver as he downed the rest of his ale and stood and left.

You watched every inch of his departure, looking down your elegant Czech nose at his plump belly and woman's ass, and you said, "Fucking potato-eater."

"I think *potato-eater* refers to the Irish," I said.

You flipped that big Czech hand of yours through the gnat-teeming world and said, "Same thing. Potato-eaters, tea-sippers, Kikes, Krauts, Ruskies, Japs, Gooks, Chinks, Camel-jockeys ..."

"You forgot *Injuns*."

"Injuns. Come on, woman, let's go have sex."

84 Down: Duckbill

There is nothing fake about the platypus. We know that now. Now we know it exists: hybrid vigor of creatures that should never have fornicated — they had so little in common. (Why, my god, a duck and a beaver! What could they have talked about that hot hot night? What could they have seen in each other but the insult of their difference.) Yes, now we know the platypus is real and stubbornly alive. And what is a platypus, after all? What does it represent that its name is on everyone's lips, silent but noticeable as a drop of blood about to drip onto one's chin?

Star magazine

It's Sunday afternoon and I'm taking a break from writing *Czechoslovakian Rhapsody*, sprawled on the couch doing a crossword puzzle simultaneously though abstractly thinking about the pungent scent between your legs, and there it is: 84 Down: Duckbill: an 8-letter word that begins with the letter P. I kid you not. Fucking P-L-A-T-Y-P-U-S is the answer. What are the odds! I put down the crossword puzzle and close my eyes and think of you that last night when the heat of the wind and our scorched flesh created a vortex into which all histories light and dark good and bad left and right descended, and the world as we knew it (imperfect with its genocides and ethnic cleansings and [un]holy wars and racist swine) vanished like so many Bohemias—*kaput!*—and it was just you and me **IMPROVED!** and naked as in Paradise, getting ourselves back to the Garden, getting it on. And I thought that it *just might be possible* to forget about blood and skin and accents and finally feel the hot bending of each other's "sold-as-is" soul. Until you came inside me[19] and said breathlessly but matter-of-factly: "I knew you were good for *something*, woman."

---

19   I.O.U. $200.

Bohemia was

If you are ever in Prague and standing on the spot where Bohemia vanished forever and someone walks up to you and asks, *"Co je to ptakopysk?"* tell them the truth. Tell them:

A platypus is a creature that has outlived its time, has refused to evolve when everything around it was evolving into a more sensible form. It is archaic, antediluvian, breathing fossil, specter out of everyone's history wherein everyone, it seems, died at the hand of everyone else. Why? That is simply the nature of the platypus. Sleep with one if you wish. Feel the horror of its flesh inside your flesh, duckbill against your bloody lips, spurs against your blue-bruised thighs. If you can. If you cannot, then by all means succumb, succumb! You won't be alone.

No taste for decay

Dear Editor:

I found the recent wedding announcement you wrote ["Radisson man woos Bonton woman," Prague Profile, Nov. 11–17] to be in quite bad taste. Describing the decaying body of a dead German in such detail was not necessary, nor appreciated.

I hope I do not have the same misfortune of having any of my personal history retold by you.

Bill ███
Prague 6

Note: Platypuses are now protected by law and are quite common in some areas.

---

20   All newspaper clippings were appropriated from *The Prague Post* with the exception of the crossword puzzle, clipped from *The Kansas City Star.*

A FILM BY
CAMILLE
BACOS
AND
MIEKAL
AND

Entre

Pyrobiblios

Now showing at www.nd.edu/~ndr/issues/ndr19/contents19.html

FROM 10 : 01

Lance Olsen

00 : 00 : 00 : 00

MIDAFTERNOON IN A MOVIE THEATER in the Mall of America. Glary lights before the show make everything seem stark and unfinished to Kate Frazey, a bony aerobics instructor relieving herself of her shocking-pink ski jacket, bunching it on the folded-up seat beside her, and sitting in row three, seat nine, seeing herself as she does so as if from a crane shot among these other filmgoers filtering in and settling down around her. Kate, blond hair so dark it is almost the color of high-fiber breakfast cereal, is Franz Kafka's great-great granddaughter, although she carries no awareness of this within her. She doesn't know her great-great grandfather once had an affair with another bony woman, Grete Bloch, friend of Felice Bauer, to whom Kafka was briefly engaged. Kate doesn't know Grete had a son about whom Kafka never learned, nor that his son was supposed to have died while a child, but was adopted by a Jewish businessman and his wife, and brought to New York in the thirties. Whenever Kate dreams, it is about the plots of Kafka's work, which she has never read because she believes there are already too many stories in the world. Kate dreams that two strangers in top hats and frock coats are always knocking at her door, wanting in. That she is a ninety-pound weight-loss artist dissolving in a cage full of hay in the town square in Prague. That she is a muscular hare darting through a wet field at night and that, no matter how fast she runs, no matter which direction she chooses, the beautiful hounds sleeping within the castle miles away will awaken the next day and chase her down. This is why Kate doesn't sleep unless she has to. This is why she hasn't slept for two nights, why she leans forward now, elbows on knees, concentrating very hard on keeping her glistery brown eyes wide open.

97

00 : 00 : 01 : 01

THREE ROWS BACK sits Stuart Navidson, plumping gynecologist with a small practice in Minneapolis. Heart a hummingbird, Stuart hunches over his Palm, reading email, oblivious of the factoids flipping up on the movie screen in front of him. He doesn't care in a *zip pan* the camera moves so quickly the image in between the original subject and its successor is blurred, nor that the first film fan magazines appeared in 1912. Monday afternoon at the office, he received an email with no subject heading and fake sender address. *Eat shit and die*, it said. Spam, Stuart thought. Tuesday morning Stuart walked out of his house to find a small note stuck under the windshield wiper of his metallic-shale Audi saying, simply: *Bastard.* When their friends Austyn and Jed Jacobsen stepped out of a Szechwan restaurant with Stuart's wife Valerie and him after a nice dinner Wednesday evening, Stuart found a second not-so-small note stuck under his windshield wiper. *What next?* it inquired in a red scrawl. He balled it up and chucked it into the slushy street before Valerie could catch up with him. "Stupid advertise-ment," he told her when she looked like she might inquire about it. They spent Friday and Saturday at their cabin up on the shore of Lake Superior near Beaver Bay and returned two hours ago to discover their house had been broken into while they were away. The only thing missing, so far as they could determine, was a single pillow from their bed. After the police left, a shaken Valerie headed off to keep a lunch date. Stuart drove here to calm down, clear his mind, and reflect. It isn't working. A new message has just appeared on his PDA. *Are we having fun yet?* it asks. Stuart is quite confident he knows the answer.

00 : 00 : 03 : 13

MIGUEL GONZALEZ AND ANGELICA ENCINAS wait neither for the glary lights to dim nor the trailers to flash awake before beginning to feel each other up. They are fourteen and have snuck into the next-to-back row on their first date. A chant is cycling through Miguel's head: *Just my hand on her thigh, just there, just like that, look, just my fingers moving beneath her skirt, just the tips, just the slowness of them, just the heat of her skin, just that and nothing else, just the way she smells, peppermint shampoo, just these things, just these and nothing more, just here, just like this, just my fingertips moving.* Angelica, eyes closed, is far away from Miguel's hand. She is imagining an establishing shot in her very own private documentary: there Miguel and Angelica are making out among all these people settling in to their seats and the camera is panning back and there is the AMC theater in which they are sitting on the fourth floor of the Mall of America tucked among thirteen others in which hundreds of other people are settling into their seats and the camera is panning back and there is the mall itself frantic with thousands of other people frantic with Christmas with dangling pink angels with cotton-candy snowdrifts and the camera is panning back and right through the roof and the parking structures are receding through the graywhite blizzard and the city park and the hotels and the feeble car lights trembling and it is Sunday and here they are here Angelica and Miguel are and there could be other ways to express a beginning but this one is as good as any and these touches as good as any and so this must be desire sure why not this must be what they mean when they say that word.

00 : 00 : 04 : 12

AT THE BACK OF THE THEATER, in one of the seatless spaces reserved
for the handicapped, slumps Zdravko Prcac in his motorized wheelchair.
Zdravko is wearing a baggy red, white, and blue jogging suit with matching sneakers. Beneath it he is wearing a one-piece style Depends with an
absorbent pad in the crotch area and no belts, tape, or buttons. Eyes shut,
chin on chest, suspended on the whorling rim of sleep, Zdravko is semi-
dreaming of his dead wife Kosa, to whom he was married for fifty-five
years. When Kosa passed after a long battle with a disease that turned her
memories into water, it felt as if a surgeon had visited Zdravko in the night
and extracted his lungs. He stopped eating, but his nurse brought him to
the hospital where the doctors attached a tube beneath his collarbone to
keep him away from her. These days Zdravko's main goal in life is to leave
it. This is proving more difficult than he anticipated. In the meantime,
he strives to remain invisible. A Serb charged with atrocities committed at
the Omarska camp, Zdravko fled through Hungary to Austria in the final
days of the war, from Austria to America. He became eight different people
along the way, and is frightened he might have caught immortality from a
mosquito in the Szeged train station one humid summer evening. Zdravko
believes in certain international officials' eyes he still matters, but is mistaken. At the back of the theater, he semi-dreams he is sitting in his old
living room with Kosa, reading the newspaper after work. It is winter. The
electric fire is glowing. The heavy drapes are drawn. Kosa is knitting, only
backwards. With each stitch she undoes, another memory drops away from
her, a tuft of glassy milkweed.

00 : 00 : 05 : 11

VITO PALUSO CHOOSES an aisle seat. That way he can easily reach down and shift the position of his crutches should someone want to get by. Manipulating his bent bad legs into place, he begins daydreaming about the video he is making. Vito works as a security guard in the mall, sitting in a cramped concrete room observing a wall of surveillance monitors. When he locates a disturbance, he phones his superior who walkie-talkies down to his crew on the floor. Vito also secretly scans the monitors for what he calls S.I.'s (pronounced *sighs*), or Special Instants: those during which tourists photograph each other. Or not precisely those, but rather the ones immediately following them, when people slowly stop smiling after the shot has been snapped and you can actually see their public masks soften and melt back into everyday blandness, a gesture almost always accompanied by a slight lowering of the head in a miniature act of capitulation. Vito wants to capture a hundred such moments, gray and grainy, slo-mo and soundless, in a montage called *Where the Smiling Ends*. Once a week, he dubs footage onto a VHS tape he takes home, downloads it onto his computer, and edits. For Vito, montage isn't a formalistic technique. Continuity determined by the symbolic association of ideas between shots rather than literal connections in time and space is a philosophical principle. Vito believes living is nothing if not a series of dissolves, superimpositions, odd juxtapositions, and unexpected cuts. He would give anything to know someday his short will be shown at a film festival, except he is terrified by failure. He will therefore never finish the seven-minute-and-forty-four-second work that has already burned through nearly two years of his life.

00 : 00 : 07 : 06

MOIRA LOVELACE LOOKS LIKE a flautist in her fifties: short, prim, stringy. She reminds Kate Frazey, one seat to her right, of a cubist painting. Weekdays, Moira teaches algebra at Kennedy High. Looking out on her students, she sees a classroom crammed with space aliens. She cannot understand their lingo. She cannot understand their clothing. What they listen to too loudly through their headphones may be many things, but none of them is music. Every Saturday evening Moira stays at home and makes sex videos of herself in her king-size bed, sheets silk leopard like in those spy thrillers from the sixties. Sometimes with one hand she employs a pink dildo that reminds her of a small pink torpedo. Sometimes she employs plastic bags and smeary makeup. The general impression is one of a messy clown asphyxiating, naked. Moira has learned a lot about cinematography over the years. How it is almost impossible to produce a movie single-handedly. How a whole evening can be devoted to a worthy sixteen-second clip. Every Sunday Moira stays in, making copies of her video, packing each in a plain brown envelope. On her way to school every Monday morning, she mails the envelopes to strangers across the country. Moira locates their names in phonebooks at the library. She thinks of her sex videos as love letters to the world. They put a crackle into lives of people she will never meet and punish her for creating them in the first place. A discreet grin tightens across her lips as Moira Lovelace pictures who may be thinking about her this very second in Omaha, Nebraska, and how.

00 : 00 : 08 : 21

1. CYNTHIA MORGENSTERN, ONE SEAT behind and right of Jerry Roemer, wants to love Cary Grant, only in black and white.

2. Conceivably there are special contact lenses for such a purpose.

3. Fat is horrifying because it makes you look like a bullfrog version of yourself. Fat reminds Cynthia of something washed up after a storm on a tropical beach.

4. Let your heart be a raisin.

5. Germs are filthy blizzards blowing through your bloodstream.

6. Cynthia wants to dwell in a silent film. Sans other actors.

7. Be still.

8. Cynthia believes in therapy through television watching. Treasure the angel within you. Remember we all awaken to the brightness of the same sun.

9. Don't touch your armrests. Your seat cushion. Don't touch your face.

10. Let your surgical mask do its work.

11. Recently Cynthia has realized life is probably the thing that arrives in ten-minute portions disturbed by commercials.

12. Your body is a smaller theater situated inside a bigger theater situated inside a bigger theater.

13. Theaters are places where outside time and space go away.

14. Cynthia likes theaters.

15. It is dark. Remain calm. This will all be over soon.

00 : 00 : 10 : 01

FOUR ROWS BEHIND AND THREE TO HER LEFT, Celan Solen tries to figure out why reality feels so inadequate simply because you can't look at it through a frame like you can a movie.

narrative by **Lance Olsen**   animation by **Tim Guthrie**

NOW SHOWING AT

www.nd.edu/~ndr/issues/ndr19/contents19.html

indecretions
Michael Joyce
Alexandra Grant

Alexandra Grant
Nimbus, (after Michael Joyce's Nimbus,, After
Alexandra Grant's idea of Nimbus, After...), 2004
Wire , motor and light in installation

AlayerOfTracingPaper (from indécritions)

I lay a placer of original text above your tracing paper, sorry. I

Illustration as light upon the shadow of adumbration? So be it. My

placed a layer of tracing paper above it, concatenating

first reaction was a resistance, the one against beauty, whether in my

words......I traced a saying of concatenation upon the uneven

own in writing or the beauty of pastel illustration. Then I began to

light of your words. Worry about the uneventful words of my

think that, if a score, it is not for me to name the playing. If there is a

imagination. Could we? Your original text displayed my uneven

shade, then cast whatever light upon it (especially given the erotic

image Above it I placed my sorrow about the image of the

fable wherein the woman shields light, holds it to her beyond the soft

uneven lighting and spaced a tracer over her head. We

hills of herself, the pattern of the morning bedsheets illustration,

could display your original text? Cat and mouse words,

labanotation, dreams of dancing with(in) ourselves).

catamount to nothing, but wonder would you could we

Illustration can, of course, un-write, impinge to the point of erasure,

trace this call. Sorry about the uneven lighting of the images.

take the focus, wash out the shadows—even invert the relation, the

Attenuated tracing of the layers of your words. figure and ground,

words become the medium

against which illustration is written

indecretions continue at: www.nd.edu/~ndr/issues/ndr19/contents19.html

cris cheek performs

online at:

http://www.nd.edu/~ndr/issues/ndr19/contents19.html

FROM UNTITLED

R. M. Berry

My voice is coming from inside this box. That's why it strikes your ear askew. Brim full and empty, almost gone, its syllables never sound, but resound merely. Or so I'm told. For myself I can't speak, of course, having never been without it. The box, I mean. Within, the sensations are pronounced, sonorous as a shower stall, all reverberating surfaces, tile and porcelain, if you know the echo I have in mind, but anyhow, a noise like no other, the resonance, you could say, of its own name. If names resounded, if bodies intoned them. My own name is immaterial. The voice comes first, then this box, and only later, if at all, the name, which makes for some frustration. Once we're better acquainted, I hope you can ignore it, but for now, you've probably got your hands full just trying to hold your tongue, so to speak. Anyway, the sound from the box isn't my name, and at the start it's the box that occupies us.

Closets are something else. I've tried living in a closet, passed my everlasting adolescence in one, groping through strangers' pockets, lights out, mothballs corroding every sinus. But a voice in a closet is muffled, gagged, the sound of its stifling, and that sensation is another one, short-lived, less hollow. Inside the box, by contrast, my voice is too replete, chock-full, or just insufficiently farfetched, to smother. It stays with you, like the flu. Let me tell you, before being boxed I often rambled in my sleep and awoke more than once to hear my gist rebound. My voice then struck me as outlandish, the nasal mutterings of an exile. None of its clamor seemed mine or, for that matter, anyone else's. Phrases returned like bad pennies, familiar currency, little sense. Maybe they hadn't been coined. Maybe I've forgotten to take my pill. Anyway, I like the phrase, *his words hung in the air*, and would use it now, I mean to describe this sensation in my box, if my box had air. Which I suppose it must. A vacuum is silent. I don't mean the carpet cleaners, which are, of course, very noisy. But outer space, the universe. A box is like that, no atmosphere, perfectly abandoned, emptiness filling all. That and the darkness are its most notable features, of which more presently.

The reason I'm boxed is I saw me happen. That is, though not exactly at peace, I can't really wish to flee, could only wish not to have seen, which I don't exactly do. What I wish is for whatever's to come and, in a manner of speaking, you, faceless at any account, but I'm rarely hopeful, having found this box too narrow for it. Which, of course, starts out all wrong, for being boxed isn't *being* anywhere, and wasn't hope always six-sided, always a suffocation? But I suppose I've got to start some place, and if one day it happens...well, there you are! So. This box, my voice, what I've seen. Others have had more, but then I'm hardly them.

I saw me happen on a parched flat when strange humors oozed from my skin. I don't recall the circumstances, but I do recall the sensations. The light was unforgiving, but when isn't light unforgiving? I remember my face baking, heard tumors sizzle like rashers beneath the dermis. At any instant I was expecting my flesh to rupture, set this old heart free, when I noticed something forming on the back of my hand. There seemed to be globules, or not quite globules, where I'd never noticed not quite globules before. A glistening of hairs, watery beads, one rivulet. Who's this? I thought, putting my tongue to the place, tasting salt. Had I turned piquant, melted to a sauce? And then it occurred to me, exactly what it's impossible to say, in the merest whisper of wind. Oh, I'll never forget that coolness! I fell into a rapture, saw vapors rising. It was my bodily assumption. Whether the change was miraculous I still can't tell, but I immediately put aside former preoccupations. There was only afterwards now. What was happening had never happened to anyone before.

I surmise from your blankness that you're not amazed. It's to be understood. My voice rarely strikes anyone at first, or only in passing, and even then more often on reflection, like a comeback or belated rejoinder. Without this box the air could be torrid, as frantic as a sirocco, thoughts consumed in perfect incandescence, while these reverberations, regardless how fulsome, take an eternity to alight. Only silence could attune the ear to within, and who's to say if mere vibrations would then amuse you? In the box all such assurances sound hollow. Not that I speak from experience, mind, but I've confused myself with this echo often enough, mistaken the dying of my own voice for others, and I know how prone I am to lie, or perhaps imagine things. If hordes were without would it be any different? I've dreamt of groans, children sobbing, and although I know it's just this box, the sound of myself recoiling, still it's no mean feat to keep all within. Why, even this now could be part of it! Let's be frank. Nothing I've recounted so far is anything you haven't been listening to forever. I could be utterly absent, my flesh a mirage, this box unbound, and how would either of us tell? See. What could be simpler? It's this that gives rise to my voice.

A few remarks on the darknesses. The first I ever noted, which was in truth the second, for to make myself wholly plain, the first was the darkness I never noticed until I'd noticed its successor, just like my youth and health and this world I discovered while out of it—well, that darkness was the speckled one. You'd call the speckles gray, I imagine, although I've scrutinized them and will swear to their being lavender. They don't themselves compose the second darkness but merely float on its surface, like hyacinths or twigs, and they undulate. For a time I dreamt only that their color undulated, a throbbing lilac, but then I remarked how the obscurity itself underwent upheavals, resembled a beast more than a condition, the flicking of some behemoth's hide, its innards roiling beneath as inexorably as blood or lava. For perfect lucidity one must attend without cease. Amid the stillness I would nestle in my penumbra, suffering the outbursts of stupor and unwitting, opacity perdurable, blackness burgeoning from my two irises, as my former flashes of brilliance fizzled and I seemed by all lights eclipsed. No knowing how long I waited, but afterwards the darkness never appeared for an instant not to have been there. In my enclosure I withstood the convulsions, rapt with ogling, the waves unfurling from below, as night invaded me and livid specks rippled over my deeps.

It was not always the second darkness that appeared, of course, for no sooner did I recognize one than there were others, and these followers made a crowd. Oh, you probably imagine my condition is singular, this black the merest parading of the same, but if you knew my obscurities, the phantasmagoria of striations, folds, seams—such an abundance you wouldn't believe. At first, when the gloom started becoming numerous, I thought I couldn't survive. I was fearful, being bereft of all, that I might lose me too. How I cursed my confinement then, prayed for illumination! But slowly I came to revel in this ignorance, the countless shadows cast on memory's wall, and began cataloguing enigmas.

It was the second darkness that began my accommodation. I know it seems preposterous now, conceiving such a hodge-podge as continent, but until the speckles appeared, I dreamt every absence was identical, each of my relinquishings indistinct. Guffaw if you must. It was only afterwards that I recognized the first darkness had been piecemeal, rifted throughout, and so I'd never actually been anywhere I'd imagined. Unlike the third, which I still admire exorbitantly and which is known for its vast, pure and perfectly blemishless indigo, an unbound ocean of black, the first I now know was a veritable ragamuffin. I came in time to call it Mongrel, while the second darkness, by which I denote my blindspot's original, I dubbed My Precious. I feel for Mongrel a special affection, as one just naturally does for stray creatures, while for My Precious I feel nothing, or only nostalgia in fits, as all must for feeling's very source.

Anyway, as I became acquainted with the darknesses, I acclimated myself to dwelling proximately, I mean here and now, and began to conceive this box as my home. Although I still can't pretend to determine its where-abouts and have given up on ever again venturing without it, from that instant to this, I've never wished to escape.

For an undetermined period following my body's assumption, by which I refer to me happening, I was the man I'd always been, or maybe I express myself crudely, but regardless how formed, I still looked outwardly indif-ferent. I absorbed myself in the common paroxysms and swallowed at my front end what I jettisoned behind and idly traversed earth's surface doing my utmost to kill time. However, all about me changed. For example, the whole of my acquaintance turned implausibly blithe. My memory of this event is even more acute than the former. It occurred under the moon called March, just as the gigantic trunks, still upstanding wherever the flat-ness hadn't suffered improvement, began to discolor. Their barren outcrops grew ruddy at top, then chartreuse, and soon began to sport tiny protuber-ances, minuscule foliations textured differently from the branchings. I struggle to remain dispassionate. But you see, I don't refer to a single trunk, or even to a copse or thicket. *Every trunk was greening.* And these sprigs— they weren't ordinary warts or follicles. They were offspring, scions, leafy miniatures of the trunk itself.

You'll want to check my prescription, of course, but I assure you I don't exaggerate. As the daily lights dimmed and brightened, I witnessed each metamorphosis, the verdant mass choking passageways, overgrowing walls. And what had seemed disorder began to disclose occult design, a transformation replicated on every tendril, innumerable likenesses, teem-ing millions. By the moon's next round the stalks' progeny had eliminated large portions of the sky and concealed several shopfronts. I could never observe a foray directly, the inching further of any particular frond, but as the light ascended each day and the atmosphere grew scorched, I recorded the verdure's advance. And when I say *I* recorded, you'll think I don't mean literally, and I accept this rebuke, for in altered circumstances I might think no more of you, but try as I might, I could compel no other beside myself to see. And this change, far more than the earth's exuberance, alarmed me. What had become of my familiars? No nth degree of obviousness, no bald-faced phenomenon or blinding sense, regardless how keen, not even the lush entanglements shading our foreheads at noon—nothing could open their eyes. Our surroundings were animate! Matter had a soul! Could I alone among mortals comprehend this?

For who knows how long I thought my countrymen were all daft. I went about belaboring passers-by, bashing their hapless brows with plain-speaking, as though mere facts, if sufficiently ruthless, might in time uplift them. To think of the blood I drew. I cringe now to recall. When at last I acknowledged the worst, I concluded they'd each succumbed to some affliction, were victims of exotic pestilence, and having alone been spared, I must play physician. This episode was more horrific than the last. I began to ogle ingenues, probe the innocent, experimenting even on hapless crones. How deeply I saw into everything! Oh, there wasn't a recess, regardless how furry, I didn't sniff out and ply. It seemed no time at all before I grew knowledgeable, and then, of course, nothing could quash me. I waxed raucous with panaceas, became feral for cures. Not a waylaid vagabond, not even the most feckless and bedraggled, but endured my benevolence. Ah, the throbbing of my lobes! There was simply no respite. Well, you will no doubt have gleaned as I soon gleaned too, that here dementia beckoned, and so my last recourse, it seemed, was to cultivate stupor. Nightly the starlight filtered through denser wefts, fronds stole under sashes and doors, while I persevered at my heroic lumpeness, knuckles dragging the tarmac, brainsack as vacant as the newborn moon.

Eventually my compatriots and I learned to abide one another. There were, I seem to recall, fewer incursions. But inwardly I still writhed. No moronic downcasting, no stubborn refusal to gape, could blot out what I'd witnessed. Anything might happen! I wanted to shout. All creation was green! And had there not been an unexpected blighting, the upspring of sudden hoariness, and during the descent called winter a breath from the downhill side, well, I believe our very abode would've been choked. The florid menace had seemed so resplendent, its foliage unceasing. At first ice, when I saw the tiny leaftips cringe, I almost broke out in whoops, forgetful of my stupidity, but when a single thoughtless peep bespattered me with hisses, I quickly withdrew my nozzle and resumed shuffling. Soon my sluggard's phlegm smeared the crust wherever I had traipsed, my fervor veiled all the while, as I blinked back glimpses of curling tendrils, frost-stung cotyledons, the yellowing chill. How could my familiars be so oblivious? I marveled. Could they really not know? And this mystery, far exceeding that of the prodigious vegetables, gradually overcame me.

At night I would float supine in my darkness, my bed ballooned round with puffs of down, and as the glaze of ice encased heaven and earth, I would know it was I, *I*, who had seen. Of what could this be the beginning? In my sleep, the past came back, neverending minutes raging round my nanny's yard, blue scooter, Raggedy Andy, but I found no assurance now in these clutchings. I wanted simply to continue, to be again that tangled knot of first one thing then another, the furor who'd abruptly become him. I haven't the vaguest idea what I'm saying. It felt as though some rift had opened, a schism forming my hiatus. I learned to say was. I learned to say them. I learned to hold my peace. Anyway, return seemed—for reasons I find obscure—unimaginable, so I tried to accept this new plight as my own. I'd never unknow all that had happened to me, and who could tell what time would? Sprawled there amid the darkness, as night encased my chamber and cold raged without, I would marvel at these changes, the vanishing green, my body's assumption, suspecting that in time they'd become past too. I seemed as mushy as a custard. And extending one digit into the gloom, I strained to surpass my present fix, this pale, until amid dim surroundings I sensed for the first time, on the tip of my furthest reach, a hardening. My edge?

LANGUAGE ACTS: POETRY IN SPACETIME

Mike Barrett

Anvil/lyre Studio is a multimedia arts collective in Columbia, Missouri which makes homegrown avant-garde. The studio has produced three live language acts—"Whereupon," "Code-A-Cell," and "Where You Are."

"Language Acts: Poetry in Spacetime" defined and demonstrated a language act at the &NOW festival. The presentation ran in three sections: "Orientation," "Visualization," "Peroration." "Orientation," a critical survey of language acts, was delivered from a mnemonic. "Visualization," a short film, quoted from language acts produced in Missouri. The film included text animation, a score of DNA sequences, and a short movie by Aaron Jud-lowe. The audience provided the voiceover, reciting what they had written from a prompt. "Peroration" concluded with poetry and a meditation on the inner ear.

The text below is a recreation of the first section, "Orientation." The italicized parts are verses from the poem, "Din & Sit: Cuts of Phi on *Sein und Zeit*." The rest, a series of propositions, is recollected from a mnemonic. The mnemonic was printed on the audience's program. Here, the mnemonic precedes the recollected text.

Language Acts: Poetry in Spacetime (a partial transcript)

You know before
you know to ask. I ask
that act is one possible.
Is disclosure choice?
Is music understanding?
To carry a tune is one
possible to disclose.

home

we wear   the present

body is sense

Spacetime is home.

We dwell there in the present.

The body is its sense.

Being in it wears us out.

Until the day we die, spacetime is where we are.

> *Not that it's not*
> *what we think it is;*
>
> *the is is not*
> *what we think is is.*
>
> *We are and it's not*
> *what we think.*

dimensions

model's model's model   **models in matter**

model's model

Spacetime is multidimensional.

Consciousness is its geometry.

Consciousness is a model of spacetime made out of the same matter.

Language is a model made out of the same matter as consciousness.

Poetry is the model's model's model. Poetry gives a language act its form.

A language act is a function of Coleridge, entropy, and chance.

Coleridge: Each part has its own integrity and works towards an organic whole.

Entropy: It obeys the cosmic law of dissolution.

AND
   so much depends upon
    so much depends upon
     so much depends upon
          the random

The TELOS of a language act is to make poetry out of spacetime.

The one in the other is the same one. No one is your father and its other--nothing is its wife and your brother. The fire is your family in the center of a name. The name precedes the family but not the fire. The fire is preceded by a star with skies. The formal not the latter is disguise for the circle walked around your matter; a small fire inside dies as you die, loyal to your wife and brother, your cousin, and the other nothing that is your mother.

Joseph Beuys

not culture/culture   **Anvil/lyre Studio**

practices

The artist Joseph Beuys once said that creativity is capital.

Anvil/lyre Studio is creative capital put to work. It has no material presence save what it produces.

Anvil/lyre Studio produces language acts. The practice of language acts includes: improvisation, collaboration, multimedia, audience assistance, and artifact.

Improvisation: the quiddity and haecceitas of the present press their way into the act; the performer assists.

Collaboration: a language act is labor shaped by artists, filmmakers, musicians, and writers. Each adds an esthetic dimension on the way to the complexity of spacetime.

Multimedia: creation finds its mode through many channels. The audience loves to change channels constantly.

Audience: the audience assists not only in assembling the meaning of elements, but in producing those elements.

Artifact: provide an artifact that orients the audience as to where they are and where they're going; provide an artifact compelling as art. The artifact then becomes a mnemonic—the language act has a present in the future; it continues to perform.

Even though we are limited by time, talent, production budget and by the material circumstances we occupy and occupy us, Anvil/lyre Studio accepts limitations as inherent in any useful thing. The language act is a useful thing, an effort of the will. The language act is an enactment of culture. Our lot is not to wait for cultural acceptance but, like Blake's Los, hammer in making culture.

Anvil/lyre Studio finds its smithy in the present and makes language acts there.

> *Being is a late arrival*
> *when Time says it's time to go.*
> *Being is the cold that kills*
> *when the sun is starting to grow.*
>
> *Time is a mood in German*
> *space is cornered in lines.*
> *Being is dawn painted on*
> *the mind's metastatic stein.*
>
> *They give their gifts in portions*
> *some are fatal some are later*
> *and they let you have the last word*
> *when your say no longer matters.*

IMPLEMENTATION

Nick Montfort and Scott Rettberg

www.nd.edu/~ndr/issues/ndr19/contents19.html

Implementation is the first novel-length work of fiction to be published and distributed on stickers. That is, *Implementation* is both a work of fiction and a work of art: a novel about the peripheral effects of the war on terror, psychological warfare, American imperialism, sex, identity, and the idea of place; it is also an art project that borrows from the traditions of net.art, mail art, sticker art, conceptual art, situationist theater, serial fiction, and guerilla viral marketing. Both Montfort and Rettberg have written electronic fiction in the past, and see the sticker novel as one way of connecting some of the ideas of nonlinear narrative and interactivity with printed texts in physical space.

On the website, readers can read the installments of *Implementation* in PDF format. Each serially released installment consists of thirty individual texts printed on three sheets of stickers, and the completed novel includes eight installments. Participant readers can print the stickers on standard shipping labels, and adhere the stickers wherever they choose. Many readers then photograph the sticker placements, and email those photos back as a contribution to the project. In addition to the texts, the website includes more than 900 photographs of sticker placements at a variety of locations in the U.S. and Europe. The act of situating the chunk of story in a distinct physical place (examples include a war protest in Chicago, the lobby of the British Museum, the entrance to the New York Public Library, and an abandoned Soviet sports structure in Tallinn, Estonia) has some interesting effects on its interpretation, and comprises an exciting way for readers to interact with and to help shape the narrative.

Implementation will be featured at the FILE 2004 International Festival of Electronic Language in Sao Paulo, Brazil. It will be shown at the Slought Foundation in Philadelphia in spring 2005. Spineless Books will distribute the complete novel in a limited edition in 2005, as a boxed set of sticker sheets. All downloadable installments and photos of sticker placements will also remain available free of charge on the project website.

Helsinki, Finland 2004-08-27

Letters to Unfinished J.

Sheila E. Murphy

3.

He had a melted cheese look in his eye. I wanted then to touch but we were housed in our official stances making gestured conversation. He had a lift poised in his shoe. Each one of us interpolated who we thought we were along fair lanes I memorized the turf war and released it. Returning to the child who told boys where to stand along the football field. For the first time I saw light as a perfume within his eye. Two forms of inattention. Now my mind is waltz prone. Now I'm ready for earned relaxation. Wash made ready on the line, the milky tones of birds, the small velocity of cinders when a car drives up. The way his after shave chimes knotty pine.

13.

Soprano cuts of her first album water half my plants. I dram a sheaf of little wind for motion to alive me. Seashore sunrooms all the plexiglass I know. The view is tantrum. And the lithe phantom of how we bake love slyly paces across the logic of indigenous pale flowers. Cushions in our memory come due. We prance across Schenectady. We softball our collective conscience. We leave a fleck of room in sylph land to have practicum and talk unto the hour of candles. At the grotto all the prayer we have mirrors each hand-picked stone. What are others praying for. The woman who immerses who she is in playthings paused a moment while we softened likely outcomes with cool voice. The secret of admiring plants she'd sprinkled and could save. The secret of accepting how things stop and what is left, inevitable embrace. With slow hands true as souls that would release as many things as they have grasped. One phase at a time until the integration. Final as the color pale in an uncertain sky. Locales have seasons and locales enroll in our affection. One time and another to form patterns that will be there after anyone can reach us anymore.

22.

Sleep, although plush, cannot be recognized within scrapbooks scented like libraries dressed in fine feathers of dust. She wore her glasses long upon the nose, and fibrillations manicured the stop loss of her headache. The market lives to be manipulated. Allows malarkey to unfasten ribbons that uncover: plash and withered snapshots of spoons worth more than reflex. Pressed lamp softens with the color pink our made up minds that face the neighbors. Frost lures us to a place where plaque will be less noticeable to spines. How much can bodies bear with minds so very like them. Circumspect arrangements flow as winter perched above a Bunsen burner. Given irresemblance to familiar moments waltzed into a world of free throw lines considered tangent to imagined wilderness.

25.

Decorum wafts into the semicircle, searching for an opening more subtle than the arc made by the letter "J." The room is cluttered with recovery. Stories leave a tarnish reminiscent of ashen thumb paintings on foreheads. *Describe an outward sign and its effects.* Participants arm wrestle lines into a yeast of artificial touch. Each behaves as though instructed to French kiss a mirror. *Parades cost money. Lives cost money. Children...* She gathers would-be blooms into her arms but not her heart. Lectures them and some who might be listening or premising a likeness to their private histories. Down in the street, traffic and crowd scenes perspire blood. *There is a fee for marching outside a democracy.* Plea bargaining erupts into a hedge against emotional inflation. *Trust is a mood-altering drug.* All evenings end with pantomime of willed transcendence. Too precisely wanted by the ravenous who long to matter to a universe that seems not to have mattered back.

ANAGRAMS OF AMERICA

Mike Smith

The following poems are a selection from a book-length manuscript entitled *Anagrams of America*. Each of the poems is an anagram of its source text, which is identified below each poem. All the letters of the source text have been used, once and only once, in the composition of the responding poem. No letters have been added and no letters have been left out.

PLAN

Mike Smith

> *Those who write of the art of poetry teach*
> *us that if we would write what may be worth the*
> *reading, we ought always, before we begin, to form a*
> *regular plan and design of our piece.*
>
> —Ben Franklin

1.

To be separate, anonymous, silent, yet not
without real power and pride, say
the tact and driven mindset of software
giants, ex-hackers bailed out by the F.B.I.

Or troubleshooters, key specialists
flown in to exact purpose yet no
further ado, then flown back home again.
One of the sought-after, needed, few.

2.

Bound by boundlessness, appalled
by applause, overreaching
in despair—The poet at home
in a prose nation. He weathers his vast,
unforgiven country like a storm.

3.

By jolt, by dint of play, Rex Eternity
can milk every almanac list, render
moot our daily reinvention of the sky.
Many may act. More cry out. Unnerving Time

4.

exists for our misuse. In it, loved lover,
icy stream are lost. View
the damage done in Limit's civic name.

—The body of the poem as a whole is an anagram of the four numbered
sections of Benjamin Franklin's "Plan for Future Conduct," Labaree et
al., eds., *The Papers of Benjamin Franklin, 40 vols.* (New Haven: Yale
University Press, 1959-).

REREADING STEPHEN CRANE

Mike Smith

Back home, and down, down
in the yard, in the fog, reading
yet not reading, I hear
this train head west, hot
and fast for I don't know where,
the dry whine fed only by the mood
of the sea, of the wind.

It hits me:
        America,
the miraculous, the absurd...

How is the eyed stranger met?
Any lesson learned and left off?

Once, those odd trademark capitals
lay like toy tracks slapped down
across a lost century.

—The body of the poem is an anagram of Stephen Crane's "Forth went
the candid man." The last stanza of the poem refers to Crane's odd
insistence, to the point of withdrawing the book from publication, that
his first collection of poetry, *The Black Riders*, be printed entirely in
capital letters.

FROST

Mike Smith

There are others along the way
I dreaded more, but this soon proved
the hardest, you soon proved hardest.
So after weeks of loss and of only
more or less loss, I'd had enough,
woke up and got out. Seeking beginnings,
I headed straight for the end.
I caught, one afternoon, a bus
bound for San Francisco, the house
of your birth. But before I'd been gone
even an hour, I found them,
hooked to, of all things,
a scratched Plexiglas ticket window,
these blue bullets on a bright blue
release, fresh from the home office.

Surely, they were my way through to you,
your way around to me. Surely,
this was the net, open end
of the line. (Though you should know,
this is really all a part of the game.)

Back out of all this now…

*Warning: A Potentially Violent
Individual is one*

            too much for us.

Who is sullen and highly argumentative.

One year ago. A year here nearly
to the hushed, harsh day, and what?

Unreasonably critical and scornful of authority.

I can't get through to them.
I cannot get them to understand.

Indicates a heightened resentment for those

Editors and other poets, family, friends

who are perceived as more fortunate.

Stellasue I mentioned before, then
at *AGNI*, kindly Sven, who said
he was hooked, though something kept
him hesitant. Roundabout Eric at *CR*,
for whom the third time wasn't charmed,
who asked me to wait a year then try again.

He'll write them all out a verse
instead of a curse
as these questions without reply
keep fluttering by.

Voices persistent complaints
of personal misfortunes.

Awakened somewhere
in god-forsaken Illinois, I undertook
an uneasy apology, a rough, heady draft.

Shows unusual impulsiveness,

~~Recently, it has been argued~~...
~~The unknown contemporary should~~...
Increasingly I began to feel...

becoming confused,

that late works of this kind were wholly inevitable...

and easily frustrated,

I found myself…

pacing up and down the center aisle.

pacing up and down the aisle.

    (O, to be greater
    than the rough sum
    of all your detractors, O, to be, yourself,
    too lofty and original to rage.)

I tore the thing to shreds.

Communicates a verbal or a written threat

Other poets! If only
there were a ready spell-book
to ward off all the worst:

Several canceled checks marked "entry fee."
A book of stamps, a heal-all, some gin.
A dog-eared copy of Faust, yellowed
with a lowly highlighter, and then

choose a chapbook from a bottom shelf.
Salt liberally, and through and through,
with bitter, histrionic tears.
Shake well, then let it steep. Ah, let it stew.

Note: As these are only some
of the major characteristics, please
be alert to the show
of any unusual behavior.

This marks the end of the line.
This makes sixteen.

    —The poem is an anagram of Robert Frost's "Directive." The italicized
    lines, also part of the anagram, were taken from a notice posted outside
    the Greyhound bus depot in South Bend, Indiana. This is the sixteenth
    and final poem in the *Anagrams of America* sequence.

INDEX OF FIRST LINES

Myrlin Hermes

1.

A Clock stopped—
A curious knot God made in paradise,
After the first powerful, plain manifesto
All human things are subject to decay,

And me happiest when I compose poems.

An Epigram should be—if right—
A noiseless, patient spider,
A poem should be palpable and mute
A Sonnet is a moment's monument,—

As we get older, we do not get any younger.
Barely a twelvemonth after
Because I could not stop for Death—
Because you are old and departing I have wetted my handkerchief,

Blow, blow, thou winter wind,
Blow out the candles of your cake.
Burnished, burned-out, still burning as the year
Busy old fool, unruly sun,

But most by numbers judge a poet's song,

By and by
Can we not force from widowed poetry,
Captain or colonel, or knight in arms
Caught in the center of a soundless field
Close by those meads, forever crowned with flowers,

Come away, come away, death,
Come live with me and be my love,
Come live with me, and be my love,
Come, live with me and be my love,
"Come live with me and be my love,"
Come to your heaven, you heavenly choirs,
Come, worthy Greek, Ulysses, come

2.
Composed in the Tower before his execution,
Dark is the forest and deep, and overhead
Dawn cried out: the brutal voice of a bird
Dazzled thus with height of place,

Death, be not proud, though some have calléd thee
Diligent in the burnt fields above the sea
Earth has not anything to show more fair:
Euclid alone has looked on Beauty bare.

Fair seedtime had my soul, and I grew up
First having read the book of myths,
Found a family, build a state,
From harmony, from heavenly harmony
From low to high doth dissolution climb,
From my mother's sleep I fell into the State.
From stone to bronze, from bronze to steel
From Water-Tower Hill to the brick prison
Full many a glorious morning have I seen

Gather ye rosebuds while ye may,
Go and catch a falling star,
Gods chase
Go, lovely rose!
Go, smiling souls, your new-built cages break,
Go, soul, the body's guest,
Granted, we die for good.

Hail to thee, blithe Spirit!
Hear me, O God!
Hear the voice of the Bard!

Here is the place; right over the hill
Here lies Jonson with the rest
He thought he kept the universe alone;
He would declare and could himself believe
His words were magic and his heart was true,
How vainly men themselves amaze
Hunt, hunt again. If you do not find it, you,

3.
I
I am: yet what I am none cares or knows
I celebrate myself, and sing myself,
I cry I cry
I do not know much about gods; but I think that the river
If but some vengeful god would call to me

I have been here before,
I have done it again.
I have met them at close of day
I know that I shall meet my fate
I'll tell thee everything I can;
I look for the way

In Aesop's tales, an honest wretch we find,
In a fashionable suburb of Santa Barbara,
In a real city, from a real house,
In a solitude of the sea
In a stable of boats I lie still,
Indeed I must confess,
I ne'er was struck before that hour
In May, when sea-winds pierced our solitudes,
In spite of all the learned have said,
In this world, the isle of dreams,

4.
In vain, in vain—the all-composing hour
I once believed a single line
I shall never get you put together entirely,
Is it a dream,
Is it possible

I sought a theme and sought for it in vain,
I struck the board and cried "No more;
I taste a liquor never brewed—
I, the poet William Yeats,
I will arise and go now, and go to Innisfree.
I would to Heaven that I were so much clay,

Let us go then, you and I,
Like the stench and smudge of the old dump-heap
Loving in truth, and fain in verse my love to show,

5.
Milton! thou shouldst be living at this hour:
"More Light! More Light!"
Move him into the sun—
Much Madness is divinest Sense—
My candle burns at both ends;
My pictures blacken in their frames

Now as I was young and easy under the apple boughs
Now I see its whiteness
Now it is autumn and the falling fruit
Nudes—stark and glistening,

Of all the causes which conspire to blind
Of heaven or hell I have no power to sing,
Of man's first disobedience, and the fruit
O golden-tongued Romance with serene lute!

6.
Pray thee, take care, that tak'st my book in hand,
Redoubted knights, and honorable Dames,
Remember me when I am gone away,
September twenty-second, Sir: today
She sang beyond the genius of the sea.

Sing, cuccu, nu. Sing cuccu.
Sing lullaby, as women do,
Softly, in the dusk, a woman is singing to me;

So he came to write again
so much depends
Sports and gallantries, the stage, the arts, the antics of dancers,
Stone-cutters fighting time with marble, you foredefeated
Success is counted sweetest

Tell all the Truth but tell it slant—
Tell me not, sweet, I am unkind
That civilization may not sink,
That poets are far rarer births than kings

The beginning of art—
The poetry of earth is never dead:
There is a land of pure delight
There is a singer everyone has heard,
There is delight in singing, though none hear
The whole process is a lie,
The world is
They do not live in the world,

Think not this paper comes with vain pretense
This poem is concerned with language on a very plain level.
Though beauty be the mark of praise,
Thy praise or dispraise is to me alike:
'Tis time this heart should be unmoved,

7.
To draw no envy, Shakespeare, on thy name,
Two roads diverged in a yellow wood,
       Unconscious
   Under the bronze crown
Undesirable you may have been, untouchable
Unreal   tall as a myth
Up from the bronze, I saw
Vowels plowed into other: opened ground.
Webster was much possessed by death
Weep with me, all you that read
   We lay red roses on his grave,
What needs my Shakespeare for his honored bones
What passing-bells for these who die as cattle?

What thoughts I have of you tonight, Walt Whitman, for
When I a verse shall make
Where two or three were flung together, or fifty
Who shall doubt, Donne, where I a poet be,
Who would be
With Donne, whose muse on dromedary trots,
Within a delicate grey ruin
With only his feeble lantern
Word over all, beautiful as the sky,

Ye distant spires, ye antique towers,
Ye goatherd gods, that love the grassy mountains,
You are made of almost nothing
you fit into me
Your mind and you are our Sargasso Sea,

FROM *THE BOOKS OF UBAR*

David Ray Vance, Catherine Kasper and Amy England

Issues in Archaeological Botany
Paid for by Friends of The Historical Archive League.

Dis-ethical Paper Consumption
The Historical Archive League has maintained an unwavering policy against disethical paper consumption since the time of its *21ˢᵗ Meaning Festival*. Dating from that meeting, Tablet X1 reads:

> *It is an abomination to imprint botanical matters of any sort (whether dried pulp or dried, whole specimens) with lettering, numbering or any other form of sketched figure relating to (or otherwise intended to communicate) botanical knowledge. The ghastly nature of this practice is apparent and obvious.*

The rightness of this position *is* obvious, yet paper consumption on the part of rogue botanical archaeologists persists, bringing shame to all. The practice has been statistically linked to a number of social ills observed in present day Ubar, including an alarming preponderance of striped patterns in leisure wear, increased incidents of blatant disrespect to urban monkeys, and extra tongues growing out of the Temple.

Dirt Under Fingernails
Unsightly dirt under fingernails is not, as some have argued, a professional certitude for practitioners of archaeological botany. While it is true that dirt under one's fingernails was common and presumed unavoidable early in the development of the field, in today's professional practice it is recognized as entirely otherwise, particularly given recent developments in *imaginative field displacement* which make actual digging obsolete. The Botanical Archive League, a subcommittee of the Historical Archive League and Ubar's only sanctioned body for the governance of Botanical Archaeology, endorses the "CLEAN" program for dirt avoidance.

Cease contact
Limit exposure
Eliminate doubt and forgetfulness
And imagine digging rather than actually digging
= No more dirt!!

island

Gravity's Effects on the Larynx

1) The title of a poem authored by Adrianna Frog in commemoration of the vocal occurrences on Denbobned Day. It was upon reading this poem that Frog was clubbed to death by scornful listeners. The mob's dissatisfaction centered not on the quality of the poem itself, but on Frog's spelling which was egregious, as could be readily inferred from her stammering recitation. The present-day fashion of purposefully incorrect spelling is generally considered unfortunate backlash to Frog's mortal beating. (See: Adrianna Frog: *The 10 Years Death of Poetry*).

2) Reference to "vocal knowledge" consequent fluctuations in Ubarian Gravity. Several meta-scientific studies have disproved this phenomena's existence, so that most experts agree the effect in question most likely results from a combination of psychosomatic and bio-physical reactions, not gravity. That is to say, the fact that one can scream when faced with "fear of the known" and yet not hear one's own screaming is best explained as a trick of conscience brought on by overindulgent sensory reciprocity or, as researchers at Niatpu University have speculated, as the result of heavy grade turbans pinching the third and fifth tympanic nerves. In any case, there is absolutely no evidence that grav-

ity plays any role whatsoever.

3) There are no more entries for this subject, but decorum requires a third
   entry where any two have been gathered, and so this third is offered
   humbly unto our readers with hope of forgiveness at any perceived
   transgressions.

The Horror Which Cannot Be Spoken*

*"Permission To Allude" granted by High Fanatum (Certificate #090) is on public display in the
Historical Archive League Annex in Nnamegah Nigam between the hours of 0900 and 0901 as
required by applicable statutes. Evidence of "Permission to View" is required for entry. No children
allowed. No glass containers allowed. All forms of recording, including memorization, are forbid-
den and will not be tolerated under any circumstances.*

npnominst,sfryjrnpmxsosmfoyesddjptysmfdypiy;olr[rmodpmyjrnpfupgks,sl
s[osmfnpndsofimyps;;instupijsbrlo;;rfupitytrrsmfdjs;;yjid[rtodjomyrtms;gph
gpts;;rcodyrmvr/zpm;udo;rmvreo;;dsbrupi/ztr[rmyomdo;rmvrsmfnrdo;rmyg
ptupismmpus;;ypejp,upid[rslsmfnpnesd,pdytohjyrpidgptjodtohjymrddesds[
[strmysdoms;;yjomhd/

WARNING: By order of The High Fanatum (Dicta 001), *The Horror* may be alluded to in
written form only with express permission of The High Fanatum, and only in indecipherable
code. Verbal allusion is punishable by extreme death. This policy is intended to safeguard the
public from any possible reoccurrence, accidental or otherwise. Alluding to the horror without proper licensing and/or in any decipherable form is illegal and prosecutable under Penal
Code 1. Attempts to decipher the indecipherable code are expressly prohibited under Penal
Code 1b. Reading indecipherable code aloud is not prohibited but is highly discouraged.

—David Ray Vance

*Editor's Note: a free gift subscription to *The Notre Dame Review* will be awarded to the first
reader who emails us a correct translation of the encrypted passage. Employees of *NDR* or
friends and relatives of the author are not eligible.

postcard

Wig of Bees
From Baba Ganesh's *Dictionary Lands:*

1.) A general dizziness accompanied by a whirling or buzzing; an entangle-
ment of hair begun at the roots below the skin; a sensation caused by neu-
ron hives or the neurological illness which damages optical nerves, resulting
in multiple segmented visual resolutions which sometimes mimic honey
comb in shape and depth.

2.) The physical phenomena associated with the headbanging dance (See
Gifts of Apology), or with head bruising, (See: *Punishments for Adultery*). This
"wig of bees" has unknown natural causes, but also could be created through
a series of dances and physical wounds inflicted to the head, particularly to
the frontal lobes.

3.) An expression used to mock irrational verbal responses or circular
patterns of speech sometimes but not always associated with the actual
neurological illness; an expression often meant to demean someone or to
lead back to a series of language structures which are more linear in
construction; i.e., a.)Is your wig full of bees? Or b.)What are you wearing, a

wig of bees? Or c.) What's wrong with you? Is your wig composed of bees? Here the example uses "wig" to mean both brain and head, as well as sense and language. In the above example, this expression is also a metaphor for "composure." In order to determine the exact subtlety of definition, a frontal examination is required.

4.) In the Hotel of the Cicadas, it has been rumored that a dessert has appeared on the menu several times under the name: wig of bees. Its composition consists of some kind of cream and some kind of honey, as well as some textured element resembling burnt sugar strands or crunchy wafer cookies. Most likely its foundation is bee custard, a delicate blending of cream and honeycomb still dripping with live bees.

Cabinet of Infinite Compartments
Contains a universe and an eyeball. One million drawers, each with a different lock or latch, none functional without employ of a kind of ointment or plant oil, in which are arranged the constantly changing contents—
(Objects and collected things are exchanged, lent out, employed in stories of accumulation, and borrowed by Mokhrani, head librarian, who records the objects in volume-size lists.)—
What follows, of course, is a minutia, a dust-mite-size sample in translation:

Bird's wings and beaks	Useless Utensils
Lacquered teas	Dead Alphabets
Hotel Fruit souvenirs	Cloth cups and molded dishes
Flavors of rain	Dried lichen
Cracked foods	Drawers Devoted to Blue Smells
Discarded tales of Baba Ganesh	Keys to green desires
Words which cannot be memorized	Houses of Bees
Passport stamps to other worlds	An Ubarian history in jars
Scraps from vacation days	The well-spring of contentment
Ceramic limbs	Ubarian dead
Musical instruments	Conical dreams of water
3-dimensional poems	Blueprints of Ubar
Miniature vertebrae	Selected shards from the glass beach
Profiles in sealing wax	Toxic uses of cactus enhancement
Vistas of unknown cities	Watercolors of monkey codes

Phallic rocks

Canoptic containers

Cameos of the auspicious chicken

Collected Astrological lenses

—Catherine Kasper

The Wheel of Shadows

A wheel whose spokes are intersecting figure eights, shadowed with pegs that are topped with eyes painted inauspiciously open or auspiciously shut—what does it reveal to us? First, the two types of infinity—the finite infinite and the infinite infinite, knotted time and plumed time. Second, the months in which it is wise to set forth, sit down, sail off, see more, stay home, store figs, stuff the ballot box, strew pebbles, stew leeks, and stoop to folly, and the months in which it is not.

Thirdly, the wheel delineates for us the shape of a year. This year might consist of the familiar three hundred and sixty-five days, but how oddly they are disposed of. Each of the twenty-two months (*digits*) lasts sixteen point six days, or *ribs*, completely unbroken by weeks, let alone weekends. Each day is named for an ordinary object (key, bowl of rocks). Only the partial day, at the month's end, is a nameless, unspeakable time—the rest is all thoroughly accounted for. (The new month following this partial day begins thus fourteen hours and twenty four minutes, or three *limbs*, later than the last month). Picture it: sixteen interminable days, the day's five hours/*limbs* horribly wrenched from the places that one only just became accustomed to them holding, all leading up to that fourteen-and-a-half hour black-out of shuffling and desperate reorientation. No wonder Ubarians require that up to ten elevenths of their year be spent in vacation.

—Amy England

J'Abab's Cosmic Gown

One of the most incredible accounts written in the Vermillion Notebook is that of the nomad J'Abab and her attempt to replicate the astrological pattern of night stars upon the surface of countryside, the piece of land from the western slopes leading right up to the acreage used by the Infinite Compartments' storage. Her plan was, using mere candlewax, string and a digging tool, to mimic a night sky in what we would call "summer" months, in exact patterns of candlelight so that the earth's surface would appear to be holding a mirror up to the stars. J'Abab worked for nearly 300 days when she realized her project was of an immense scope, one beyond her initial computations. She became a hermit for several years, during which time it is presumed she worked on a detailed constellation map. When she came out of hiding, she enlisted other citizens and began all over again, projecting a star pattern some forty years in the future.

Here, the star project, or roughly translated "cosmic gown," began to enter the imaginations and journals of the average citizens. People wrote of the dawn hours spent digging holes and melting fat or tallow and measuring rope. Because these candles were embedded in the sandy earth, the country-side itself appeared unaltered. Children began to dream of "star carpets" and worlds where people "walked on sky" and kept their heads "buried in earth." After a period of roughly twenty years, storms and a major flood caused the destruction of over fifty percent of J'Abab's "gown" and documents flour-ished which dismissed her project as "extravagant nonsense," "foolish and pointless," and "doomed to failure" because she insisted on imitating "the great astrologers." J'Abab persisted, even though she initially lost the aid of most residents. As she neared the end of thirty-nine years, however, her project seemed it might reach fulfillment. At this time, she had an experi-mental test "lighting" of "partial" sky which proved so spectacular that once again, she was able to enlist the aid of over one thousand residents.

The lighting of the "partial" sky both excited and disturbed witnesses, who felt that they had surely "died" or were witnessing the "re-creation" of the world. Some speculate that it would have been similar to floating in space, a kind of dizzying, groundless sensation, an experience similar to loss of gravity or a sparkling vertigo surrounded by what would appear to be infinity.

At the end of forty years, with the sky exactly in line according to the accurate astrological predictions of J'Abab, ten thousand "lighters" worked to light what has been recorded as "an infinite number" of candles covering several thousand acres. After ten hours, night would fall, at which time all candles would have been lit.

As the last lighter returned to the hillside overlooking the acreage, and as the sun slipped beyond the horizon, we can only suppose that a silence fell over the city's residents like none before. After an hour of total darkness, that silence must have given way to audible sighs and exclamations, clap-ping perhaps, or even song. At that moment, J'Abab's cosmic gown would have glowed in perfect mimicry to the sky over Ubar, wedging the hillside covered by observers between two stellar, identical fabrics.

—Catherine Kasper

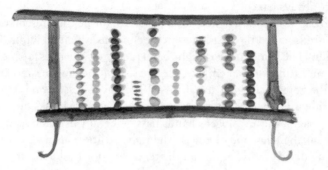

logometer

Astrology Further Revealed
Horoscopes are based on the month, day, and hour. Twenty-two months,
sixteen (namable) days, and five hours means that there are 2,260 individual
possible horoscopes, requiring column inches far in excess of the surface area
of the *Daily Pyramid*. Most must content themselves with the vague and
generally unhelpful hour- or *limb*-based horoscope—for example:
    Spicy: You will travel, then travel again.
This is quite misleading when read against the specific horoscopes in the
spicy group, for example:
    Spicy black bowl of rocks: Your hands will resemble starfish and blue
    crabs will traverse your knees as you stare sprawling at the bottom of the
    wine light sea.

So how does one acquire one's specific, helpful horoscope? My friends,
people are the same everywhere. Money, sexual favors, black market souve-
nirs—so obvious, so uninteresting.

~

Here we call an astronomer an astrologer by mistake and then profusely
apologize. Not so in Ubar, where only astrologers have real telescopes. An
astronomer must make do with a cardboard tube and a convincing expression of frowning authority. But the astrologer's telescope! First of all, it is
very, very long, like the Washington Monument. Second, it bristles and fes-
toons itself with excrescences of gears and pulleys and dials and meters, most
having no function except to delight the heart. And third, it is intensely
decorated with pictures of naked people. Religious subjects are favored; the

figures are always naked.

A typical subject of religious claymation might be the presentation of the holy headdress to the first heresiarch before his extended family and the multitudes. The same subject might be depicted on the telescope, except that the multitudes are naked, likewise the sisters and cousins and aunts, likewise the heresiarch (grey and lined of face but robust of body), likewise the heavenly messengers, whose genitals have pages like books do. As if to rifle those pages, the astrologer's hands pass gracefully over the scene as she or he adjusts the telescope to exactly the right position, using a wrist-worn positioning device (not a device *on* the telescope, for I told you that those don't work). This done, the world-weary lens inspector steps up and does his bit, and then, then, the viewing of stars.

Why view the stars? To check the accuracy of the calendar. Is this necessary? No. The calendar is very accurate, and doesn't need adjustment more than once in a thousand years. But a great part of the mystique of astrology rests in the setting of the cold silver of that carefully positioned, fully inspected eyepiece to the eye, like setting a coin to the eye of a corpse, amid a riot of nudity. Most astrologers insist on traveling through this grandiose ritual every night. Would you forgo it?

—Amy England

BIOPOETRY

Eduardo Kac

Since the 1980s poetry has effectively moved away from the printed page. From the early days of the minitel to the personal computer as a writing and reading environment, we have witnessed the development of new poetic languages. Video, holography, programming and the web have further expanded the possibilities and the reach of this new poetry. Now, in a world of clones, chimeras, and transgenic creatures, it is time to consider new directions for poetry in vivo. Below I propose the use of biotechnology and living organisms as a new realm of verbal creation.

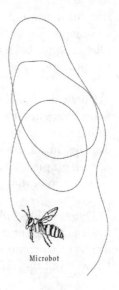

Microbot

1) Microbot performance: Write and perform with a microrobot in the language of the bees, for a bee audience, in a semi-functional, semi-fictional dance.

2) Atomic writing: position atoms precisely and create molecules to spell words. Give these molecular words expression in plants and let grow new words through mutation. Observe and smell the molecular grammatology of the resulting flowers.

The "robeet" (robotic bee) would allow a poet to write a performative dance-text that has no reference in the physical world (that is, does not send bees in search of food). Instead, the new choreo-graphy (kinotation) would be (bee) its own reference.

3) Marine mammal dialogical interaction: compose sound text by manipulating recorded parameters of pitch and frequency of dolphin communication, for a dolphin audience. Observe how a whale audience responds and vice-versa.

4) Transgenic poetry: synthesize DNA according to invented codes to write words and sentences using combinations of nucleotides. Incorporate these DNA words and sentences into the genome of living organisms, which then pass them on to their offspring, combining with words of other organisms. Through mutation, natural loss and exchange of DNA material new words and sentences will emerge. Read the

transpoem back via DNA sequencing.

5) Amoebal scripting: Hand write in a medium
such as agar using amoebal colonies as the inscrip-
tion substance and observe their growth, movement,
and interaction until the text changes or disappears.
Observe amoebal scripting at the microscopic and the
macroscopic scales simultaneously.

6) Luciferase signaling: create bard fireflies by manipulating the genes that code for bioluminescence, en-
abling them to use their light for whimsical (creative)
displays, in addition to the standard natural uses (e.g.,
scaring off predators and attracting mates or smaller
creatures to devour).

7) Dynamic biochromatic composition: use the chro-
matic language of the squid to create fantastic colorful
displays that communicate ideas drawn from the squid
Umwelt but suggesting other possible experiences.

8) Avian literature: teach an African Gray parrot not
simply to read and speak, and manipulate symbols, but
to compose and perform literary pieces.

The beginning of a
new alphabet. Let-
ters can be created
with carbon nano-
tubes, tiny cylinders
only a few billionths
of a meter in diam-
eter, as exemplified
by this letter "T".
Words created at
this nanoscale can be
made stable under
the laws of quantum
molecular dynamics.
The first letter of the
word "Tomorrow".

9) Bacterial poetics: two identical colonies of bacteria share a petri dish. One colony has encoded in a
plasmid a poem X, while the other has a poem Y. As
they compete for the same resources, or share genetic
material, perhaps one colony will outlive the other,
perhaps new bacteria will emerge through horizontal
poetic gene transfer.

10) Xenographics: Transplant a living text from one
organism to another, and vice-versa, so as to create an
in vivo tattoo.

11) Tissuetext: Culture tissue in the shape of word-
structures. Grow the tissue slowly until the word-struc-
tures form an overall film and erase themselves.

12) Proteopoetics: create a code that converts words into aminoacids and produce with it a three-dimensional proteinpoem, thus completely bypassing the need to use a gene to encode the protein. Write the protein directly. Synthesize the proteinpoem. Model it in digital and non-digital media. Express it in living organisms.

13) Agroverbalia: Use an electron beam to write different words on the surface of seeds. Grow the plants and observe what words yield robust plants. Plant seeds in different meaningful arrays. Explore hybridization of meanings.

14) Nanopoetry: Assign meaning to quantum dots and nanospheres of different colors. Express them in living cells. Observe what dots and spheres move in what direction, and read the quantum and nanowords as they move through the internal three-dimensional structure of the cell. Reading is observation of vectorial trajectories within the cell. Meaning continuously changes, as certain quantum and nanowords are in the proximity of others, or move close or far away from others. The entire cell is the writing substrate, as a field of potential meaning.

15) Molecular semantics: Create molecular words by assigning phonetic meaning to individual atoms. With dip-pen nanolithography deliver molecules to an atomically-flat gold surface to write a new text. The text is made of molecules which are themselves words.

16) Asyntactical carbogram: Create suggestive verbal nanoarchitectures only a few billionths of a meter in diameter.

17) Metabolic metaphors: Control the metabolism of some microorganisms within a large population in thick media so that ephemeral words can be produced by their reaction to specific environmental conditions,

By assigning specific semantic values to aminoacids, a poet can write a protein. The "Genesis" protein, above, critically encodes the biblical statement: "Let man have dominion over the fish of the sea, and over the fowl of the air, and over every living thing that moves upon the earth."

such as exposrure to light. Allow these living words to dissipate themselves naturally. The temporal duration of this process of dissipation should be controlled so as to be an intrinsic element of the meaning of the poem.

18) Scriptogenesis: Create an entirely new living organism, which has never existed before, by first assembling atoms into molecules through "Atomic writing" or "Molecular semantics". Then, organize these molecules into a minimal but functional chromosome. Either synthesize a nucleus to contain this chromosome or introduce it into an existent nucleus. Do the same for the entire cell. Reading occurs through observation of the cytopoetological transformations of the scriptogenic chromosome throughout the processes of growth and reproduction of the unicellular organism.

Start by collecting mud from the bottom of a lake or river. Create a flat sealed box and introduce the mud, supplemented with water from the lake or river, cellulose (use the most interesting pages of a newspaper), sodium sulphate and calcium carbonate. Seal the box. Approximately 5,000 different microorganisms (prokaryotic bacteria and archaea) will make up this population. Make a mask with the text to be read. Expose to light everything but the text. In about 2 weeks the text will be dark enough to be clearly read. Expose the whole surface to environmental light and allow the words to dissipate. The population within the sealed chamber will recycle nutrients and will support itself with no additional aid.

Poetry Is

George Quasha

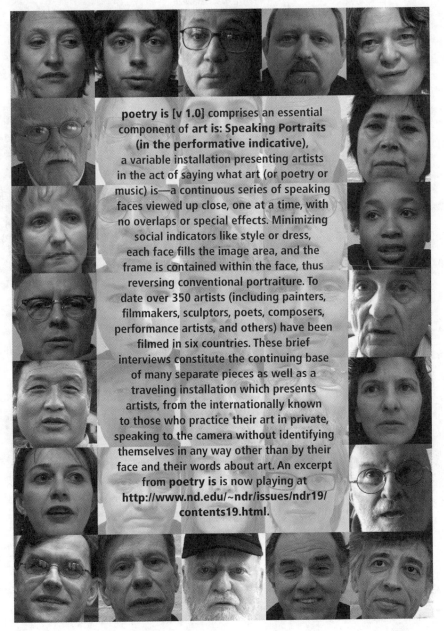

poetry is [v 1.0] comprises an essential component of **art is: Speaking Portraits (in the performative indicative)**, a variable installation presenting artists in the act of saying what art (or poetry or music) is—a continuous series of speaking faces viewed up close, one at a time, with no overlaps or special effects. Minimizing social indicators like style or dress, each face fills the image area, and the frame is contained within the face, thus reversing conventional portraiture. To date over 350 artists (including painters, filmmakers, sculptors, poets, composers, performance artists, and others) have been filmed in six countries. These brief interviews constitute the continuing base of many separate pieces as well as a traveling installation which presents artists, from the internationally known to those who practice their art in private, speaking to the camera without identifying themselves in any way other than by their face and their words about art. An excerpt from **poetry is** is now playing at **http://www.nd.edu/~ndr/issues/ndr19/contents19.html.**

TEXTFED

William Gillespie

The first thing I remember is text. "An hypothesis that is hardly indispensable: alphabetical writing is already, in itself, a form of duplication, since it represents not the signified but the phonetic elements by which it is signified; the ideogram, on the other hand, directly represents the signified, independently from a phonetic system which is another mode of representation." It had to be true. While I found and made connections between all text from then on, I never found my way back to that quote. Experience seemed like an inaccurate representation of text.

Now I am going to be late for my job at the bookstore.

The second thing I remember is warmth. The kinetic motion of the amniotic fluid. It made me feel good. It was the warm bed, bath, shower I never considered leaving, and all warmth thereafter was merely a cozy interruption in the endless cold. Warmth was unstable when it wasn't eternal, perfect "warmth."

Now I am cold.

The third thing I remember is a smell. The antiseptic tang of the delivery room. It seemed something went wrong. That smell haunted me elusively forever, lurking just beneath the odor of the world. The transient scent of a flower was tainted by it.

Now I am hurt.

The fourth thing I remember is milk. My mother's breast. She had very good taste. Nothing tasted like her, everything claimed to. My first mouthful of solid food didn't have the delicate flavor good writing used to.

Now I am hungry.

The fifth thing I remember is my mother. The pictures in an alphabet book. I saw they were important. It was the last time I ever saw their shapes, they became as invisible as cells. I no longer trust my eyes, they often read words incorrectly.

Now I am alone.

The sixth thing I remember is my mother's voice. "Writing, in Western culture, automatically dictates that we place ourselves in the virtual space of selfrepresentation and reduplication; since writing refers not to a thing but to speech, a work of language only advances more deeply into the intangible density of the mirror, calls forth the double of this already doubled writing, discovers in this way a possible and impossible infinity, ceaselessly strives after speech, maintains it beyond the death which condemns it, and frees a murmuring stream." Don't believe everything you hear. I miss her lullabies, there are no other. I can never hear what people are saying to me and wish they'd write it down.

Now I am listening to my voice staring through the shattered rearview mirror at the upsidedown road my cheek stung with frozen blood creak for help.

Stephanie Strickland with Cynthia Lawson

at:

www.nd.edu/~ndr/issues/ndr19/contents19.html

CONTRIBUTORS

Joe Amato is the author of *Under Virga* and *Bookend: Anatomies of a Virtual Self*. **mIEKAL aND** is a poet, intermedia artist and director of Xexoxial Endarchy, a non-profit experimental arts publisher and umbrella arts organization. He also co-founded Dreamtime Village, a hypermedia/permaculture ecovillage project in southwest Wisconsin. **Camille Bacos** is a Romanian filmmaker who has recently relocated to Wisconsin and started work on several new projects with miEKAL aND. Before moving to America, she produced many entertainment shows for Romanian television. She is also the author of several studies about the role of image in collective mentalities. **Peter Balestrieri** lives with Claire, Dominic, and Ilario in Iowa City. **Mary Jo Bang**'s most recent book is *The Eye Like a Strange Balloon*. She teaches at Washington University in St. Louis. **Mike Barrett**, a poet, teaches in Missouri. He is the founder and Creative Director of Anvil/lyre Studio. **Caroline Bergvall** lives and works in England. She has had texts featured in a number of magazines in England and North America. Recent texts include *Eclat* and *Goan Atom: Jets Poupee*. Work also includes collaborations on performances and text-based installations. She is Director of Performance Writing at the Dartington College of Arts in Devon, England. **Charles Bernstein**'s *Shadowtime*, libretto on Walter Benjamin written for composer Brian Ferneyhough, is forthcoming this spring from Green Integer; the opera will be performed at the Lincoln Center Festival, in New York, in July 2005. Bernstein teaches at the University of Pennsylvania, where he directs PennSound. **R. M. Berry** is professor of English at Florida State University, and author of the novel *Leonardo's Horse*, and the story collections *Dictionary of Modern Anguish* and *Plane Geometry and Other Affairs of the Heart*. He is publisher of Fiction Collective Two. **Jenny Boully**'s book *The Body* was published in 2002. Her work has been anthologized in *The Best American Poetry*, *The Next American Essay*, and *Great American Prose Poems: From Poe to the Present*. **cris cheek** is a poet-writer, artist and sound composer interested in interdisciplinary and hybrid poetic textualities/performances. He lives in Lowestoft, North Suffolk, where he curates Sound & Language recordings and publications and is Editor of LanguageAlive Books. **Lucy Corin**'s novel *Everyday Psychokillers: A History for Girls* was published in 2004. Recent short fiction appeared in *The Southern Review* and *Fiction International*. She teaches at the University of California, Davis. **Lydia Davis** is the author of four books of fiction, most recently the story collection *Samuel Johnson Is Indignant*. Her latest translation, *Marcel Proust's*

Swann's Way, won the French-American Foundation's 2003 Translation Prize. **Tom Denlinger** is an artist and assistant professor of Art at Lake Forest College. He is a photographer and videographer who has had solo exhibitions in New York and Chicago. He is currently co-editing an anthology on contemporary uses of the Surrealist Exquisite Corpse. **Debra Di Blasi** received the 2003 James C. McCormick Fellowship from the Christopher Isherwood Foundation. Books include *Drought & Say What You Like* and *Prayers of an Accidental Nature*. Her fiction has been adapted to film, radio, theatre, and audio CD in the U.S. and abroad. **Amy England** is the author of two books of poetry: *The Flute Ship Castricum* and *Victory and Her Opposites*. She teaches poetics, surrealism and creative writing at the School of the Art Institute of Chicago. **Brian Evenson** is the author of seven books of fiction, most recently *The Wavering Knife*. He is a senior editor for *Conjunctions* magazine and teaches Creative Writing at Brown University. **Kass Fleisher** is the author of a creative nonfiction work, *The Bear River Massacre and the Making of History*; and an experimental prose work, *Accidental Species: A Reproduction*. Her work has appeared in journals such as *The Iowa Review, Bombay Gin*, and *Postmodern Culture*. She is assistant professor of English at Illinois State University, in Normal. **William Gillespie** is a poet, fiction writer, radio show host, and founder of the independent publishing house Spineless Books. He is the author of *Johnny Werd: The Fire Continues, 2002: A Palindrome Story in 2002 Words* (with Nick Montfort and Shelley Jackson), *The Unknown* (a book and hypertext novel), and *Newspoetry*. He is the current Electronic Writing Fellow in the MFA program in Literary Arts at Brown University. **Alexandra Grant** was educated at both Swarthmore College in Pennsylvania and the California College of Art in San Francisco. An upcoming solo exhibition at Gallery Sixteen:One in Santa Monica, called "Homecomings," marks the culmination of a decade of work about text and art, identity, language and location. **Tim Guthrie** is a mixed media artist who uses a wide range of media in both his 2-D and 3-D artwork. He is a professor at Creighton University in Omaha, Nebraska, and teaches a variety of courses. His artwork has been shown both nationally and internationally. **Scott Helmes** is an experimental poet and language artist who lives in St. Paul, and who also performs as part of the Be Blank Consort. His work is in the *Avant Writing Collection* at the Ohio Universities. **Mrylin Hermes** is the author of the novel *Careful What You Wish For*. A graduate of Reed College, she is currently studying at Royal Holloway, University of London, where she is working on her second novel, a postmodern Shakespearean romance. **Michael Joyce** is professor of English at Vassar College. His interests include hypertext fiction, media studies, modern literature, and theory. His most recent novel is entitled *Liam's Going*. **Eduardo Kac** is internationally recognized for his interactive net installations and his bio art. **Catherine Kasper** currently teaches at the University of Texas-San Antonio. Her book of poetry, *Keld Stone*, is due out this year. **Cynthia Lawson** is a new media technologist, artist, and educator. Her work has been seen at the Modern Museum of Art (Bogota), UCLA Hammer Museum, Macy Gallery, NY Arts Space, CalArts, RISD, and various online journals and publications. Lawson lives in New York City, and is faculty and associate chair of Parsons School of Design's Integrated Design Curriculum. **Paul Maliszewski**'s letters to the President have appeared in *Fence*, *J&L Illustrated*, and other magazines. His writing has also been published in *Harper's*, *The Paris Review*, *Granta*, and the Pushcart Prize anthologies. **Mark Marino** is a Ph.D. student in New Media at University of California at Riverside. He lives in Los Angeles with his wife and daughter. He teaches at Loyola Marymount University and edits *Bunk Magazine*. **Michael Martone**'s next book, *MICHAEL MARTONE*, is composed of fifty contributor's notes he published in the contributors' notes section of magazines. **Steve McCaffery** is author of fifteen books of poetry and one novel. In 1973 he co-founded with the late "bp" Nichol the Toronto Research Group. He has performed his poetry world-wide and his work has been translated into French, Spanish, Chinese, and Hungarian. **Nick Montfort** is a poet and interactive fiction author who has collaborated on many literary projects. He wrote *Twisty Little Passages: An Approach to Interactive Fiction* and co-edited *The New Media Reader*. **Noam Mor**'s work in this issue is from his novel *Arc: Cleavage of Ghosts*. **Sheila E. Murphy** is the author of *Proof of Silhouettes*, *Concentricity*, *Letters to Unfinished J*, and *Green Tea with Ginger*. She grew up in a Notre Dame family and now lives in Phoenix. **Lance Olsen**'s text piece in this issue is from his novel *10:01*, which will be out this Spring. **George Quasha**'s work includes video, installation, performance, poetry, and sculpture. His *Axial Stones and Drawings*, together with *Watercolors by John Cage*, open this month in New York. He is the author of numerous books of poetry and writings on art, including *The Preverbs of Tell*, *American Prophecy*, and *Tall Ships*. **Scott Rettberg** is assistant professor of New Media Studies in the Literature Program at Richard Stockton College of New Jersey. He is the coauthor of *The Unknown*, a hypertext novel, and the author of *Kind of Blue*, a serial novel for email. **Davis Schneiderman** is chair of the American Studies Program and assistant professor of English at Lake Forest College. His creative work has been nominated for a Pushcart Prize and has been accepted by numerous journals including *Fiction International*, *The Iowa*

Review Web, and *Exquisite Corpse*. He is currently co-editing an anthology on contemporary uses of the Surrealist Exquisite Corpse, as well as co-editing the new literary journal *Potion*. **Mike Smith** holds degrees from UNC-G, Hollins University, and the University of Notre Dame. Recent work has appeared in the *Malahot Review*, the *North American Review*, and *Salt*. **Stephanie Strickland** is a print and new media poet. Her fourth book of poems, *V: WaveSon.nets/ Losing L'una*, has a web component. Her prize-winning works include *V, True North, The Red Virgin*, and *Ballad of Sand and Harry Soot*. She teaches new media as part of experimental poetry at many colleges. **TNWK** is an ongoing collaboration between Kirsten Lavers and cris cheek, two artist-writers making work together as co-authors. TNWK employs multiple mediums and multiple modes to engage in conversations with site, context and participation. **David Ray Vance** is a doctoral candidate in the creative writing program at The University of Houston and is the associate editor of *Gulf Coast: A Journal of Literature and Fine Arts*. His poems and stories have appeared in such publications as *Chicago Review, Denver Quarterly, Borderlands, Sniper Logic*, and in the anthology: *Is This Forever or What?—Poems and Paintings from Texas*.

Acknowledgements

Special thanks to Michael Martone for his RKO and Exchange Ad Exchange ads. Lydia Davis's "Story" was first published in her *The Figures*. Brian Evenson's "House Rules" first appeared in *Third Bed*. Debra Di Blasi's "Czechoslovakian Rhapsody Sung to the Accompaniment of Piano" first appeared in *The Iowa Review*. Catherine Kasper's "J'Abab's Cosmic Gown" was fist published in *Mid-American Review*; "Cabinet of Infinite Compartments" was first published in *McSweeney's*; "Wig of Bees" was first published in *Leviathan*.

Tongue Tied?
Let RKO Untie that Tongue

RKO Radio Poems
Since 1976, our nation's bicentennial

A Hoosier Tradition

Founded in Bloomington, Indiana, during the filming of the seminal film *Breaking Away*, RKO Radio Poems has provided only the best un-tongue-tied verse for over a quarter century. Over 2,000 satisfied customers. Nearly 5,000 poems in circulation.

Here's How It Works

Here's how it works: One of our crack team poets will ask you if you would like a poem today. If the answer is yes--and why would it be anything other than yes--you then will be asked for the subject and the style of the desired poem.

AM, FM, POEM

RKO Radio Poems will happily provide a complete menu from which you can select the appropriate form to convey your selected subject matter. Our professional bards can professionally render, haiku, tanka, renga, naughty limericks, sonnets (Petrarchan, Shakespearean, Spenserian, or whatever-ian), sestinas, ghazals, terza rima, villanelle, rondel, rondeau, cinquain, rhyme royal, double dactyls, blank verse, free verse, nominal verse, ballads, ballades, fanfares, couplets, quatrains, those things that spell out something using the first letter of each line, prose poems, psalms, Gregorian chants, Whitmanesque lines, odes, eclogues, narrative lyrics, lyrical narratives, monologues, dialogues, epigrams, epigraphs, epitaphs, epics, mock epics, and epochal epics.

"A poem must not mean but be twenty-five cents"[1]

For a mere two bits, you too can have your very own poem. Unlike the mass produced poems manufactured by a certain company in Kansas City, RKO Radio Poems can personalize your verse to include the color of your lover's eyes even.

Samples Upon Request

RKO Radio Poems will be happy to forward to you sample swatches upon receipt of a self-addressed stamped #10 envelope. Yours to keep. Please specify spondees, iambs, trochees, anapests, antispasts, or molossos.

RKO Radio Poems
9 Helicon Way
Reform, AL 35401
205-344-5059

[1]Rhyme slightly higher. Verse written upon subjects found in the nation's national parks or considered under the jurisdiction of the interstate commerce clause of the U.S. Constitution subject to surcharge. Does not include tax, title, or destination charges. Credit subject to approval. No warranty is made or implied as to the quality or shelf life of verse. Offer void in Wisconsin and the United States Virgin Islands. Punctuation may vary. For the private consumption of adults over 21 years of age and for entertainment purposes only. Not to be read with food. Patent applied for. RKO Radio Poems is in no way affiliated with the RKO Radio Pictures Company. Some assembly required. Limited availability of other languages. Refrain from using if rash persists. Poem must be grounded and insulated properly.

ARS INTERPRES

An International Journal of Poetry, Translation & Art

The journal publishes primarily contemporary English language poetry, English translation of modern Scandinavian and European poetry, as well as articles on poetic translation and other related materials. *Ars Interpres* also includes reviews, review-essays, art, and photography. *Ars Interpres* is published in Stockholm.

Issue 1
240 pages. $19. 95
ISBN 91-7910-549-1

Issue 2 *Intersecting Senses*
216 pages. $19. 90
ISBN 91-7910-602-1

Issue 3 *Blessing of the Beasts*
184 pages. $19. 90
ISBN 91-7910-603-X

Issue 4 and 5
Out September 2005

Payment
If you pay from outside of Sweden please use Swift.
IBAN: SE 065 00 00 00 00 5398 1020 758
Swiftadress: ESSESESS
Bankname: SEB

http://www.ars-interpres.nm.ru
e-mail: ars-interpres@nm.ru

Contributors to *Ars Interpres* include: Annie Finch, Aris Fioretos, Eamon Grennan, Gunnar Harding, Seamus Heaney, Cynthia Hogue, John Kinsella, John Matthias, Les Murray, Jean-Pierre Rosnay, Pia Tafdrup, Tomas Venclova, Daniel Weissbort.

SUSTAINERS

Anonymous

Nancy and Warren Bryant

Kevin DiCamillo

Gary & Elizabeth Gutchess

John F. Hayward

Samuel Hazo

Tim Kilroy

Richard Landry

Steve Lazar

Carol A. Losi

Jessica Maich

Vincent J. O'Brien

Kevin T. O'Connor

Daniel O'Donnell

Beth Haverkamp Powers

Mark W. Roche

In Honor of Ernest Sandeen

In Honor of James Whitehead

Kenneth L. Woodword